IMAGES
of America

SHEBOYGAN

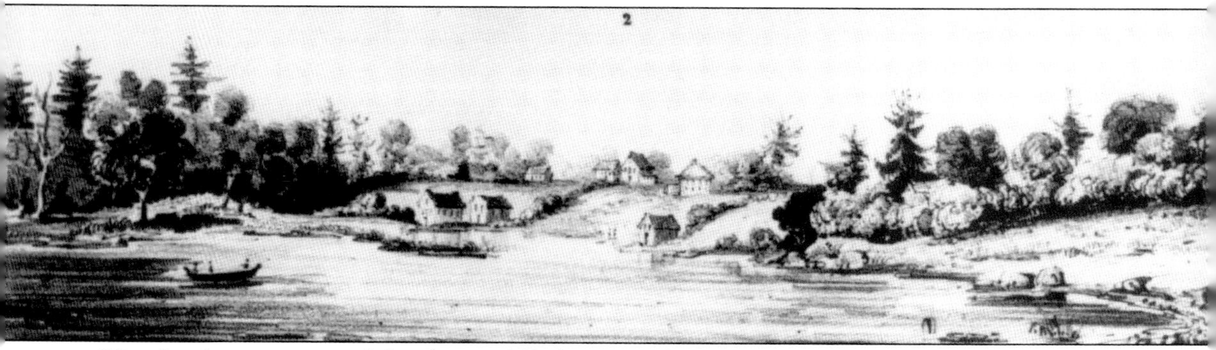

The first-known view of the shore of Sheboygan, this artist's rendering from 1838 shows the natural beauty of the setting. Located at the site where the Sheboygan River enters Lake Michigan, this natural harbor was considered the best on the western shore of the great lake. In 1835, government surveyors, after sounding and charting, predicted that a good harbor could be built with little expense. (Courtesy of Sheboygan County Historical Research Center.)

On the Cover: Young Sheboyganites enjoy a summer day at Lake Michigan. Captured near Ontario Avenue at the lakefront about 1900, this image highlights bathing costumes of the time. Women's suits typically included black, knee-length, puffed-sleeve wool dresses accessorized with long black stockings. The old lighthouse is at the far right. (Courtesy of Sheboygan County Historical Research Center.)

IMAGES
of America

SHEBOYGAN

Sheboygan County
Historical Research Center

ARCADIA
PUBLISHING

ISBN 978-0-7385-9426-2

Published by Arcadia Publishing
Charleston, South Carolina

Printed in the United States of America

Library of Congress Control Number: 2012941027

For all general information, please contact Arcadia Publishing:
Telephone 843-853-2070
Fax 843-853-0044
E-mail sales@arcadiapublishing.com
For customer service and orders:
Toll-Free 1-888-313-2665

Visit us on the Internet at www.arcadiapublishing.com

To the citizens of Sheboygan, past and present, whose inspired preservation of Sheboygan's history has created a vibrant and enduring historical community

Contents

Acknowledgments

Local history is nearly always undervalued, but if we examine it closely, we see it as the basis for all other history. This book is a group effort created by volunteers to benefit the Sheboygan County Historical Research Center (SCHRC) and to share some of the great history of the city of Sheboygan. So much history about the city of Sheboygan is available, it is impossible to contain it in one book of this type. A second and perhaps third volume will be necessary. Unless otherwise noted, all images appear courtesy of the Sheboygan County Historical Research Center. The text was written by Rosemary Eigenberger, Peter Fetterer, Janice Hildebrand, Ed Kaminsky, Dale Kuhn, Lois Landgraf, Don Lau, Katie Reilly, and Beth Dippel.

INTRODUCTION

Sheboygan, Wisconsin, situated on the picturesque western shore of Lake Michigan, is a city of contrasts and conundrums. It is a modern city facing all the challenges of today's world, ready and willing to transition into the future. At the same time, it is a city comfortable with long-established customs struggling to keep the time-honored traditions that have made it a great place to live. It is a place where people stay on the same bowling teams for decades, churches are always full and focused on the community, and everybody knows everybody else in the local taverns.

In 1995, *Reader's Digest* recognized Sheboygan as the "Best Place to Raise a Family" in the United States. Sheboygan was chosen for being a safe city, with its high levels of citizen involvement in volunteerism, church attendance, involvement in organizations, and support of community initiatives. *Money Magazine* named Sheboygan one of eight best places to retire in June 2002, referring to it as "a small town with everything," as well as the "Bratwurst Capital of the World." *Bloomberg Businessweek* named Sheboygan the "Best Place to Raise Kids in Wisconsin" in 2011.

The story of Sheboygan's settlement begins with French explorer Jean Nicolet as he passed through this area in 1635. In 1643, Louis Joliet, a Canadian explorer, and Jacques Marquette, the great Jesuit missionary and explorer, also passed this site. For the next five decades, only fur traders passed through the area, occasionally dealing with the local Native Americans. There are no further written records until 1814 when William Farnsworth, commonly acknowledged as the founder of Sheboygan, arrived. He settled permanently in the area in 1818 and established a "jackknife" or portable trading post.

In 1822, William Payne and Oliver Crocker built a sawmill at the first rapids on the Sheboygan River near today's Esslingen Park. They also built two log cabins, one of which was at the site of today's Sixth Street and Pennsylvania Avenue on the courthouse grounds. When the government finished initial surveys and placed the land for sale at Green Bay (the territorial seat) in November 1835, Farnsworth bid on the land and became co-owner of the site that included Payne and Crocker's holdings.

In 1836, Charles Cole left his native New York for Green Bay and met William Farnsworth, who encouraged Cole to visit Sheboygan and urged him to set up a mercantile and forwarding business. Cole continued on to Sheboygan and scouted the area. Pleased with what he saw, he joined Farnsworth in riding along the lakeshore to Milwaukee. The government land sales were being held in July that year, and the men intended to buy the land that would become the city of Sheboygan.

Cole purchased three lots along the Sheboygan River and hired A.G. Dye, then a resident of Fulton County, New York, to build a warehouse and 160-foot-long dock on the property. Arrangements completed, Cole returned to Cleveland for his wife, Sarah Trowbridge Cole, and family, as well as a stock of merchandise including groceries, dry goods, and hardware. The Cole family set up their business at the first hotel, the Sheboygan House, as soon as it was finished.

A severe nationwide financial panic in 1837 left the three dozen residents of Sheboygan without cash and hope. Most of the residents left over the next couple of years for more prosperous locations; some moved westward to "Sheboygan at the Falls" and two placed their houses on scows and towed them to Milwaukee. Sheboygan's residents were near starvation, and the settlement's future looked bleak. By 1839, James Farnsworth (a cousin of William Farnsworth) and his wife were the only two people left. At the time, the settlement was about three square blocks in size, bounded by Lake Michigan, today's north Sixth Street and Washington Court, and the river.

Starting in 1840, a second wave of immigration began, this one being much larger and more permanent. By the time the settlement became a village in 1846, its boundaries expanded to Superior Avenue on the north, the lake on the east, Georgia Avenue on the south, and Eighteenth Street on the west. The population had soared to nearly 300.

According to Gustave Buchen's book *Historic Sheboygan County*, in 1853, there were 1,790 dwellings, 581 farms, and 30 factories in the county, and the population was nearly 9,000, with more than 2,000 in the city of Sheboygan alone.

Native-born Americans of English descent, also known as Yankees, were the first permanent European settlers to populate Sheboygan. Most came from the state of New York and bore names like Follett, Giddings, Brown, Lyman, Moore, Kirkland, Farnsworth, Rounseville, Jenkins, and Seaman. They were entrepreneurs and businessmen, not farmers. They were hardy, intelligent, religious, and self-reliant.

Arriving next were the Irish, Dutch, and German immigrants, beginning in 1845. The great majority of emigrants from Ireland moved on to farms elsewhere in the country, but a few like Thomas Blackstock settled in the city. Blackstock was a business owner and construction superintendent of the Sheboygan and Fond du Lac Plank Road. He was president of the Phoenix Chair Company and a three-term mayor of the city, always concerned with its welfare.

The Dutch also came as early as 1845. Most moved on to live in the town of Holland, located south of Sheboygan. One prominent Hollander was Jacob Quintus, editor of the *Nieuwsbode*, a Dutch-language newspaper published in Sheboygan from 1849 to 1859. The newspaper focused on national news and worked to help transform the new Dutch immigrants into good American citizens.

The Germans came to Sheboygan in large numbers beginning in 1848. By 1860, there were 2,724 German-born residents in the city. Names like Geele, Gutsch, Foeste, Zschetzsche, Zaegel, Roenitz, Jung, Schreier, Reiss, Kohler, and Vollrath filled the newspapers, many of which were in German, with achievements and successes of those first- and second-generation immigrants.

Since about 1890, the city of Sheboygan has been blessed with smaller waves of immigrants from Russia, Slovenia, Croatia, Greece, Mexico, Laos, and Kosovo. All have helped in creating the ethnically rich populace that is Sheboygan.

One

Blazing Trails

Native Americans flourished here hundreds of years before European settlement, as evidenced by the large number of burial mounds in the area. Just south of the city lie 18 rare mounds dated from 500 to 750 AD. But by the time the first European settlers arrived, estimates show there were probably only about 1,000 Indians permanently residing in the county. Those remaining were a mixed group composed of Pottawatomie, Ojibwe, Ottawa, Ho-Chunk, and Menominee. Spread throughout the county, their villages were located on the banks of lakes and rivers, along well-worn trails, and routes of trade. The Indian settlement at Sheboygan was situated on the north bank of the Sheboygan River. These native residents were supplanted by the first wave of European settlers. William Farnsworth, born September 26, 1796, in Vermont, is considered the founder of Sheboygan. He left his mark as a promoter of the original townsite, a land speculator, public servant, and businessman who worked tirelessly to advance the growth of the village until his untimely death.

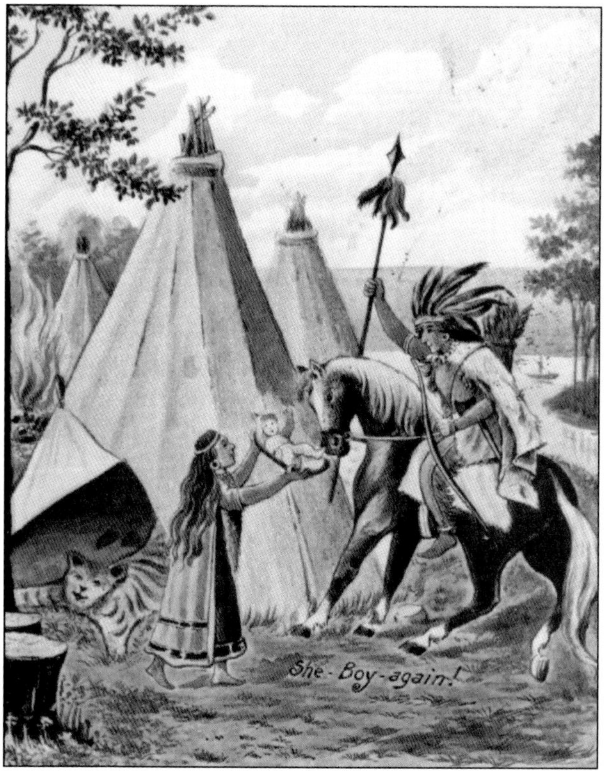

This postcard, titled "Sheboygan in Its Infancy," is one of many that humorously depict the possible origin of Sheboygan's name. This one concerns an Indian chief who had many sons but no daughters. When his wife presented him with yet another boy, she was rumored to have lamented, "She–boy–again." In reality, most authorities agree that *Sheboygan* is an Ojibwe word, but the meaning remains elusive.

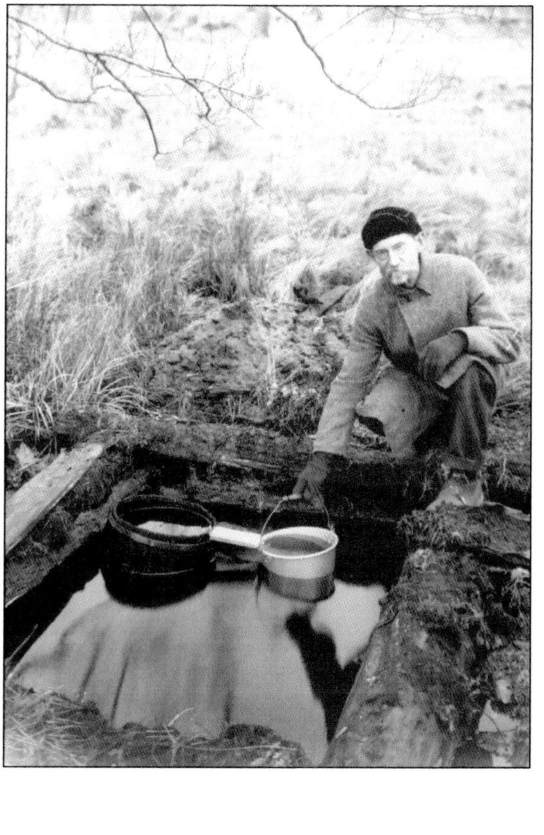

Wells such as this one were used by Native Americans as sources of fresh drinking water. Seen here is P.J. Haag (grandson of Jacob Haag, who settled in Sheboygan County in 1853). Haag found birch-bark buckets at this spring. Indians stored meat, vegetables, clothes, and trinkets in large birch-bark containers. This image was captured on December 29, 1927.

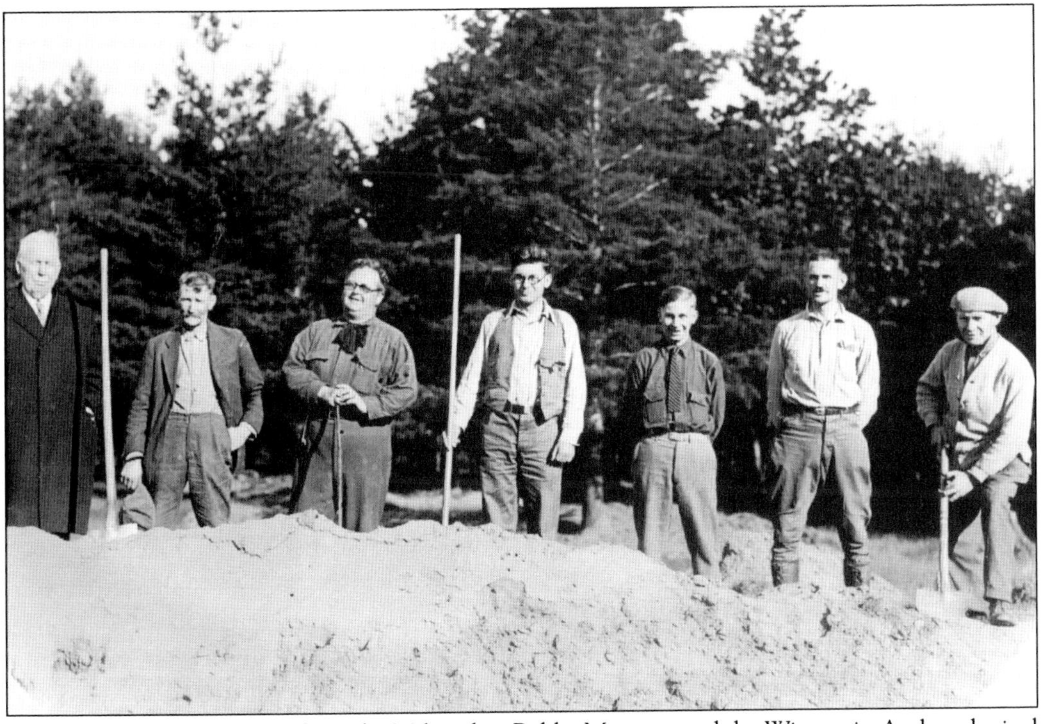

In June 1927, archaeologists from the Milwaukee Public Museum and the Wisconsin Archaeological Society conducted an excavation in what was known as the Kletzien Mound Group. Now a part of Indian Mound Park in Black River, the group originally consisted of 33 conical and effigy mounds constructed by Woodland Indians, a prehistoric culture, on 10 acres. Remarkably, many of the remains uncovered were those of men over six feet tall.

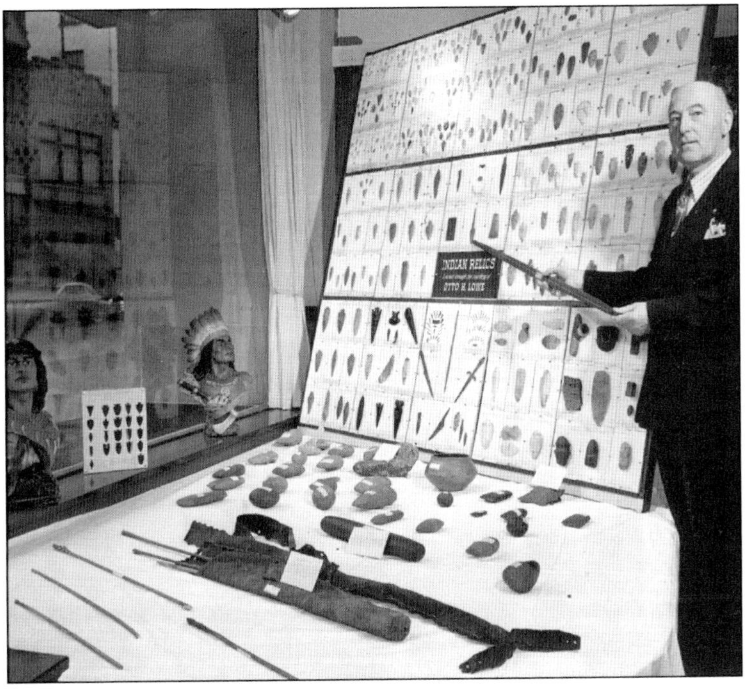

South Side Junior High School principal Otto H. Lowe is pictured here with his collection of Native American artifacts while they were on display at Citizens Bank in Sheboygan. Amateur archaeologists spent many Sunday afternoons gathering artifacts throughout the county in the late 1800s and early 1900s. This collecting and excavating of the area's mounds desecrated many important sites before a more sensitive understanding was gained by citizens of the county.

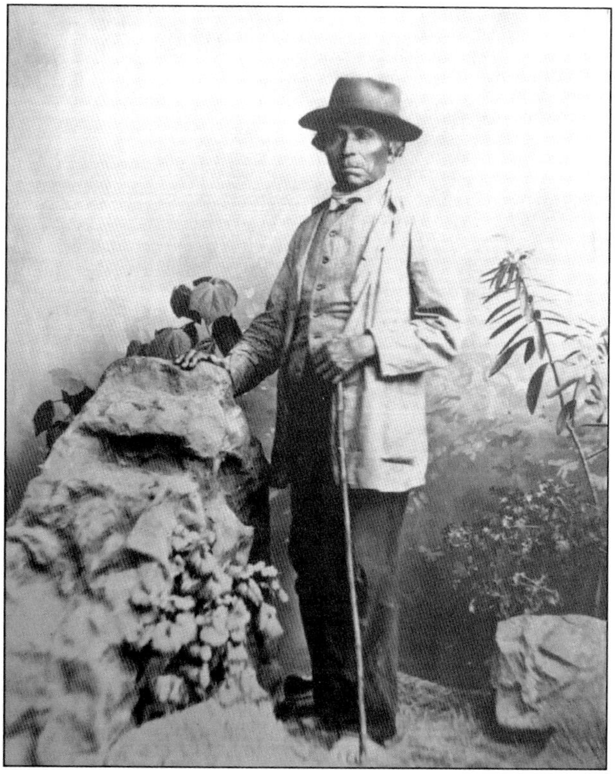

Old Solomon, a well-known Potawatomi Indian, was one of the last Native Americans to leave the county for relocation. He gifted the Henschel family, who lived just north of the Sheboygan Marsh, a dugout canoe, which is presently on display at the Sheboygan County Historical Museum. Old Solomon, who claimed to be a brother-in-law of Solomon Juneau, left in 1883 to go to the Menominee reservation in Keshena and died in 1889.

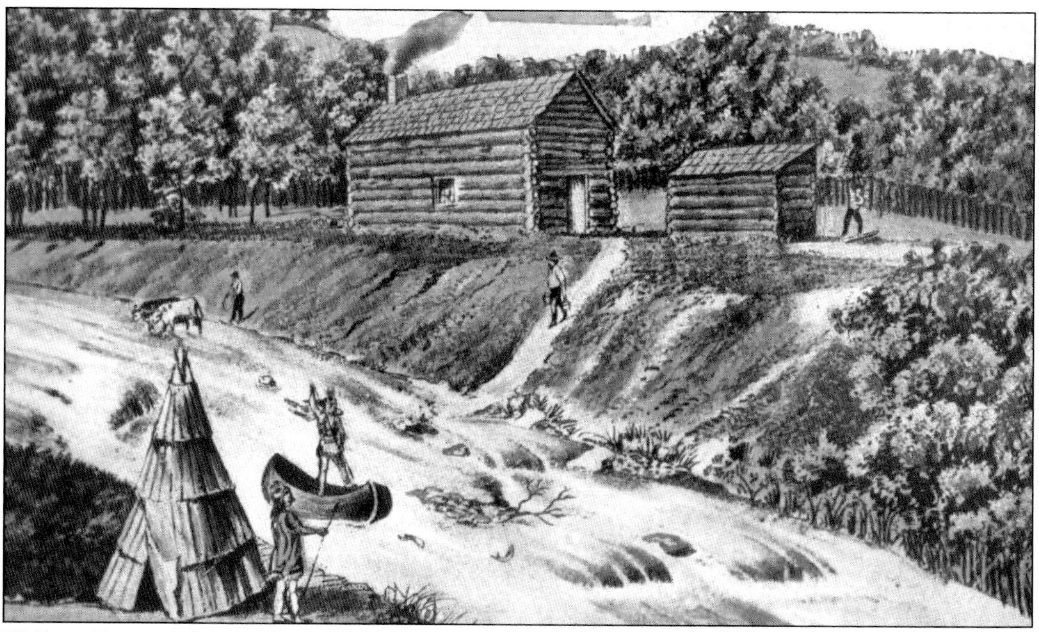

William Paine and Col. Oliver Crocker constructed the area's first sawmill on the Sheboygan River in 1834. Built at the site of the first rapids near today's Esslingen Park, this unidentified artist's rendering shows Paine's log cabin. Crocker and Paine later lost the mill and cabin to William Farnsworth because of government wrangling. The two men did not have clear title to the land, and Farnsworth bought it during a land sale.

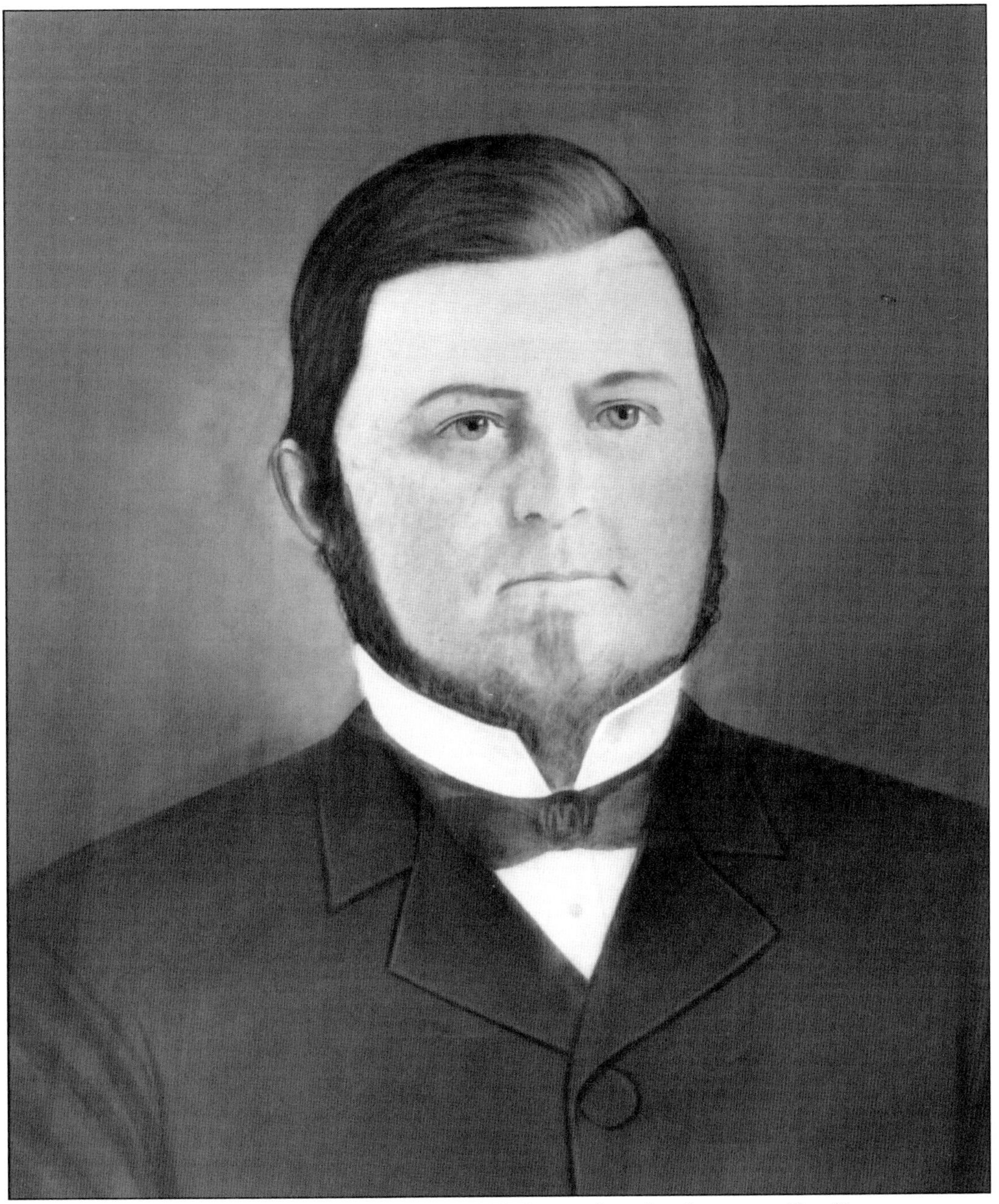

William Farnsworth set up a trading post in 1820. Soon after, the American Fur Company sent a trader of its own to put Farnsworth out of business. The trader, John Jacobs, was accompanied by his metis wife, Marie Antoinette Chevalier ("metis" is defined as a child having a French father and native mother). Farnsworth charmed Marie Antoinette and talked Jacobs out of his furs and his wife. The couple married according to Indian custom and had three children. Queen Marinette, as she was known, later divorced Farnsworth to protect her right to tribal land. Soon after the divorce, Farnsworth married Lydia Anne, the widow of his cousin James Farnsworth. James and Lydia had remained as the only inhabitants at Sheboygan when the settlement was abandoned before his death. Lydia died on October 15, 1844, and William drowned while returning from Chicago aboard the *Lady Elgin* in 1860.

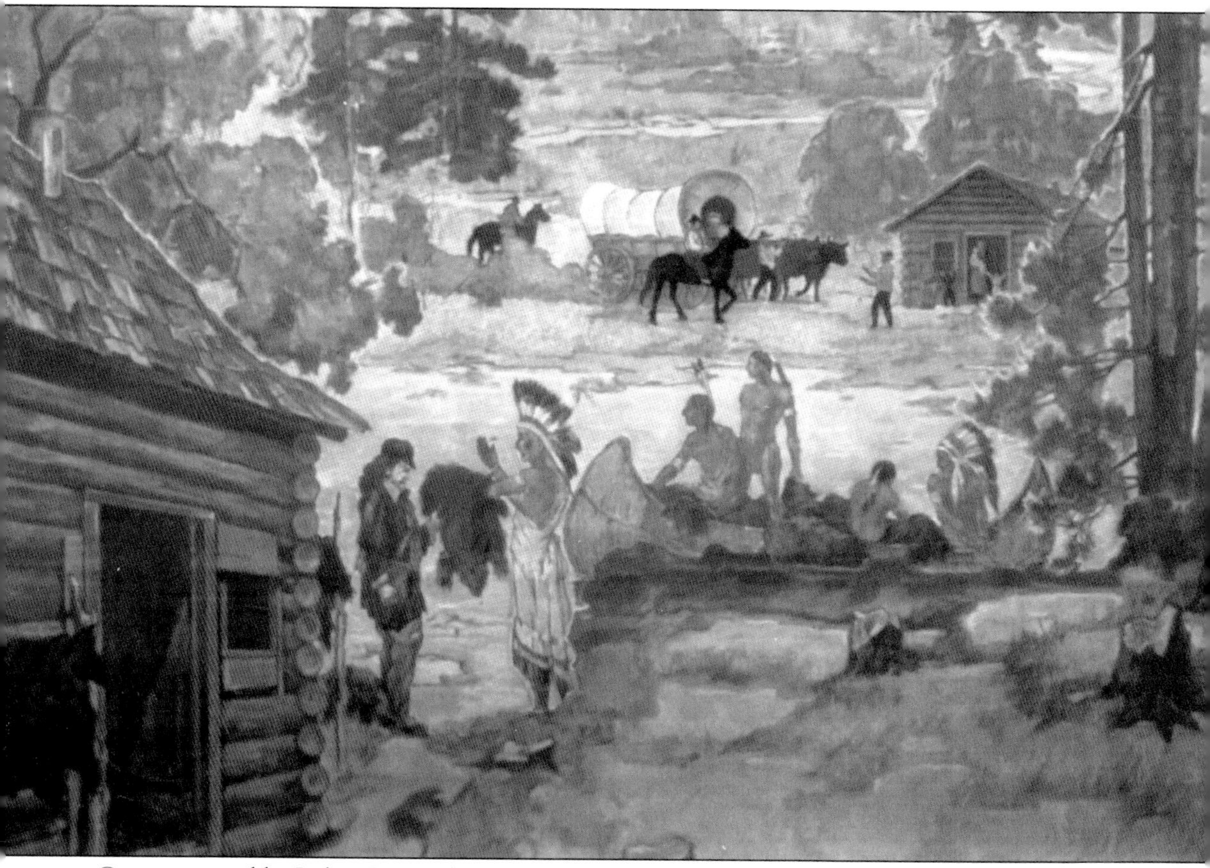

Commissioned by Judges F.H. Schlichting and Edward Voigt for the new county courthouse in 1934, this mural depicts William Farnsworth exchanging cloth and trinkets with an Indian chief for furs at the second rapids of the Sheboygan River. Painted by Chicago artist and professor G. Nordinger, it originally hung in Judge Voight's courtroom. When Schlichting became circuit judge, he moved into the courtroom with the mural. It was there for 35 years until 1969. Schlichting once quipped about the subject of the mural: "I wanted Indians; he [Voight] wanted settlers. We got both." Removed from the courthouse when the ceilings were lowered in 1969, the 12-foot-by-16-foot canvas traveled around for a number of years until Charley Kurtinitis, an acquaintance of Judge Schlichting, agreed to store it at his auction warehouse (the old Turner Hall in Plymouth). In 1985, Jan Hildebrand, a Sheboygan County Historical Research Center librarian, tracked it down and had it restored with the help of her sister Barbara Boedecker. It now graces the east wall of the library at the research center.

Two

The First 50 Years

For the first 50 years or so, much of life in Sheboygan centered on the harbor and riverfront. Started at the point where the Sheboygan River empties into Lake Michigan, the settlement of Sheboygan began to take shape in 1836, at first as a three-square-block area with one hotel, the Sheboygan House, and a post office managed by Charles Cole. At this point in the history of the area, nearly everything was a first. The first school was built in 1837 with an enrollment of 12 students. In 1843, the first store and first schooner, the *Pilot*, were built. The village of Sheboygan was incorporated in February 1846, more than two years before Wisconsin became a state. Henry Conklin was elected Sheboygan's first village president. The new government got right to work setting aside money in March 1848 for a bridge across the Sheboygan River and a well at Pennsylvania Avenue and Eighth Street. The city's first fire engine was purchased for $700. By 1849, a total of $300 was raised for the construction of a navigable harbor. In 1850, an artesian well was ordered sunk to a depth of 100 feet at $5 per foot. This was the beginning of the well at Fountain Park. By May 1851, the government was in full swing creating an ordinance to prohibit swine from running at large in the village. The first telegraph line entered the city from Milwaukee. A new jail was built, and a cemetery was laid out with the price of a plot costing $7. The village grew quickly, and in 1853, Sheboygan received its city charter. Immigrants had been streaming in since about 1847, which strained the harbor's resources, but this steady stream of new residents and workers created markets for products and services. By 1857, Sheboygan's population was at 3,500, a huge improvement over the lonely couple of James and Lydia Farnsworth, who remained in 1839. In this initial 50 years, Sheboygan grew from a wilderness to a frontier town to a thriving and somewhat cosmopolitan small city with a bright future.

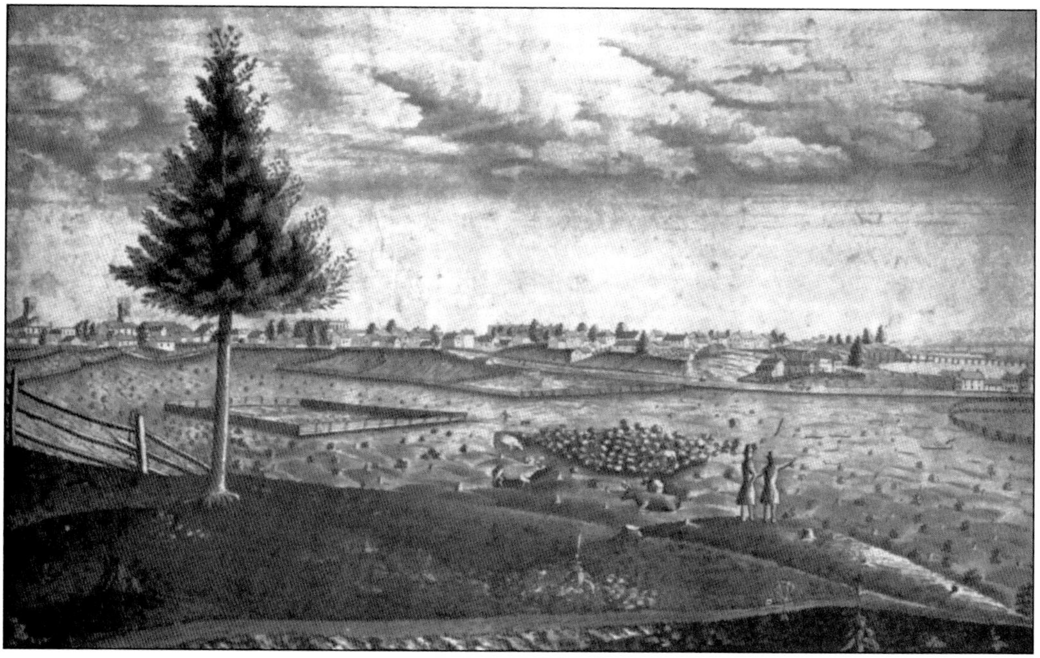

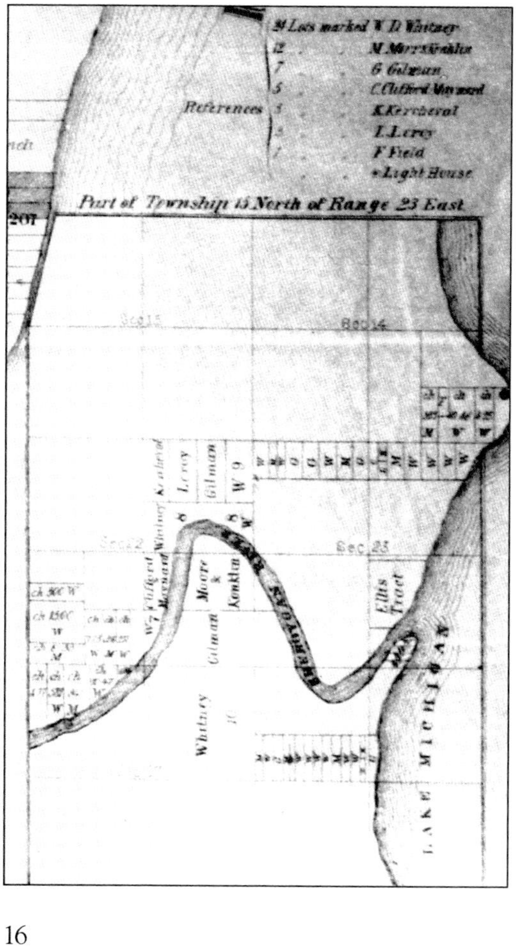

The first permanent European settlers arrived in Sheboygan in the early 1830s. The area comprising Sheboygan was platted in 1836. That year also saw the first buildings erected and the first dock and warehouse built by Asahel Dye. This view of Sheboygan, drawn by O. Kroehnke, is from the hill near Sheridan Park, the first public square, and atop one of the highest points in the city.

This early-1840s plat map of Sheboygan shows the city's first landowners. Most lots were along the Sheboygan River and Lake Michigan. As marked, lots were owned by W.D. Whitney, J. Moore and Konklin, G. Gilman, C. Clifford Maynard, K. Kercheval, L. Leroy and F. Field. The location of the first North Point lighthouse, or beacon, erected in 1838, is identified with an asterisk.

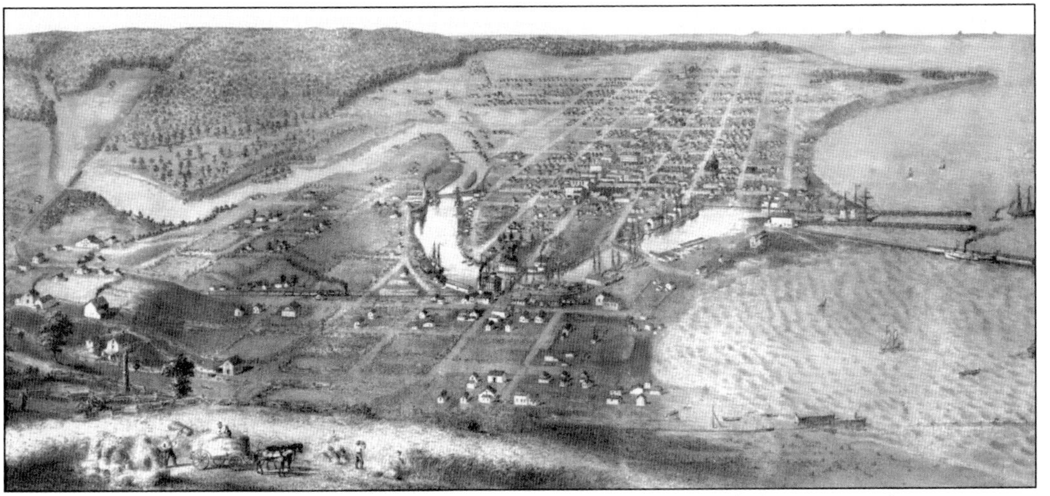

Born of Irish parents in the state of New York, Michael Lynch was Sheboygan's earliest engineer, arriving in 1842. Lynch was a bridge builder and contractor of public works. He came to Sheboygan and erected the first bridge across the Sheboygan River. He was also responsible for laying out the city's streets, grading, and all improvements made to them.

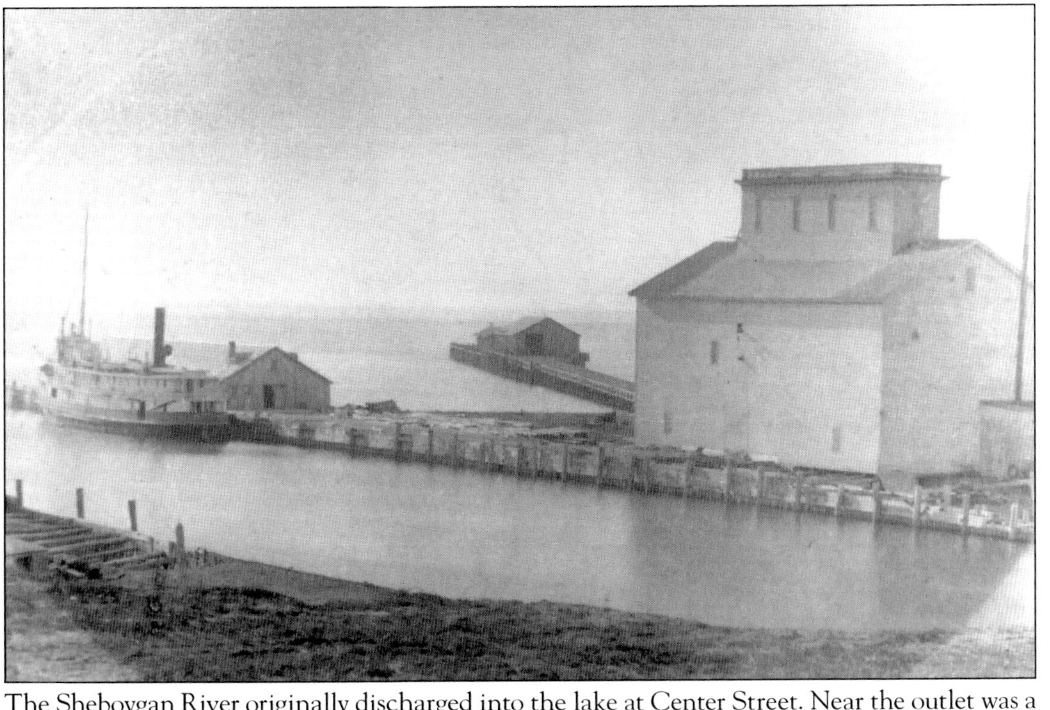

The Sheboygan River originally discharged into the lake at Center Street. Near the outlet was a narrow, sandy projection known as Kirkland's Point where Joseph Kirkland built the first grain elevator, seen here in 1865. Kirkland also extended the first pier to a length of 1,400 feet, enabling ships to load on either side. The vessel seen here is the *Messenger*, which carried flour from this port to Pentwater, Michigan, and salt on the return trip.

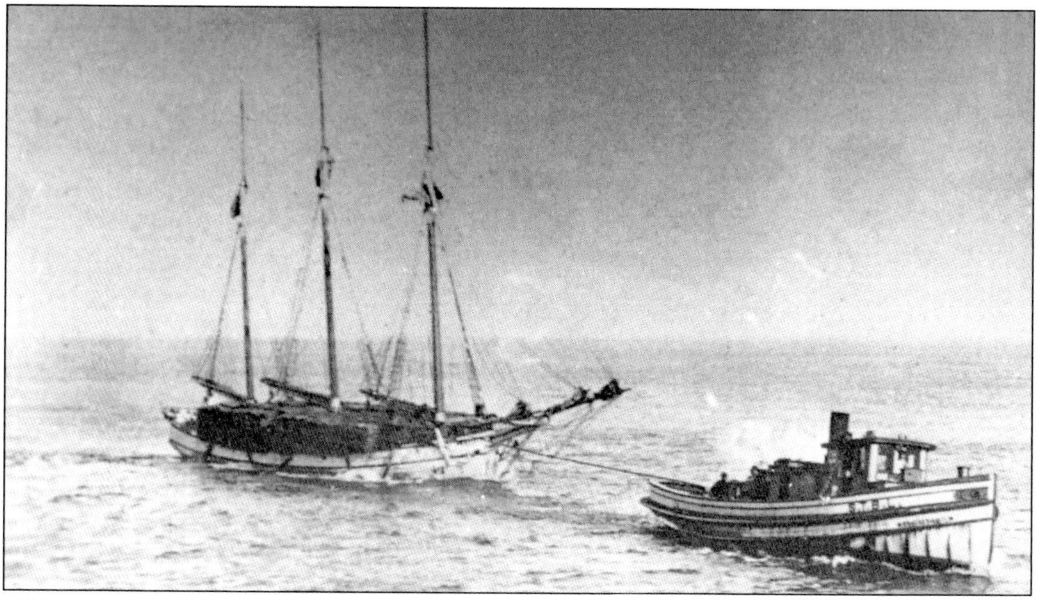

A lumber schooner is towed by the tug *Satisfaction* into deeper water from the harbor. Sheboygan County, blessed with its abundance of trees, along with rivers for waterpower, developed sawmills in the earliest days as Yankees from the east and European immigrants began developing the area's business. Those same sawmills supplied lumber, shingles, and other wood products to the fast-growing cities of Milwaukee and Chicago, as well as other markets on the Great Lakes.

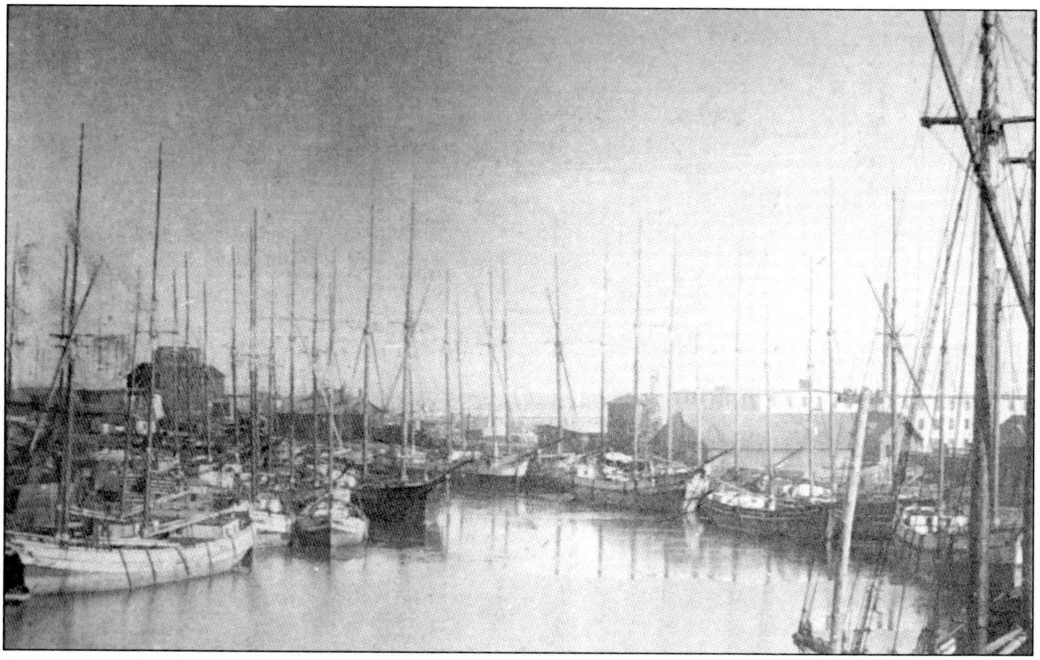

Sixteen lumber boats, most of which were owned by Sheboyganites, are tied up along the docks of the Sheboygan River east of the Eighth Street Bridge in this 1892 image. George Spratt's furniture factory is seen behind the masts at right. The large white building in the rear is the Frost Veneer factory. It was not unusual to have a dozen or more ships outside the harbor waiting for others to leave the docks.

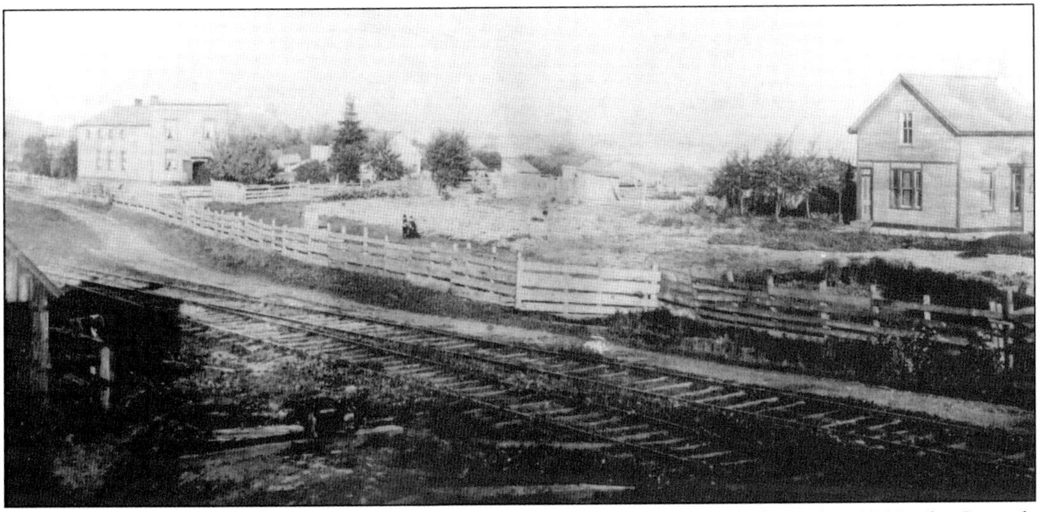

This 1870s view shows the Lake Superior House (left), constructed in the 1840s for Joseph Kirkland. The inn originally was popular with shippers, cattle buyers, and sailors. When storms lashed the big lake, heavy chains were used to anchor it to large posts. The house on the right was erected by Ernst Rosch. The railway track was built by the Sheboygan & Mississippi Railroad while Joseph Kirkland was president.

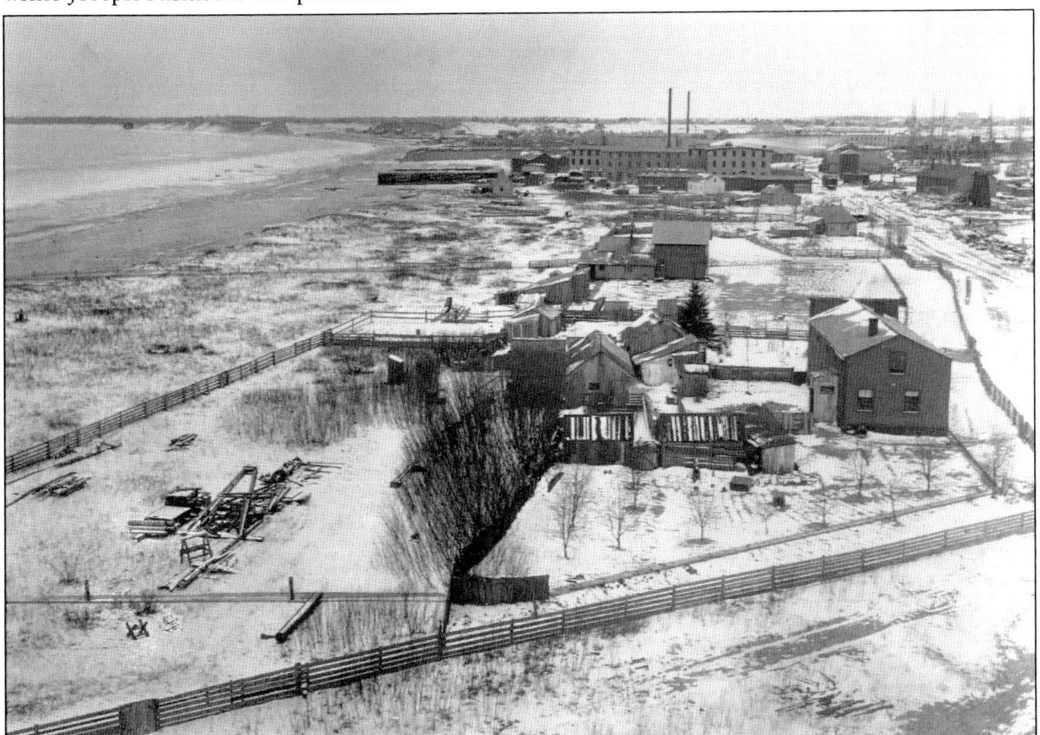

In 1847, the George Groh family settled on the peninsula at the lakefront. Their home is the small building in the center of the photograph. The family operated the Lake Superior House (right), a boardinghouse for sailors. George, a strong man, was once was seen shouldering a barrel of flour from a store on Pennsylvania Avenue, carrying it down the hill and across the old float bridge to his home without a pause or rest.

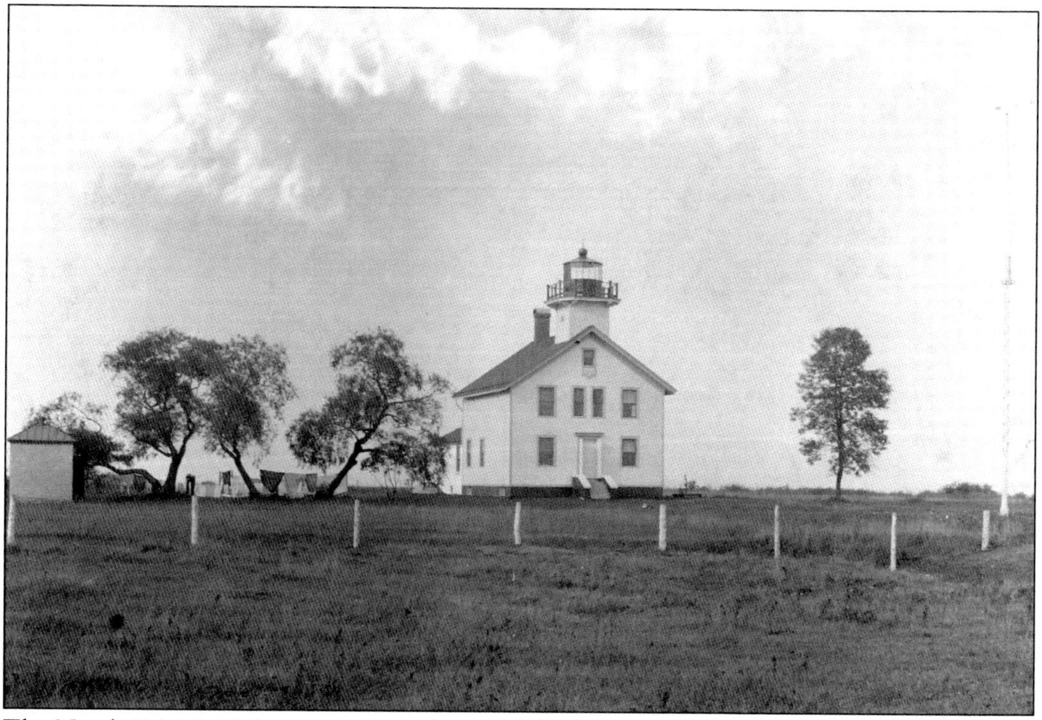

The North Point Lighthouse, seen in this c. 1885 photograph, was the second at Sheboygan. It was built about 1860 and removed from the point around 1905. Instead of guiding vessels to safety, the location of this lighthouse sometimes caused pilots unfamiliar with the shoreline to run their ships aground on the treacherous shoal that extended offshore. For that reason, it was discontinued. The building stands on Lighthouse Court today as a private home.

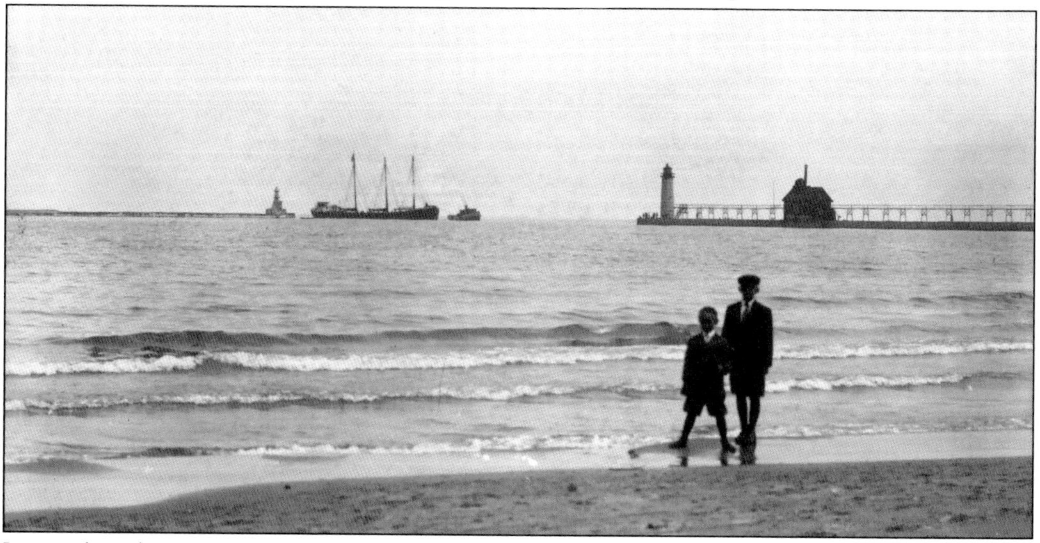

Located at the exact north-south center or midpoint of the western shore of Lake Michigan, the first beacon was installed on North Point in 1832 by the federal government. The first pier, built in 1841, extended from the north bank of the river. This c. 1920 image shows the south pier lighthouse and the north breakwater lighthouse with its cast iron lantern in the dome. A tug guides a three-master into the harbor.

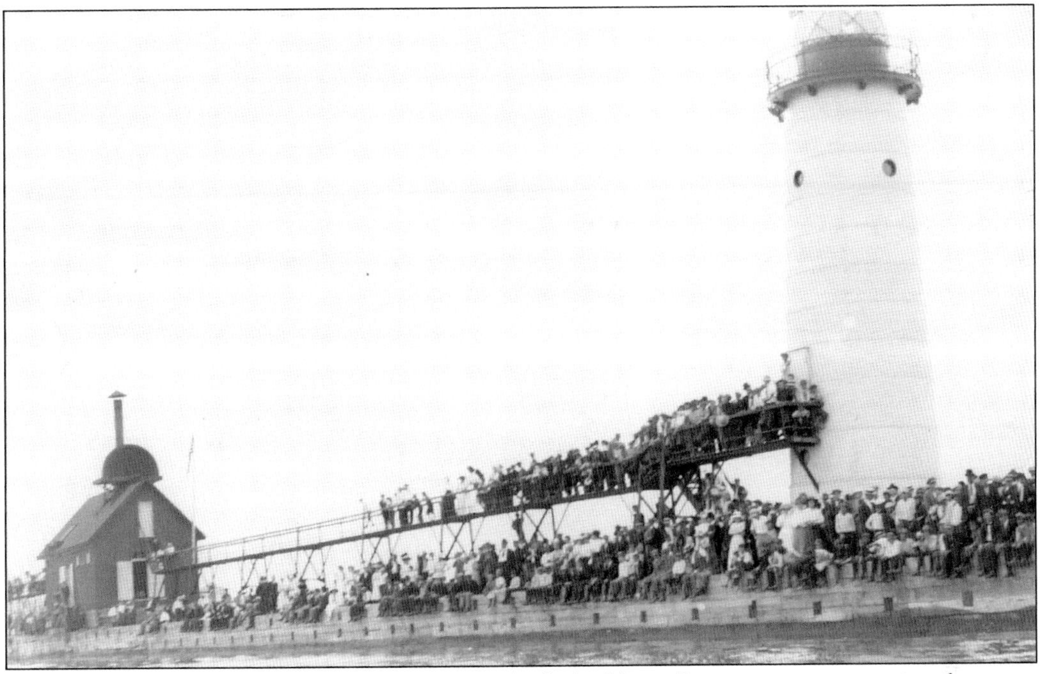

Sheboygan's south pier lighthouse, featuring a high double walkway, was an attraction for many years. The walkway was built for use by the lighthouse keeper, but it was frequently used for fun by youngsters. Seen here in 1914, hundreds of Sheboygan residents swarmed onto the old pier to watch a large fleet of sailing ships en route to Green Bay for a celebration.

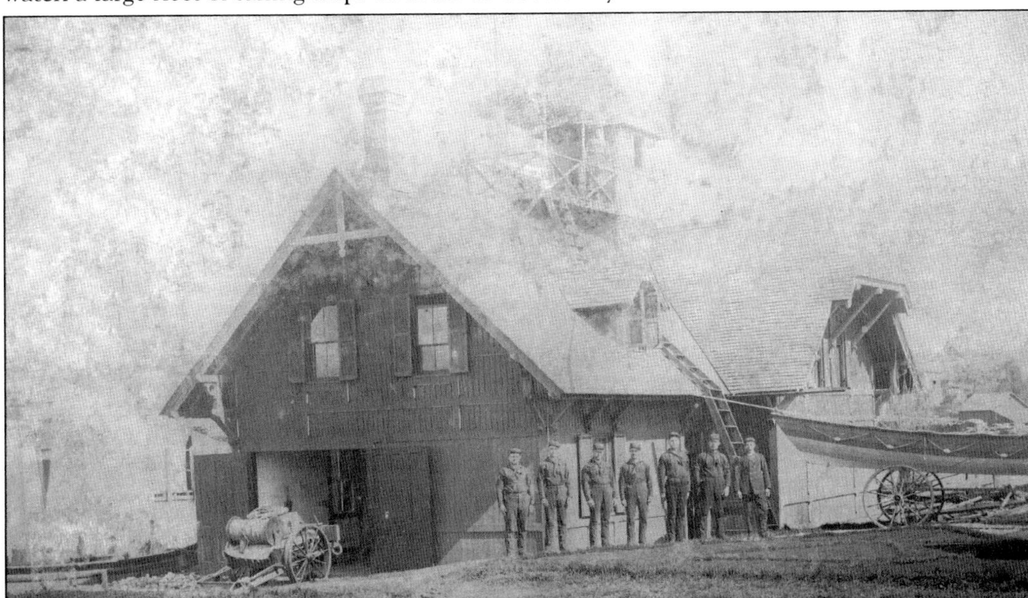

The Revenue Marine and Cutter Service was established in 1874, with Oley Groh as one of its first commanders. This first station was built along the south side of the river, just before the bend. Volunteers manned the station, walking from North Point to Georgia Avenue in search of boats in distress. In 1889, this station was abandoned. The new one was constructed at the mouth of the river.

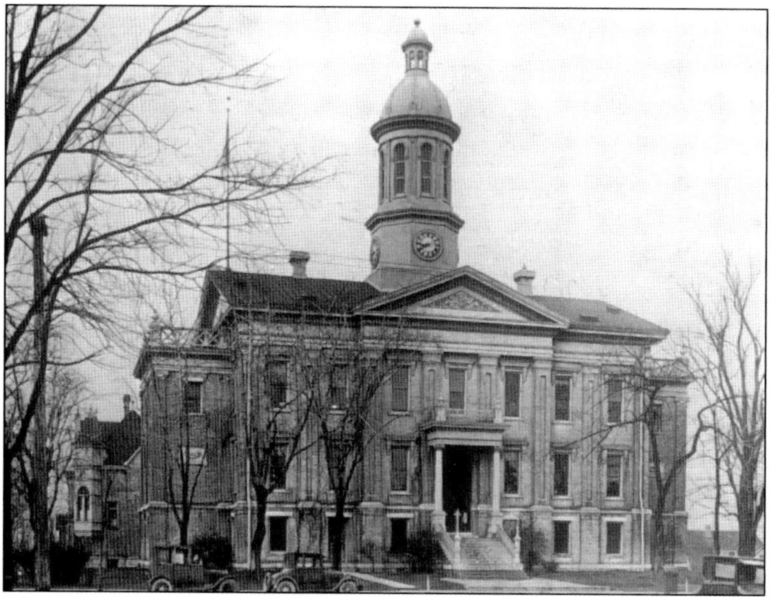

An impressive three-story courthouse was erected between 1866 and 1868 at Sixth Street and Center Avenue. It featured eight chimneys and a stately tower that supported a clock and huge bell used as a fire alarm. This building served the county for the next 65 years until 1933, when a new Art Deco–style building was constructed just north and west of the old site.

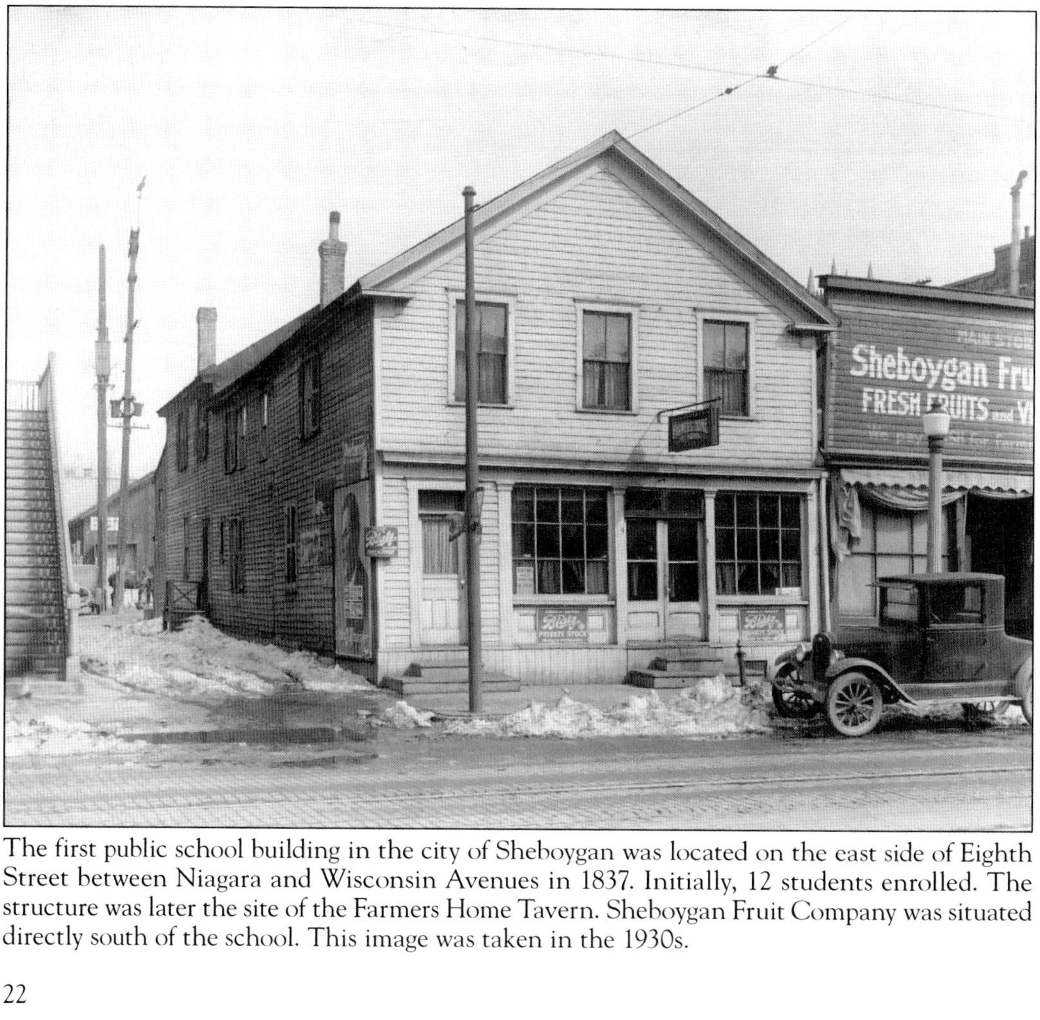

The first public school building in the city of Sheboygan was located on the east side of Eighth Street between Niagara and Wisconsin Avenues in 1837. Initially, 12 students enrolled. The structure was later the site of the Farmers Home Tavern. Sheboygan Fruit Company was situated directly south of the school. This image was taken in the 1930s.

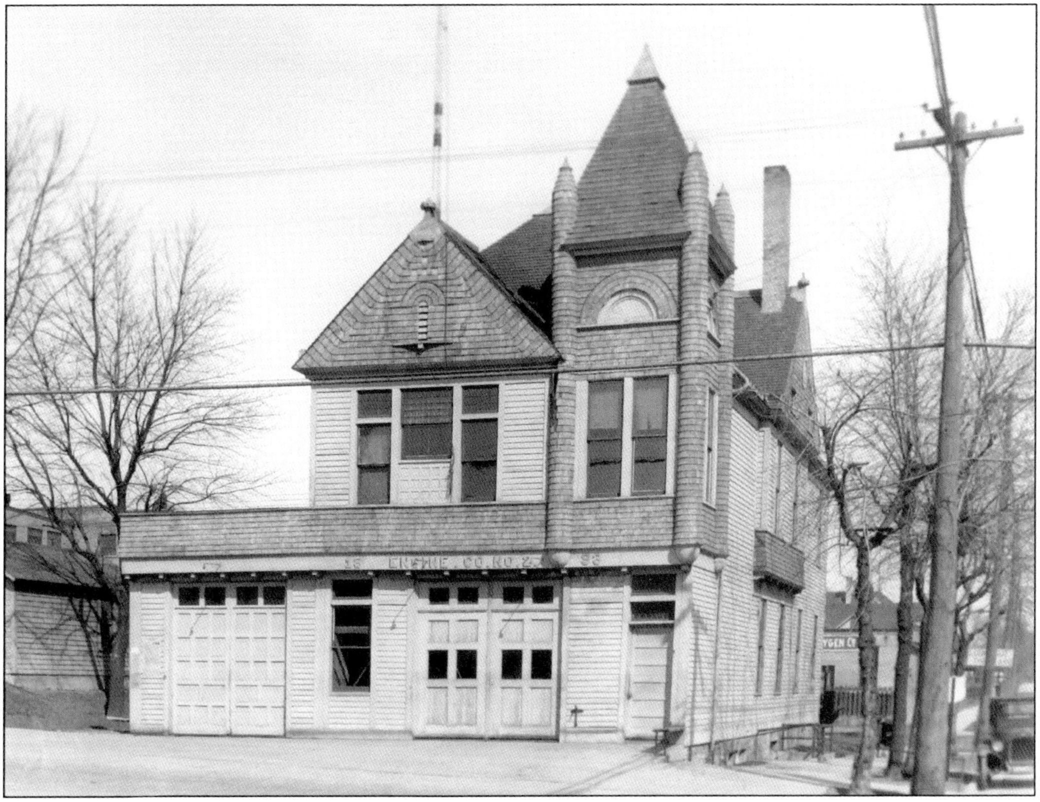

Built in 1883, this fire station, located on the northeast corner of Fourteenth Street and Indiana Avenue, was the home of Engine Company No. 2. This image is dated March 1929. In 1849, the first volunteer engine company was organized. Other companies quickly came into existence, and some of their attention-grabbing names were Deluge, Sherman, Waterwitch, Union, and Protection. While their main purpose was to fight fires, fire companies were also social clubs.

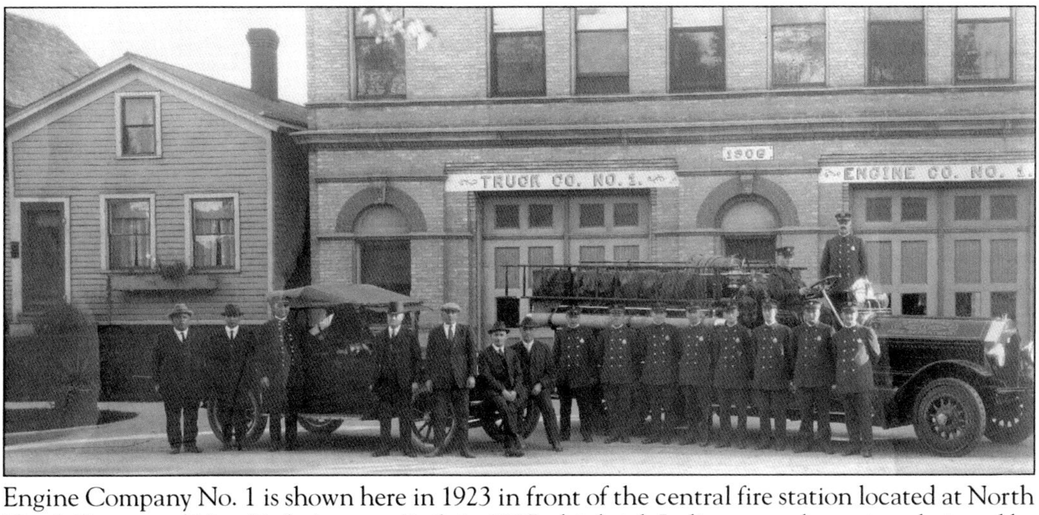

Engine Company No. 1 is shown here in 1923 in front of the central fire station located at North Ninth Street and New York Avenue. Built in 1907, this brick Italianate-style station, designed by Jacob Hilpertshauser, had stalls for horses and grain storage upstairs. The bell tower was later struck by lightning and torn down. The bell had cracked once before in 1909 and had to be repaired.

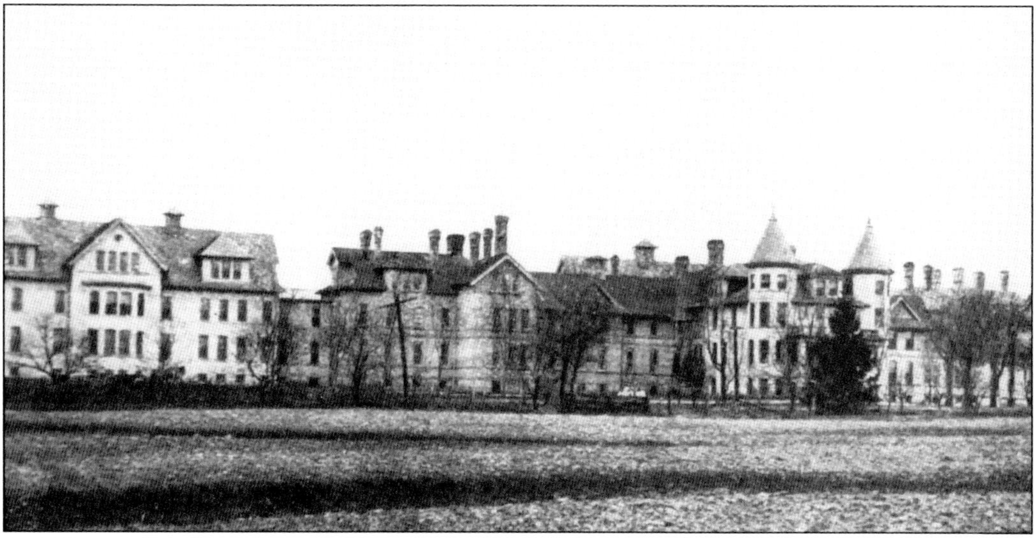

In 1878, a sum of $3,000 was set aside for building an insane asylum. Located in Winooski until a catastrophic fire broke out that killed 4 of the 17 residents, the old county hospital pictured here opened in 1882. It was closed in 1940 and razed in 1960. Located on county grounds just west of Vollrath Company and north of Kohler Memorial Drive, the abandoned building housed a German prisoner of war camp in 1945.

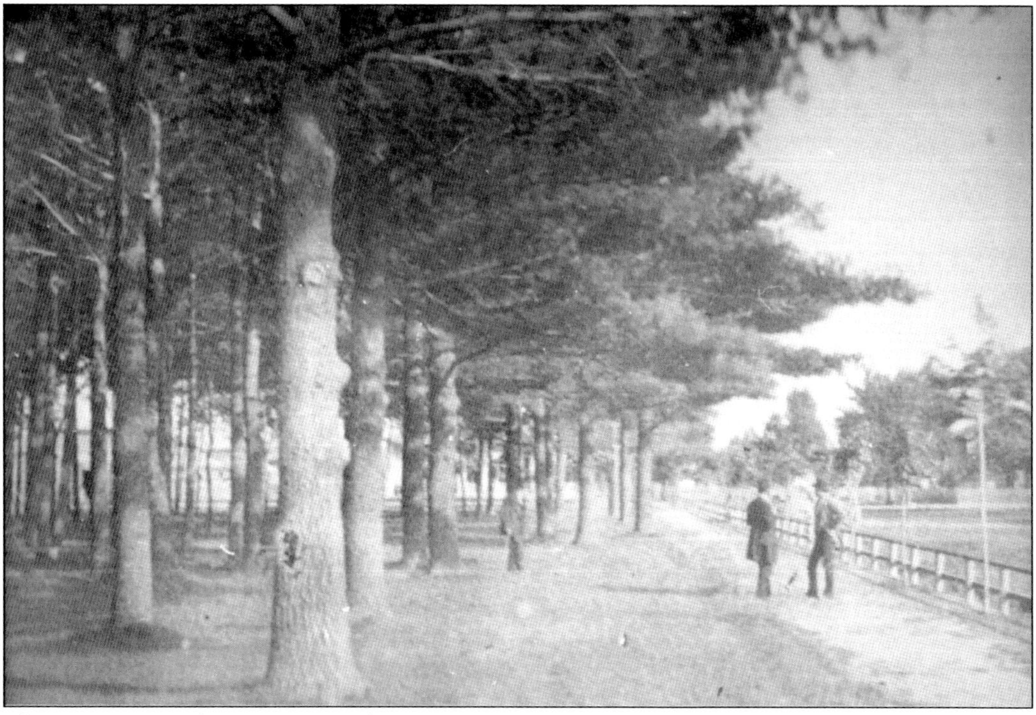

The Fountain Park area was one large pine grove consisting of the tall trees that commanded the attention of early pioneers. No point in the county, it was claimed, could boast of a prettier grove of trees. But the old trees started to show signs of age; dead limbs appeared, and the tops died, leaving nothing by skeletal remains. By 1910, woodchoppers cut down 20 trees, with more slated to go.

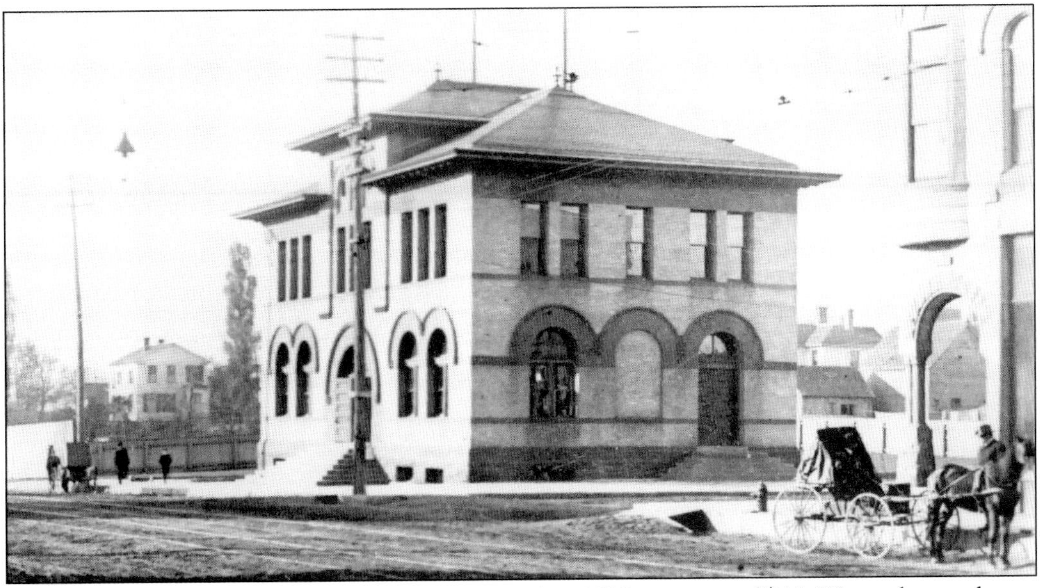

This colorful post office building was constructed in 1892 at a cost of $44,692 on the southwest corner of Jefferson Avenue and North Eighth Street. Often referred to as the old federal building, it remained in service until January 1934, when the present building at Ninth Street and Center Avenue was constructed. The building was used by the public assistance department until it was demolished in 1958.

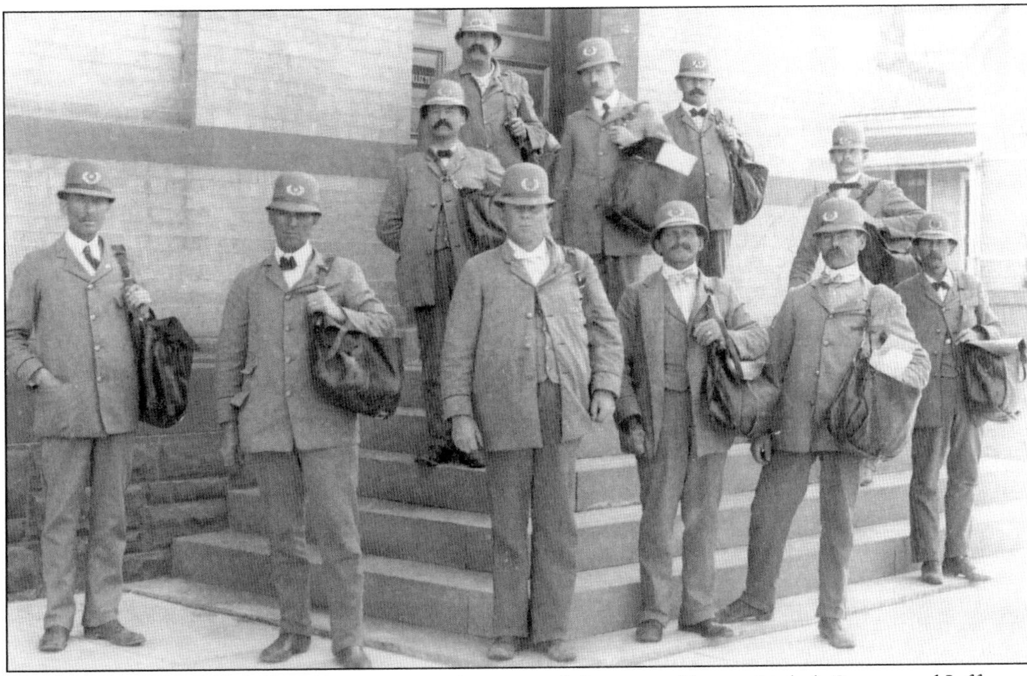

City of Sheboygan postal workers pose on the steps of the post office at Eighth Street and Jefferson Avenue in 1898. The letter carriers pictured from left to right are (first row) Fred Horstbrink, John Bertschy, Dave Merrill, Abe Moser, Al Steffen, and William Brandt; (second row) George Dusold and 77-year-old Ernst Schroeder, a Spanish-American War veteran; (third row) William Schissler, Henry Stein, and William Obigt.

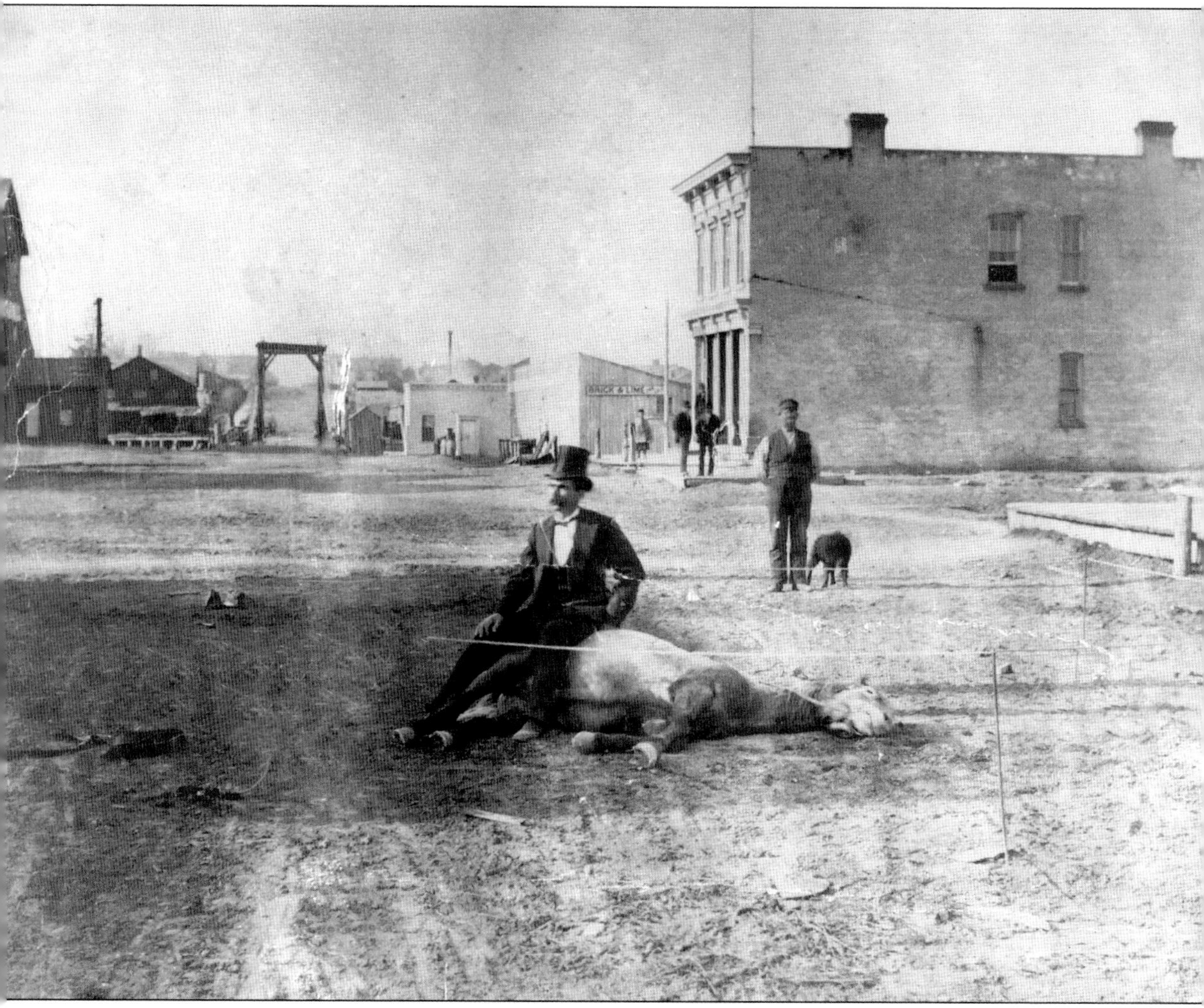

This iconic image was captured at the intersection of Griffith Street (now Eighth Street) and Indiana Avenue sometime around 1870. The photographer is unidentified but may have been George Groh. At the time, Sheboygan had an ordinance that levied a $25 fine for the abandonment of a deceased animal. That fine is nearly $700 today.

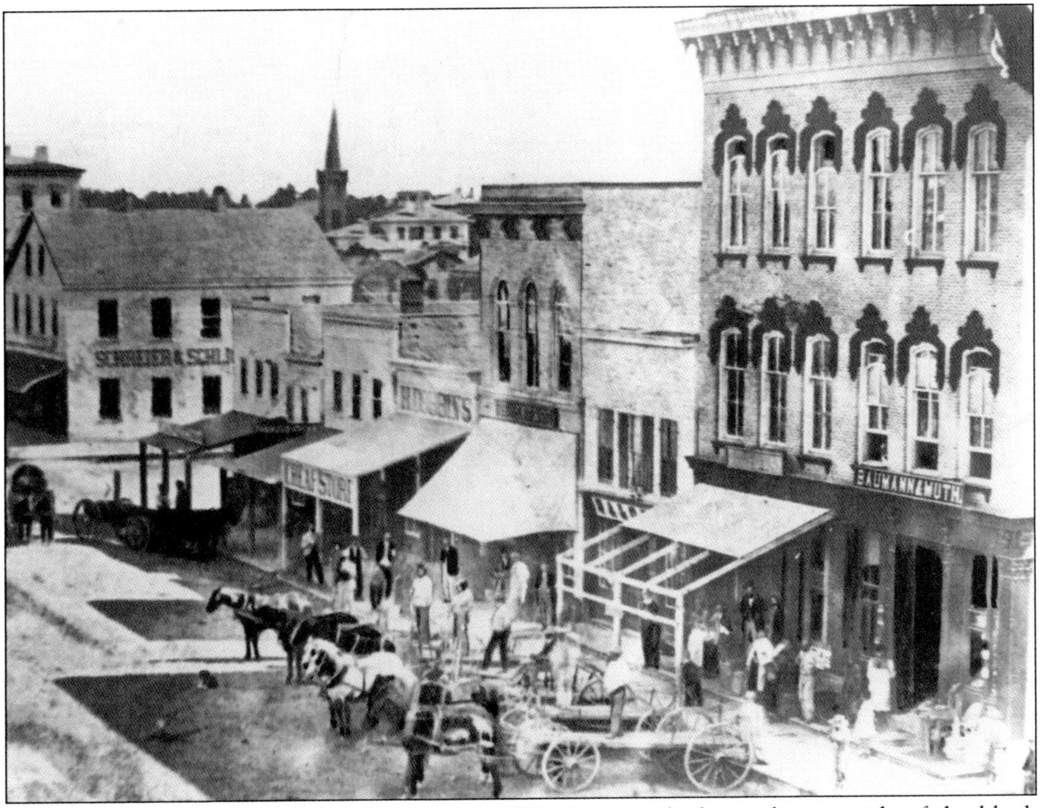

One of the first views of Eighth Street, this 1872 photograph shows the east side of the block between Center and Pennsylvania Avenues. The horse and buggy was the most popular mode of transportation at the time, although the first train entered Sheboygan from Milwaukee that same year. Streetlights were also new features in 1872, as was the appointment of J. Acker as the office courthouse clock tender.

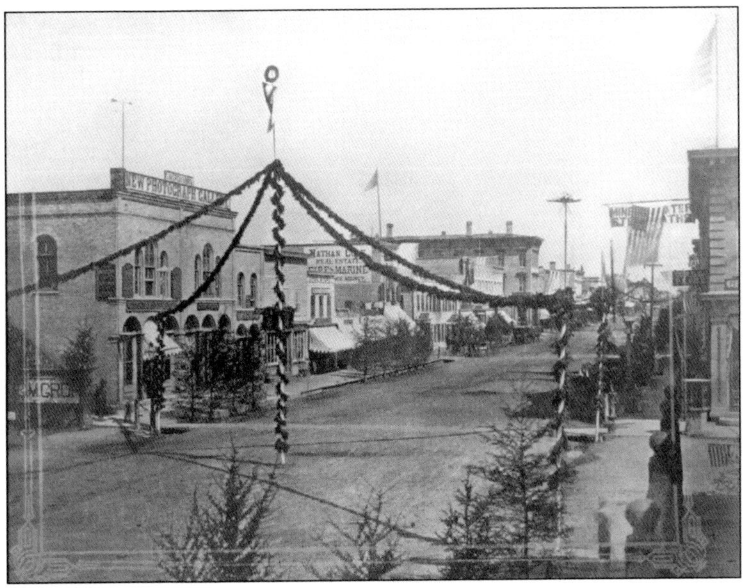

The year 1876 was celebrated all over the United States, including in Sheboygan. Eighth Street was all decked out. On May 10, 1876, all the bells in the city rang for 15 minutes in celebration of the opening of the Centennial Exposition in Philadelphia. This was the first world's fair to be held in the United States. It commemorated the 100th anniversary of the signing of the Declaration of Independence.

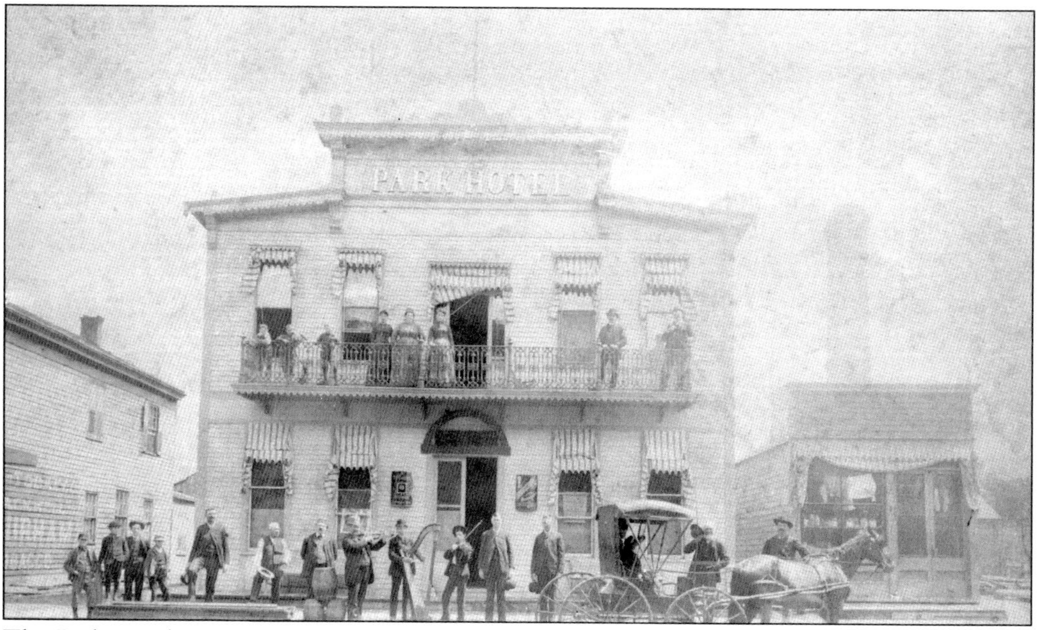

The Park Hotel, operated by Joseph Pheiler, was located on Eighth Street across from today's Fountain Park. Seen here in 1893, a local German band consisting of two violins and a harp poses in front of the establishment for a rare photograph. At left are the three Reichardt boys from Little Rock, Arkansas, and Leo and Leslie Eckhardt from Sheboygan. The hotel burned to the ground in June 1885.

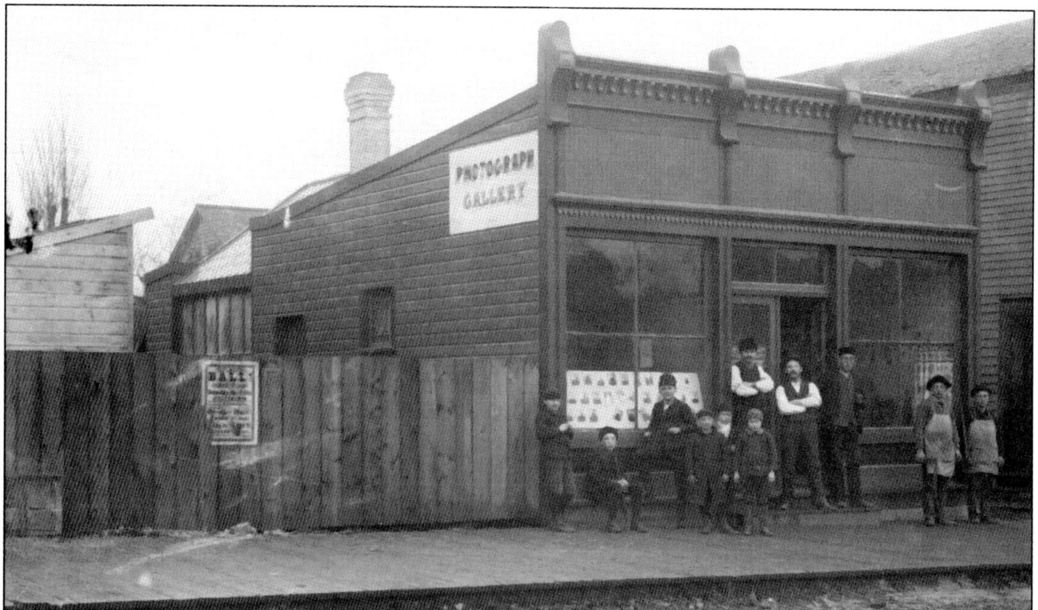

Glaeser Photographic Studio was located at Eighth Street and Jefferson Avenue. This image is dated 1891. Note the slanted panes of glass on the north side of the building, which were designed to provide the photographer with the maximum use of natural light. The poster painted on the board fence advertises a grand ball featuring the Evergreen City Guards. Examples of Glaeser's work are displayed in one of the front windows.

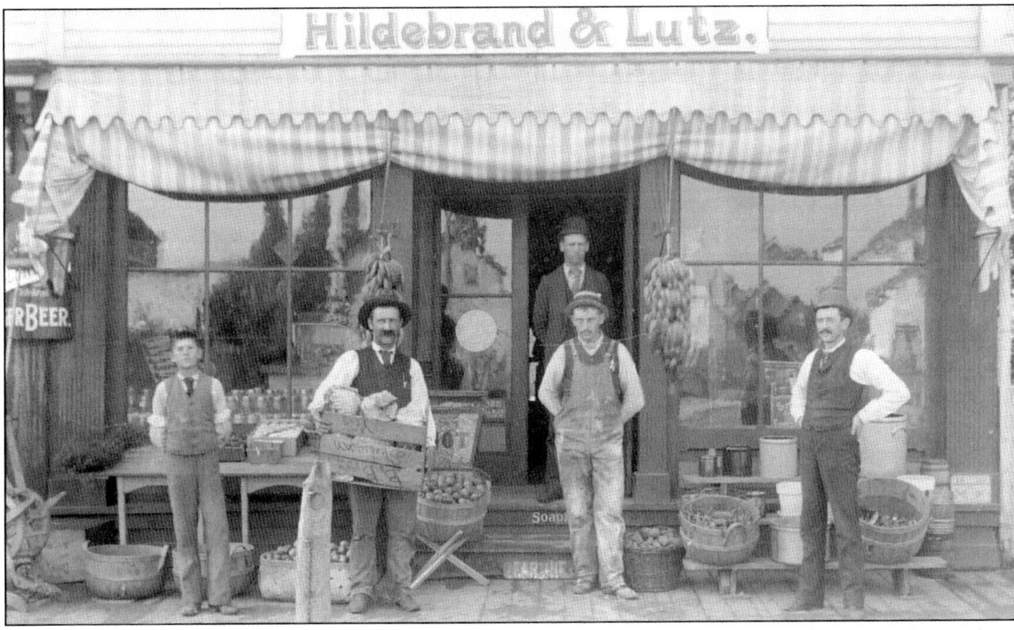

Hildebrand and Lutz Grocery, located at 1015 Michigan Avenue, was in business from about 1888 to 1902. The fresh bananas hanging outside the shop were considered a luxury of the time. Note the "B. Bros., Sheboygan, Wis" on the box of cabbage, the crocks for sauerkraut near the windows, and the fresh, hot roasted peanut machine.

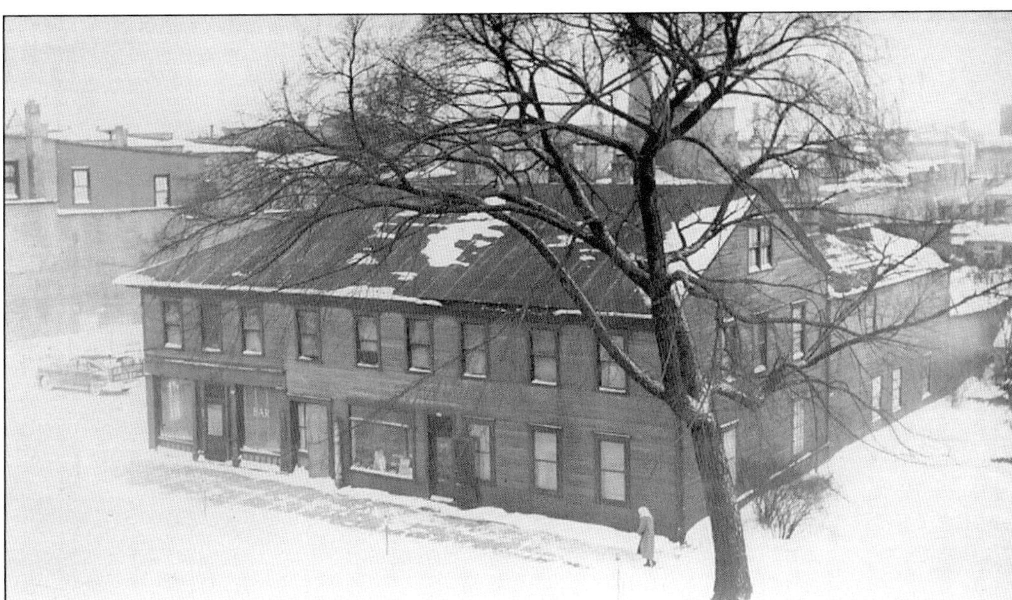

Located on Center Avenue west of Eighth Street, the old Washington House Hotel and boardinghouse stood across the street from today's city hall. Built before 1850, it was one of 11 large hotels constructed on Center Avenue to serve the incoming tide of immigrants. Everyone trudged up the hill from the pier after disembarking the ships. Center Avenue was the main street in 1850, as Eighth Street was not yet developed.

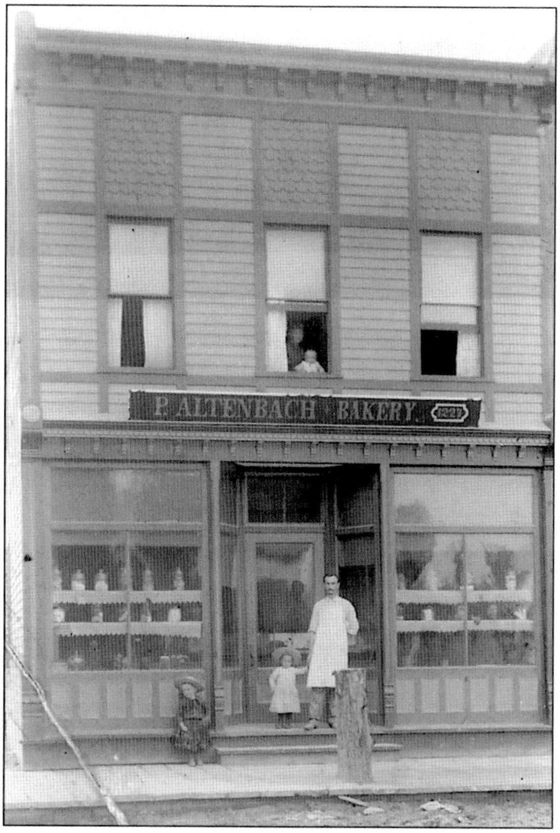

Pius and Ida Altenbach established a bakery at 1227 Superior Avenue. Pius died on January 2, 1895, of Bright's disease at the age of 38. After her husband's death, Ida continued to run the bakery to support their children. On January 24, 1898, she married Kosmos Kistner, who had emigrated from Germany in 1893. Kistner and Ida ran the business together, and the name was changed to Kistner Bakery after their wedding. Pius and two of the Altenbach children are seen here in 1892.

Pictured around 1895 is Fred Muhs with one of Kistner Bakery's horse-drawn delivery wagons. Kistner Bakery was sold in the 1920s to the Sheboygan Bakery Company. Muhs eventually established his own one-oven bakeshop in the rear of his residence on Geele Avenue in 1913.

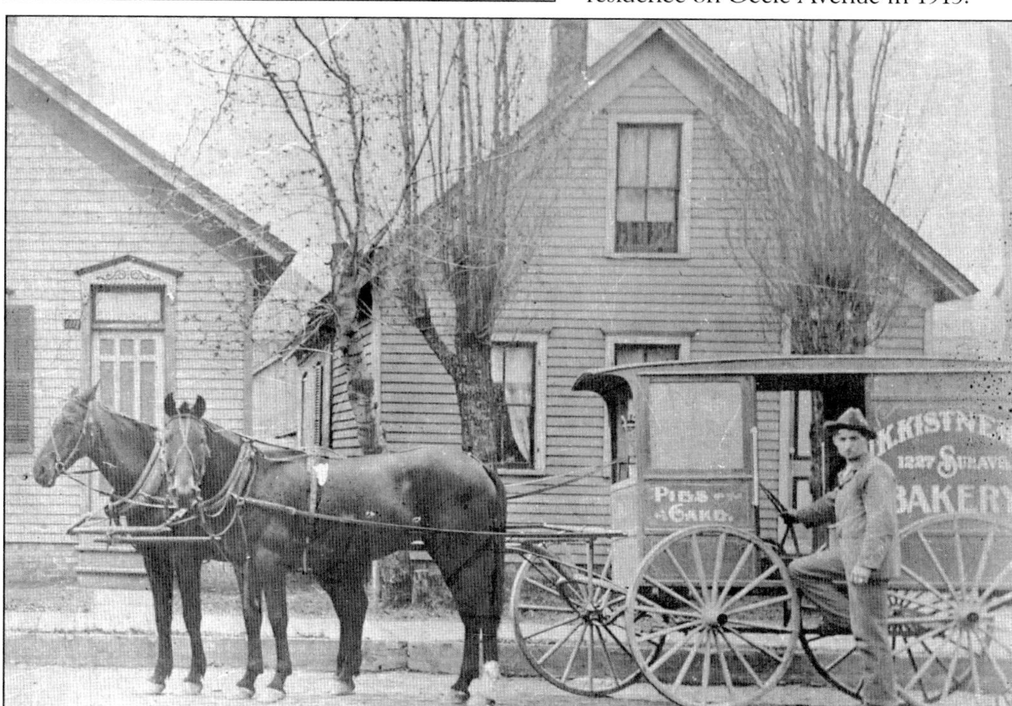

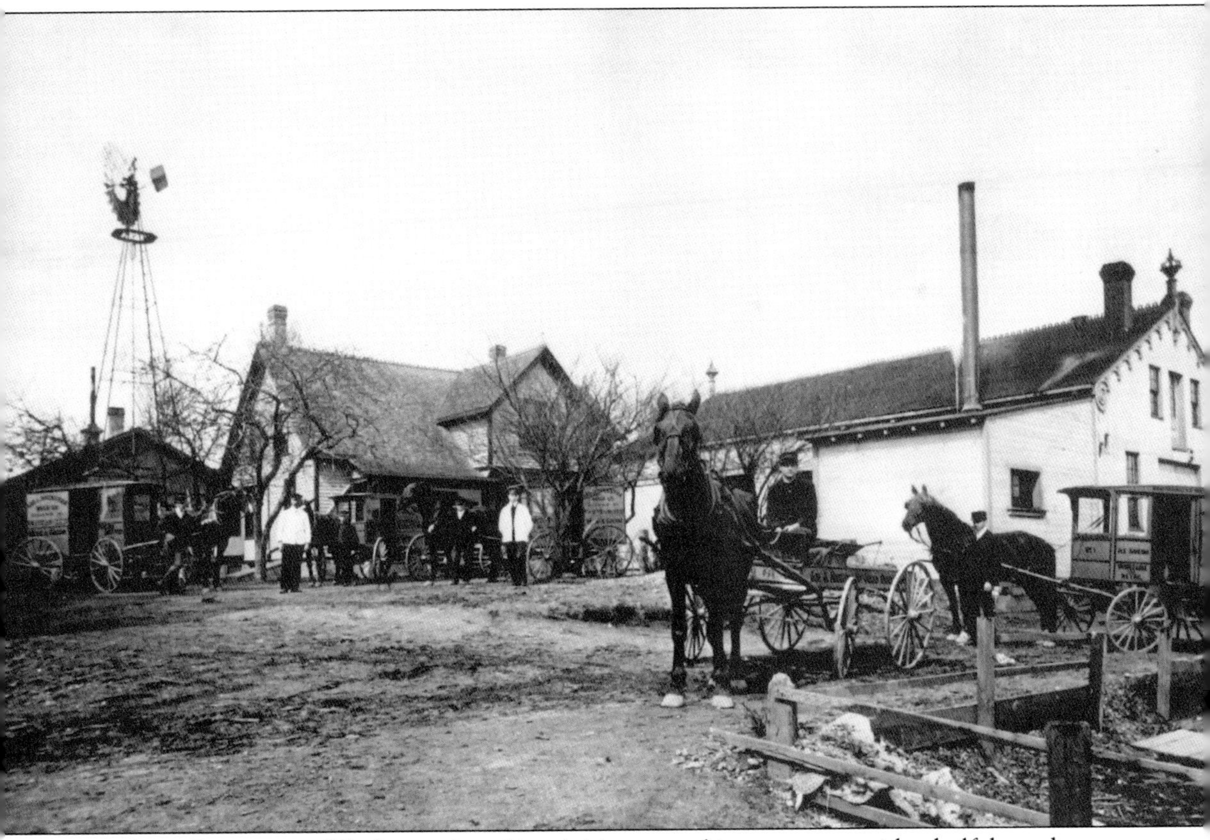

Hoekstra Dairy, one of Sheboygan's earliest dairies, served its customers with a half dozen horse-drawn delivery wagons beginning about 1895. Located on the west side of North Eleventh Street between Erie and St. Clair Avenues, George Hoekstra began his business when bottled milk was unheard of. Milk was delivered in bulk in 5- and 10-gallon cans, transferred from there into 2-gallon cans with a pouring spout, and then transferred to quarts, which were emptied directly into the customer's container. Some of the excess milk was made into cottage cheese, but the rest was given away to farmers for hog feed. The windmill, seen in the background of the photograph, provided all the power necessary for operations.

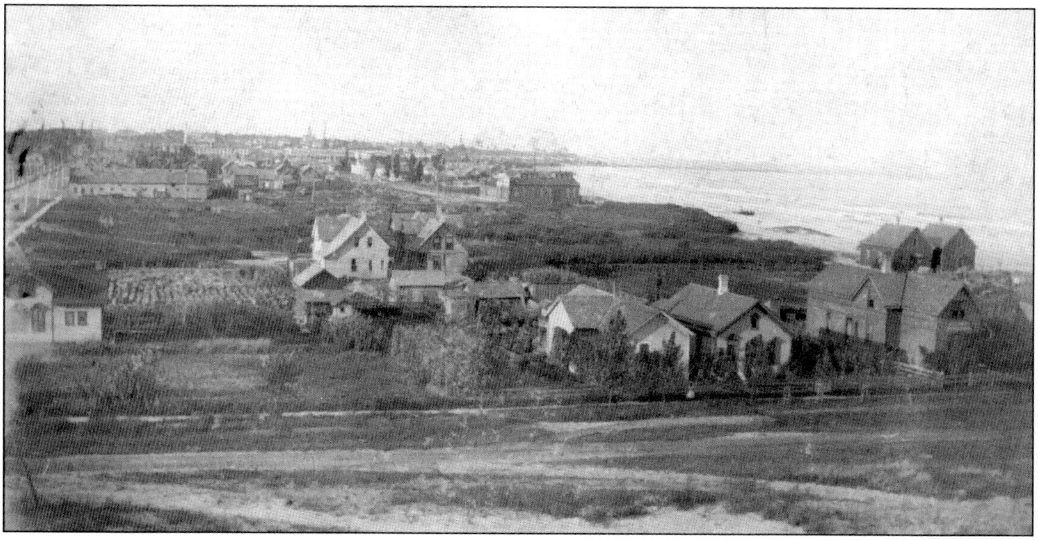

Optenberg Iron Works, seen at right center (above), was located at South Seventh and Clara Streets along the Lake Michigan shore. Established in 1893 by John Henry Optenberg, the company was a mainstay in Sheboygan's manufacturing for more than 100 years. Optenberg was recruited by David Jenkins of Jenkins Machine to come to Sheboygan from New Holstein. Optenberg Iron Works found its niche as a contractor for power and heating plants creating specialty boilers. As cheese factories spread throughout the state, the need for boilers, tanks, and smokestacks grew. During the Depression, the firm moved into the steel fabrication business, transitioning from the use of rivets to welding. The company fabricated deck sections and hatches for landing craft involved in the invasions of Africa and Sicily.

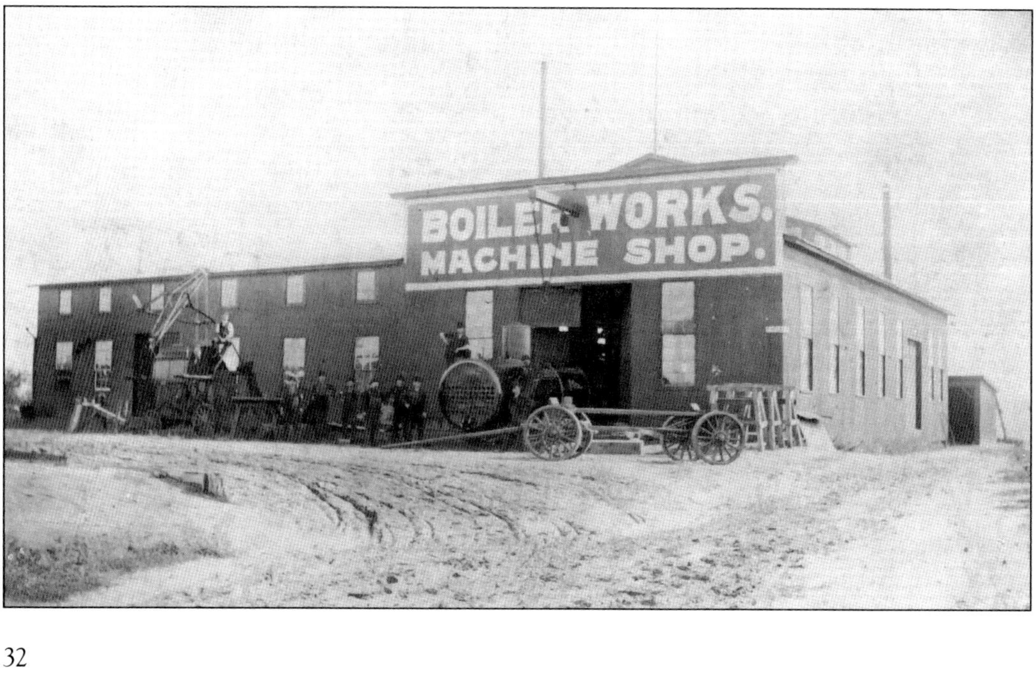

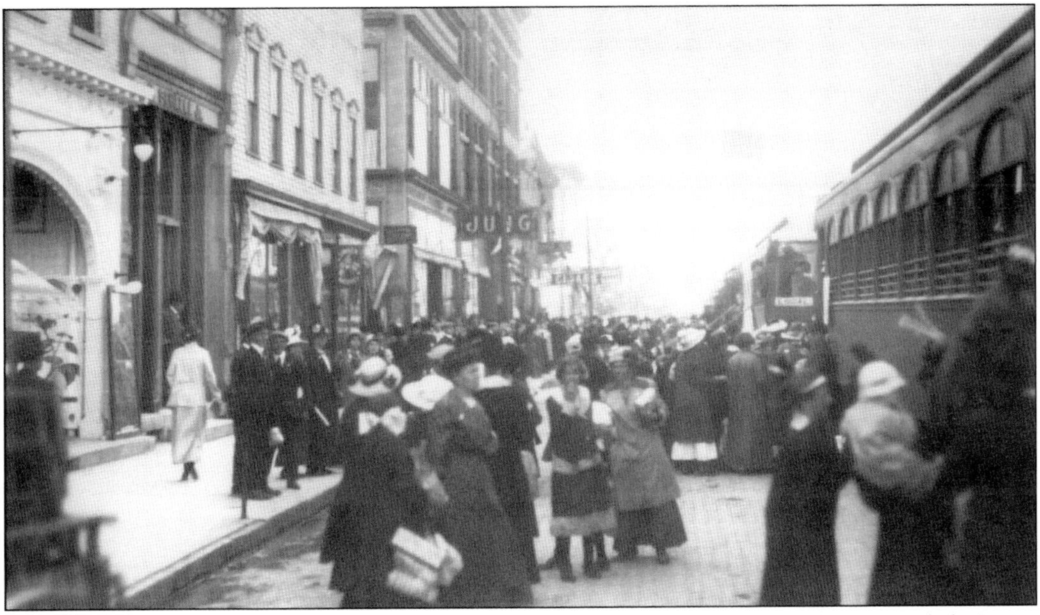

Sheboygan buzzed with people and streetcars in this c. 1910 photograph taken at Eighth Street and Wisconsin Avenue. Pictured to the left is Scheele Monument Company, and farther north is the Jung Department Store.

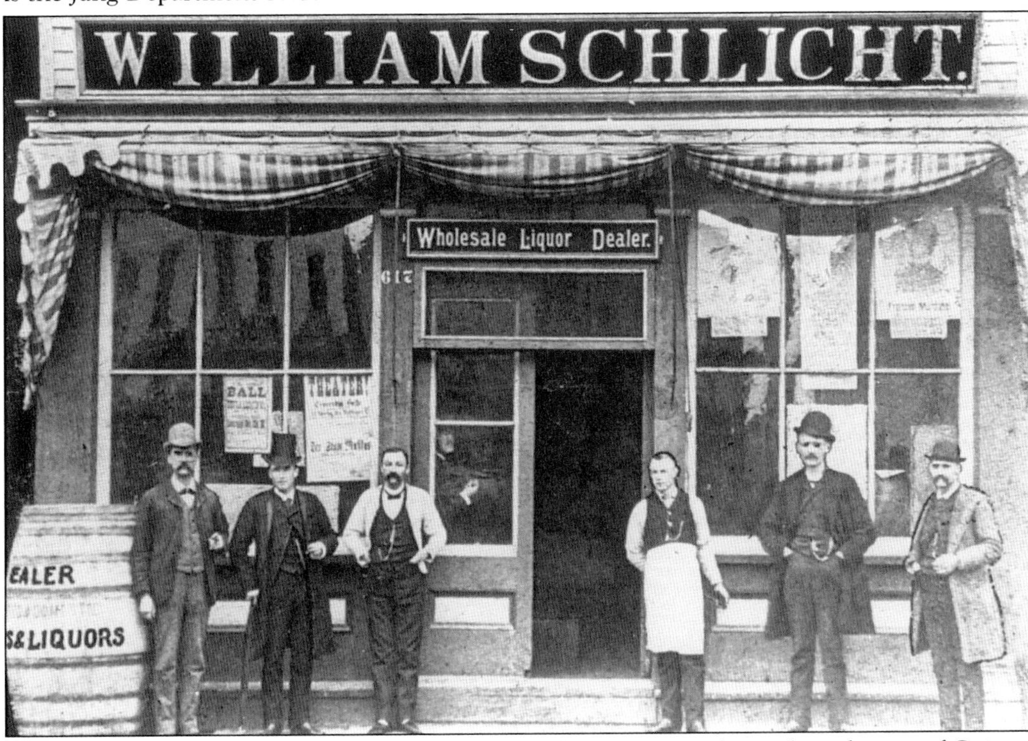

The William Schlicht wholesale liquor store and saloon was once located on the site of Citizens State Bank at 617 Eighth Street, situated between Center and New York Avenues. Schlicht was one of the city's earliest businessmen, opening his establishment in 1861. Schlicht retired from business in 1896. Born in Germantown, Washington County, Wisconsin, in 1851, he died in 1908.

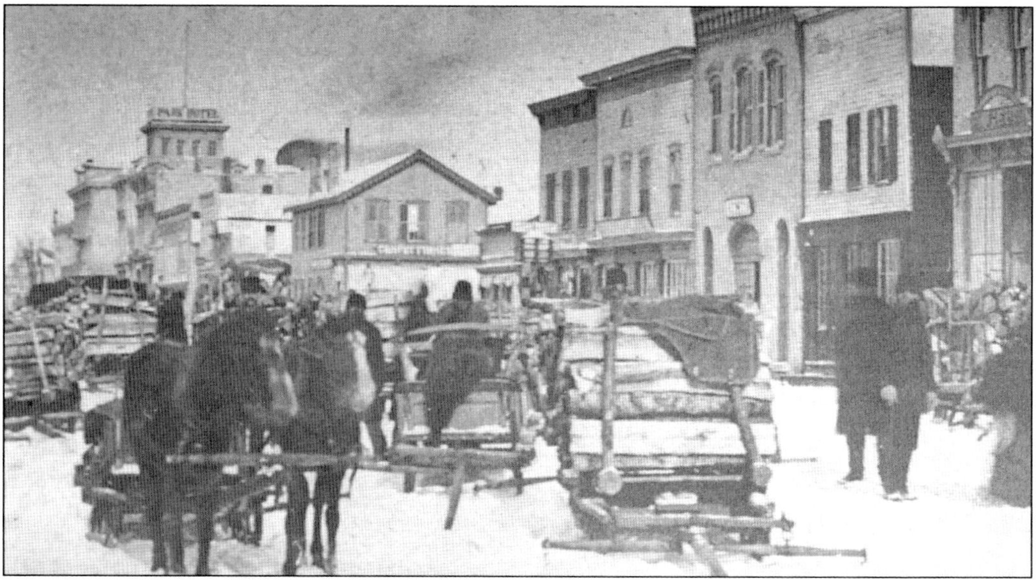

Wood auctions were commonplace during the early days of Sheboygan. Wood was used for heat, cooking, manufacturing, and much more. This image was captured during an auction that took place on Eighth Street near the Park Hotel and across from Fountain Park sometime prior to 1885. Farmers brought cords of wood via cutters and sleighs to these winter sales. A cord of wood sold for about $2.50 in 1880.

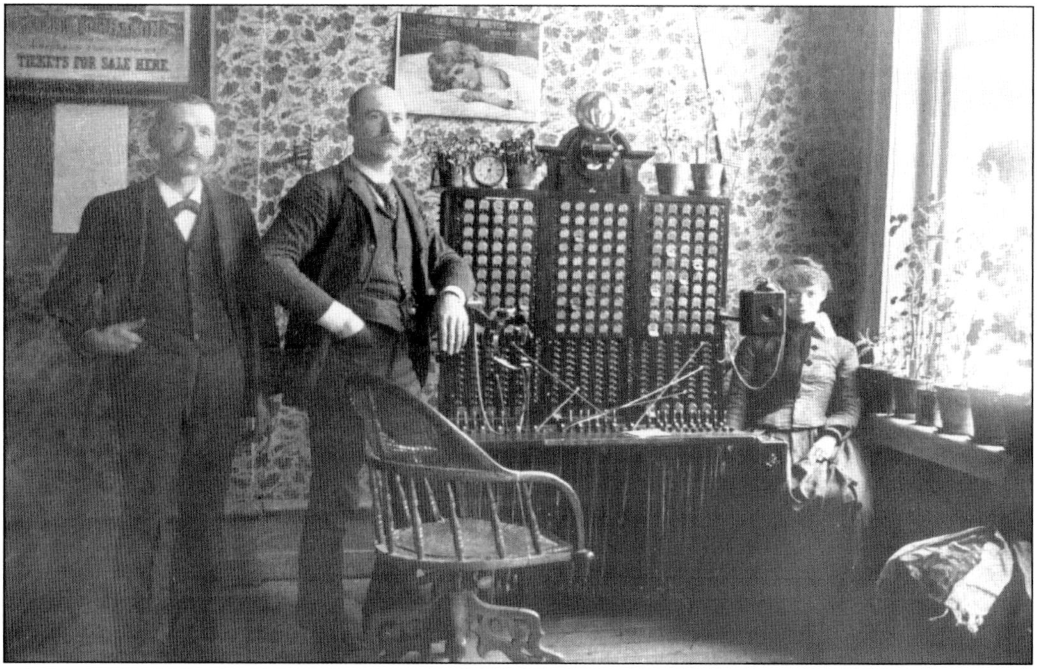

The first telephones in the city were installed in June 1881 after permission was granted to the C.H. Haskins Company to set poles and string wires. Sheboygan's first switchboard and telephone service did not get started until 1890. The Bell Telephone Company office at Pennsylvania Avenue and Eighth Street is seen here with lineman George Best (left) and manager Ed Farrell (center). The night operator at right is unidentified.

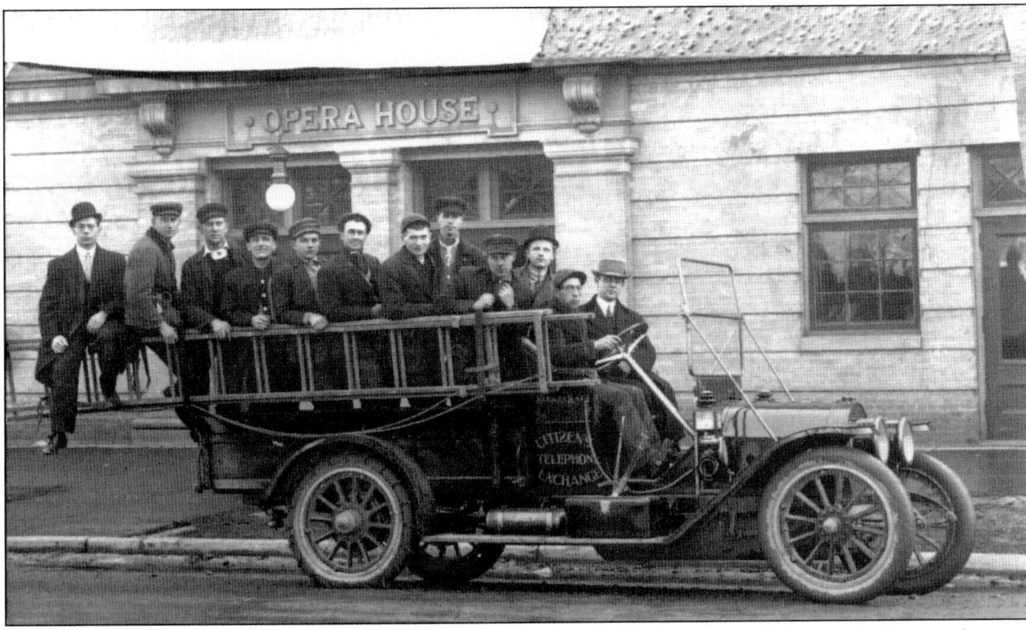

Parked in front of the old Opera House, located at New York Avenue and Seventh Street, the new Citizens Telephone Exchange Kissel Kar is filled with employees of the company. Kissel, with its motto, "Every Inch A Car," produced custom built high-quality automobiles, hearses, fire trucks, taxicabs, and utility vehicles in Hartford, Wisconsin, from 1906 to 1930.

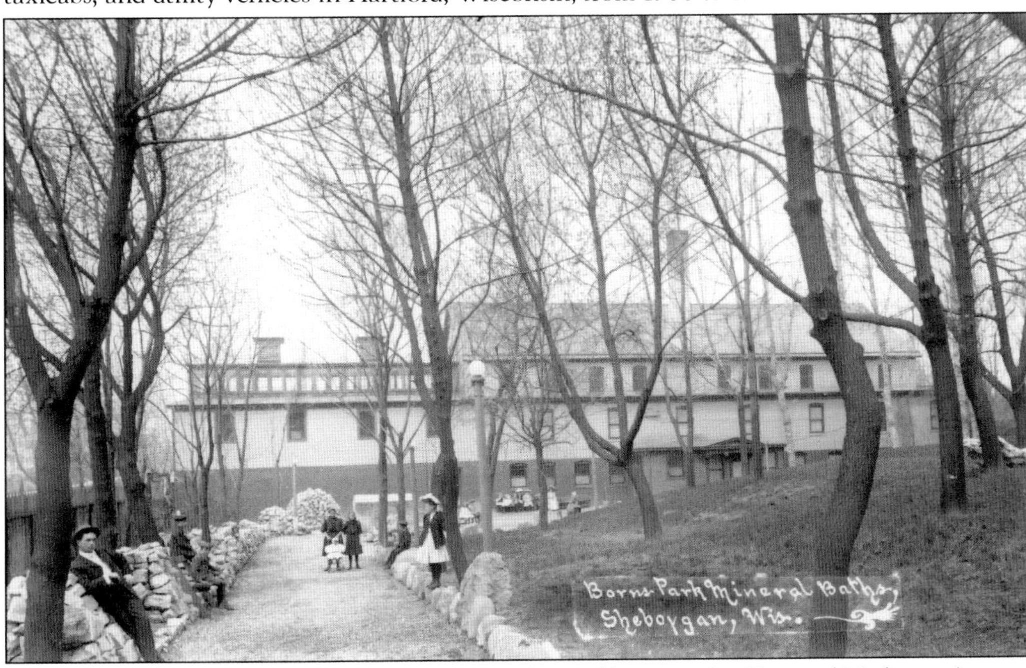

Born's Park, built in 1882 by Charles A. Born, was located between St. Clair and Michigan Avenues and Fourteenth and Fifteenth Streets. At various times, it served as a spa, natatorium, sanitarium, influenza hospital, roller rink, and monster dance hall. The business closed on February 22, 1920, but the property was not sold until 1927. The swimming pool was removed, but the building remained and became the Ninety-Nine Hall, which burned in 1988.

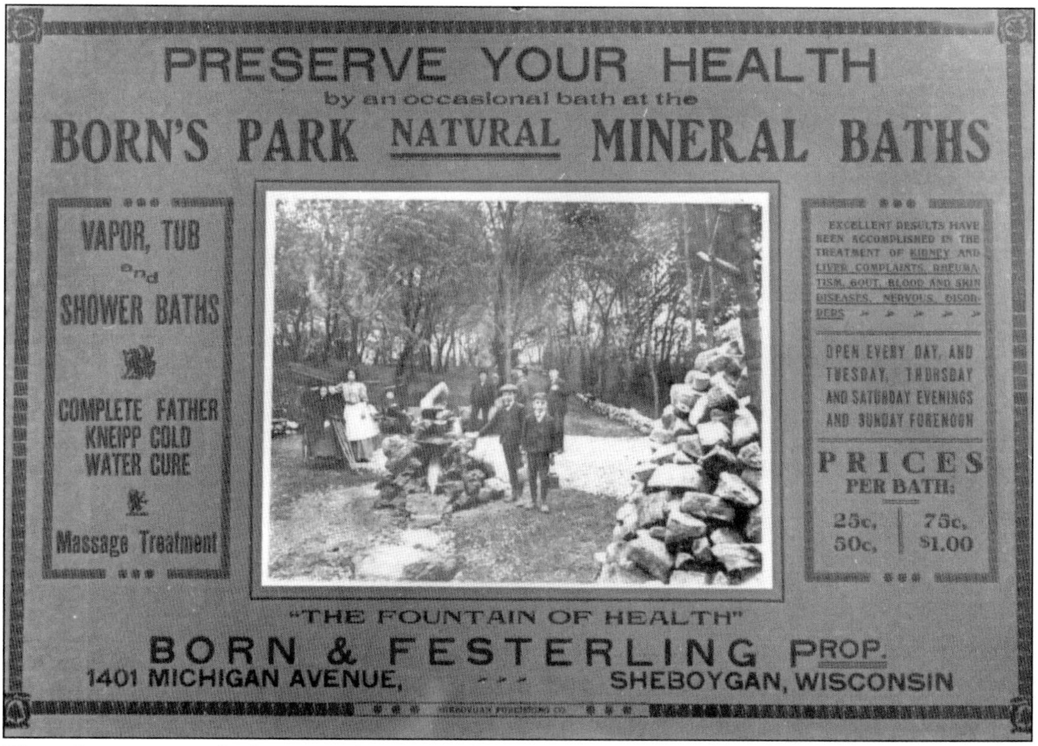

This advertisement for Born's Park promoted a time when Alfred Hotz, a graduate of the Bernard McFadden Physical Culture Institute in Battle Creek, Michigan, took over and operated the Turkish baths and massage. He was also the caretaker of the huge building and swimming pool filled with mineral water. Along with all the health programs, a band played on Sunday afternoons for the public to promote relaxation.

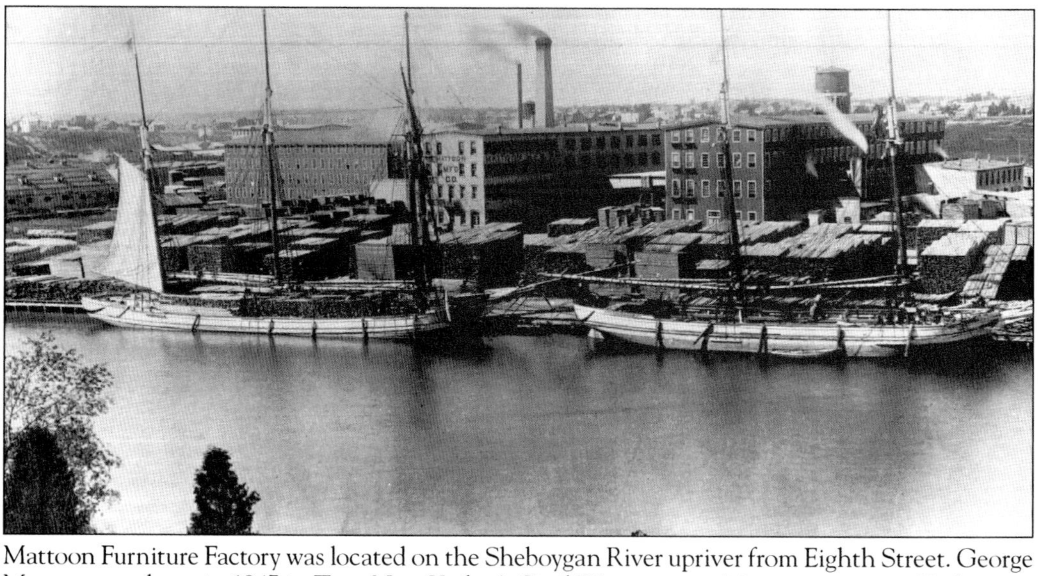

Mattoon Furniture Factory was located on the Sheboygan River upriver from Eighth Street. George Mattoon was born in 1847 in Troy, New York. A Civil War veteran, Mattoon came to Sheboygan in 1865, and in 1881, he established Mattoon Furniture with 15 workers on the north side of the river. In 1883, he moved operations across the river and built his large, successful business.

Three

Saloons and Public Houses

Saloons were welcoming places where sheepshead, skat, and cribbage were played as men talked over the problems of the day. Filled with the smells of cigar smoke and chewing tobacco, saloons were places where "a shot and a beer" was considered a mixed drink. The first saloon license in Sheboygan was issued in 1846 to Kelly Gutsch, kicking off a long and illustrious history of spirit production and consumption in the city. Sheboygan has had too many watering holes to count. One statistic said that in 1885, Sheboygan had 12,000 citizens and 390 saloons; that is one tavern for every 31 residents. It was once said that Indiana Avenue had so many taverns, it was virtually impossible to have just one drink at each establishment on the street. The bar trade kept the city government busy creating regulations to hold it in check. In August 1914, John Supuscuck, a saloonkeeper at 1211 North Ninth Street, was the first proprietor prosecuted under a new ordinance prohibiting music in saloons on Sunday mornings. He was fined $5. Also in 1914, the city council found fit to prohibit newcomers to Sheboygan from operating a saloon, as well as prevent breweries from controlling saloons conducted by private persons. No one was to be granted a saloon license unless they were a bona fide resident of the city for at least one year. In 1917, the common council adopted an ordinance prohibiting free lunches in places licensed to sell liquor. Up until 1933, drinking establishments were called saloons, but as part of the 18th Amendment, when Prohibition ended, President Roosevelt interestingly insisted that they be called taverns, and ordinances were put in place to prohibit the use of such. Whatever they are called—saloons, bars, taverns, or public houses—they are part of Sheboygan's charm.

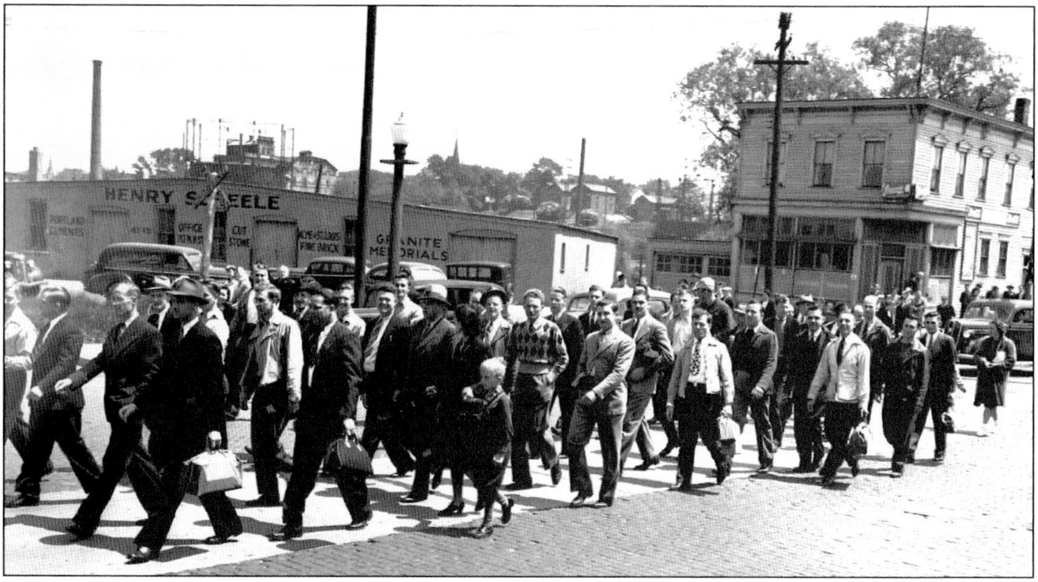

Suscha's Superbar (pictured at right, behind the men) opened in 1921. Besides being a good place to enjoy a cold beer, at one time it was also a place to buy rods, reels, and bait because of its location on the Sheboygan River at Pennsylvania Avenue. Leonard "Kelly" Gutsch, whose family established the second brewery in Wisconsin, started a bar in this building as early as 1846. Young men are seen leaving for war in this 1940s image.

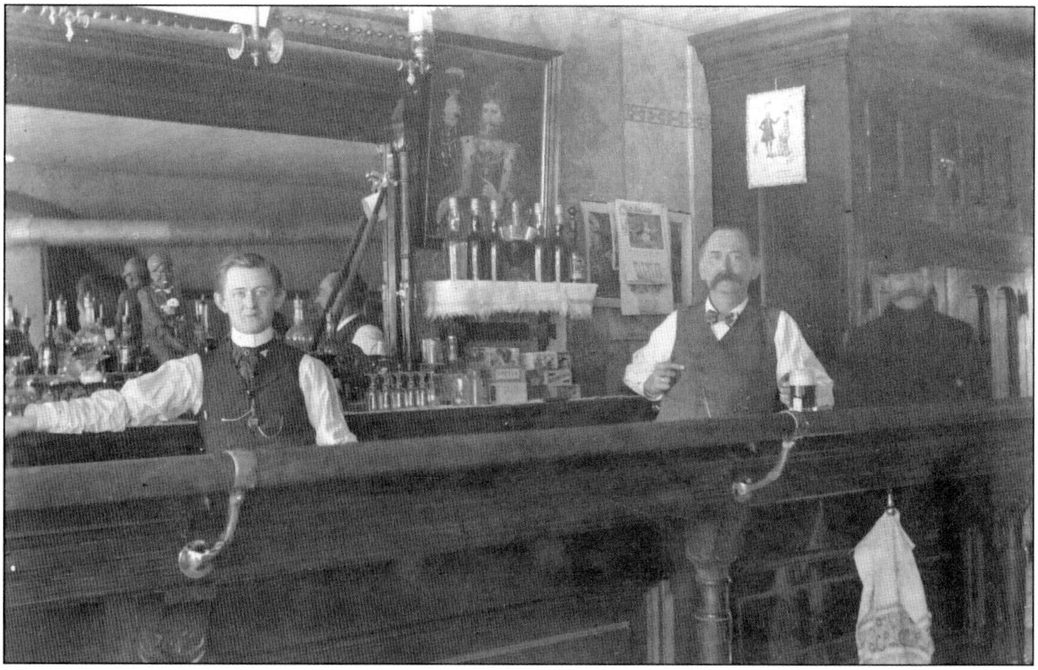

The T.L. Diestelhorst Saloon, located at 811–815 North Eighth Street, sported billiard tables, liquor, and cigars, as well as A-One Lager, which was always on draft in 1889. Bowling alleys were a drawing card, even to minors that Diestelhorst had to sometimes *raus* out of his establishment. The saloon also was advertised as an *ausspannung*, or farmer's home. Today, those addresses are home to a real estate office, a salon, and a jewelry store.

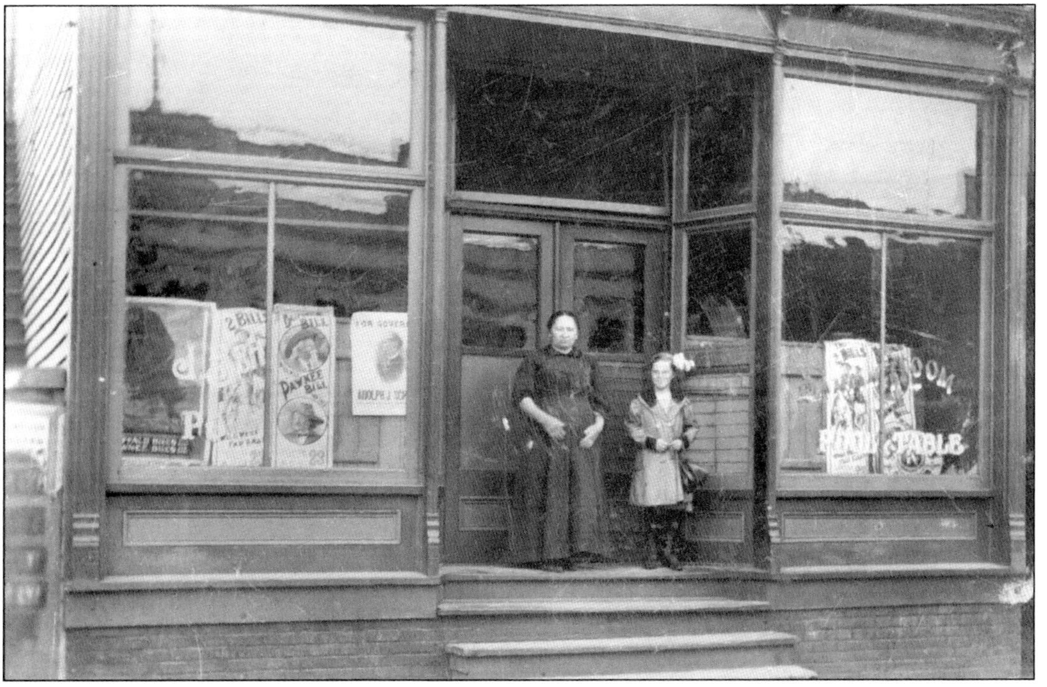

John Behrens operated the Badger State House and Slovenski Saloon at 827 Indiana Avenue, now the site of an empty lot. Besides owning the saloon and boardinghouse, he operated a grocery.

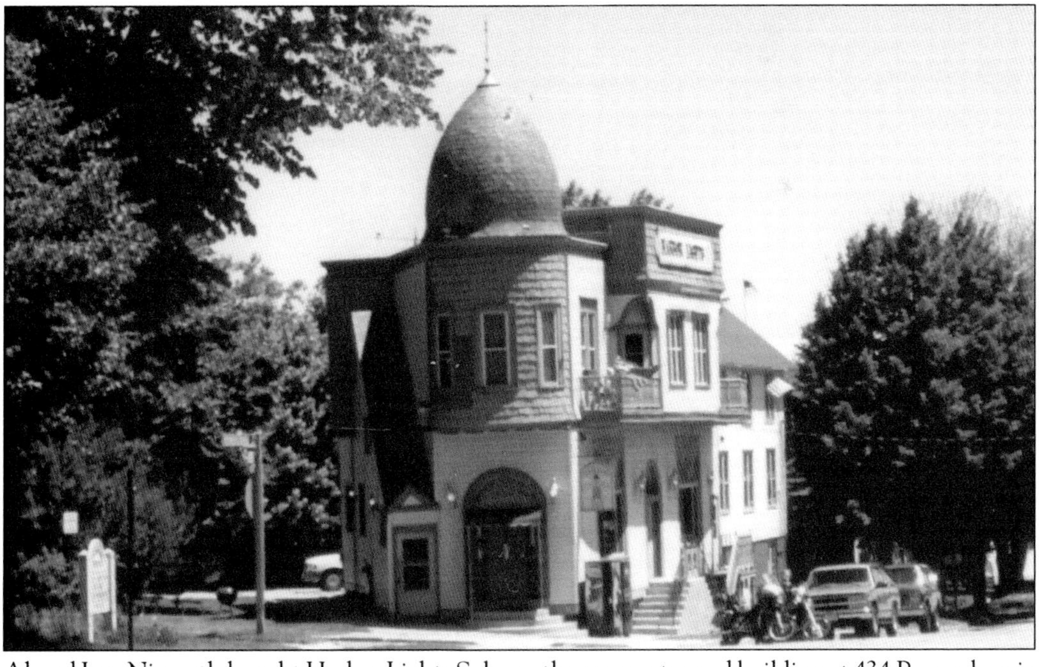

Al and Lou Niemuth bought Harbor Lights Saloon, the copper-topped building at 434 Pennsylvania Avenue, in 1975. They oversaw a major refurbishing project in 1994. Earlier owners were August Weyland, William Mueller, and John Sebanz. Peter Dinkel erected the building in 1892. This saloon was opened as the Columbia Landing Saloon, which catered to sailors who roomed next door at the Bay View House.

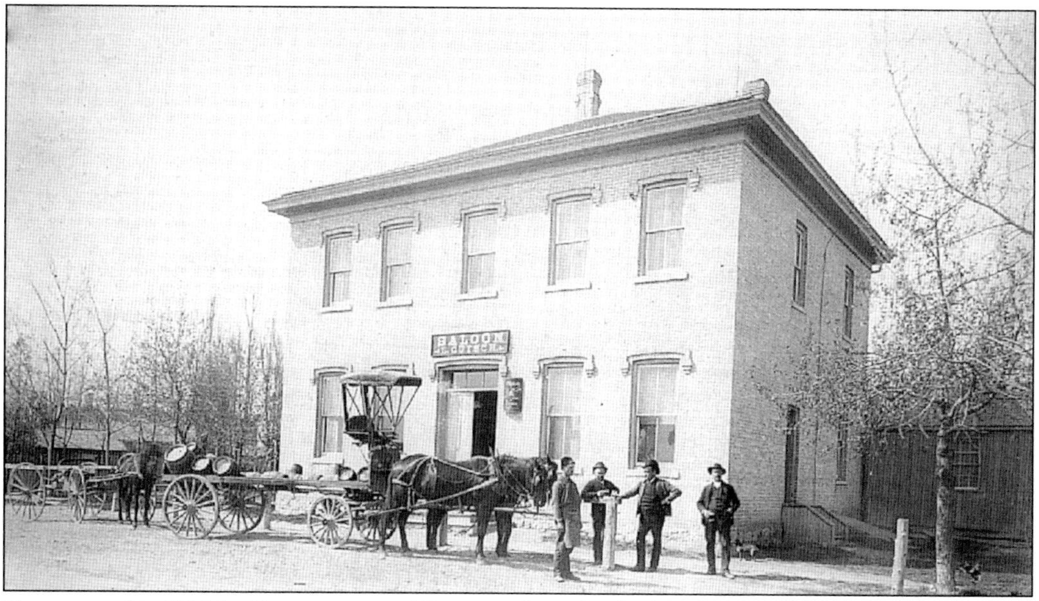

Constructed in 1891 by German native Christian Gier, this building was called Waldschloessechen, which translates to "Little Castle in the Forest," and offered rooms for rent. During Prohibition, it operated as a soda fountain. Later, the structure housed the Anton Stanskas Tavern, the Band Box Tavern, and finally, Calumet Hall. In its heyday, Calumet Hall was a popular site for weddings, roller-skating parties, and vaudeville shows.

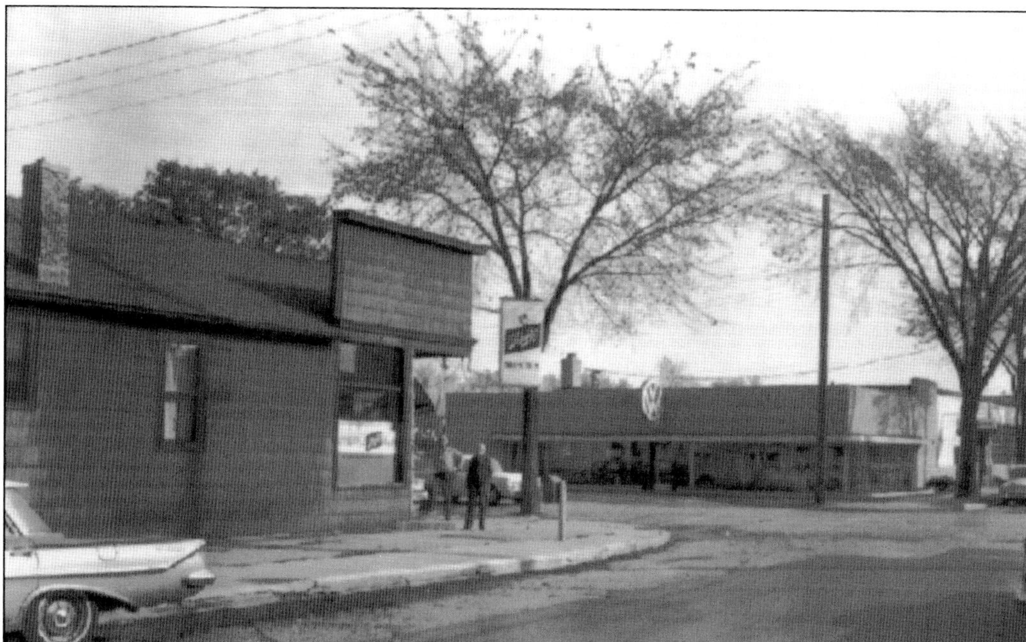

Back in 1922, when the streetcar barns were located where Motorville Auto Company used to be, Fred Mueller served soft drinks at Eighth Street and Clara Avenue. Frank J. Timm and William Krapnick were the next owners. Starting in 1932, Raymond Mosch began a more than 40-year run as owner of Mosch's Tavern. To many people, the building is still known by that name. Since 1973, it has been known as Snifters, Gary's Stop Inn, Holm'rs Bar, and Gargoyle's.

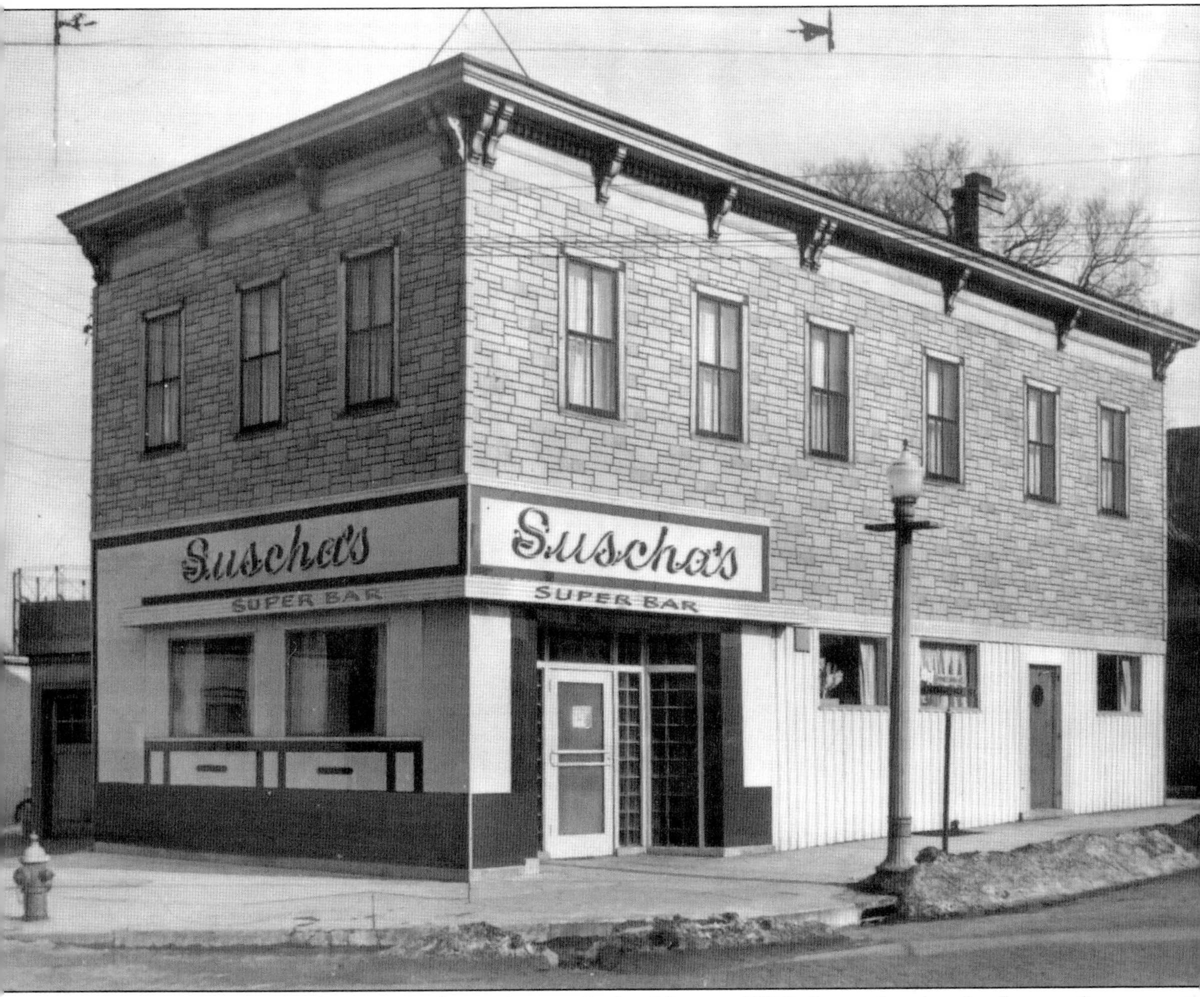

In 1907, Anton and Johanna Suscha took over the building at 933 Indiana Avenue. In short order, they opened Suscha's Meat Market, Tavern, and Boarding House. It was a gathering place for Slovenians who came to buy sausage and share news and stories of the old country. Now Zieggy's Bar, the establishment is a great place to enjoy a fish fry. Back in the 1930s and 1940s, customers would go to the refrigerator and help themselves to a beer. Polka star Frankie Yankovic considered Zieggy's his Sheboygan home. His first visit was just after World War II when he stopped in for drinks after playing a show at the Playdium. He even mentioned Mary Ziegenhorn, the owner, during an appearance on *The Tonight Show*.

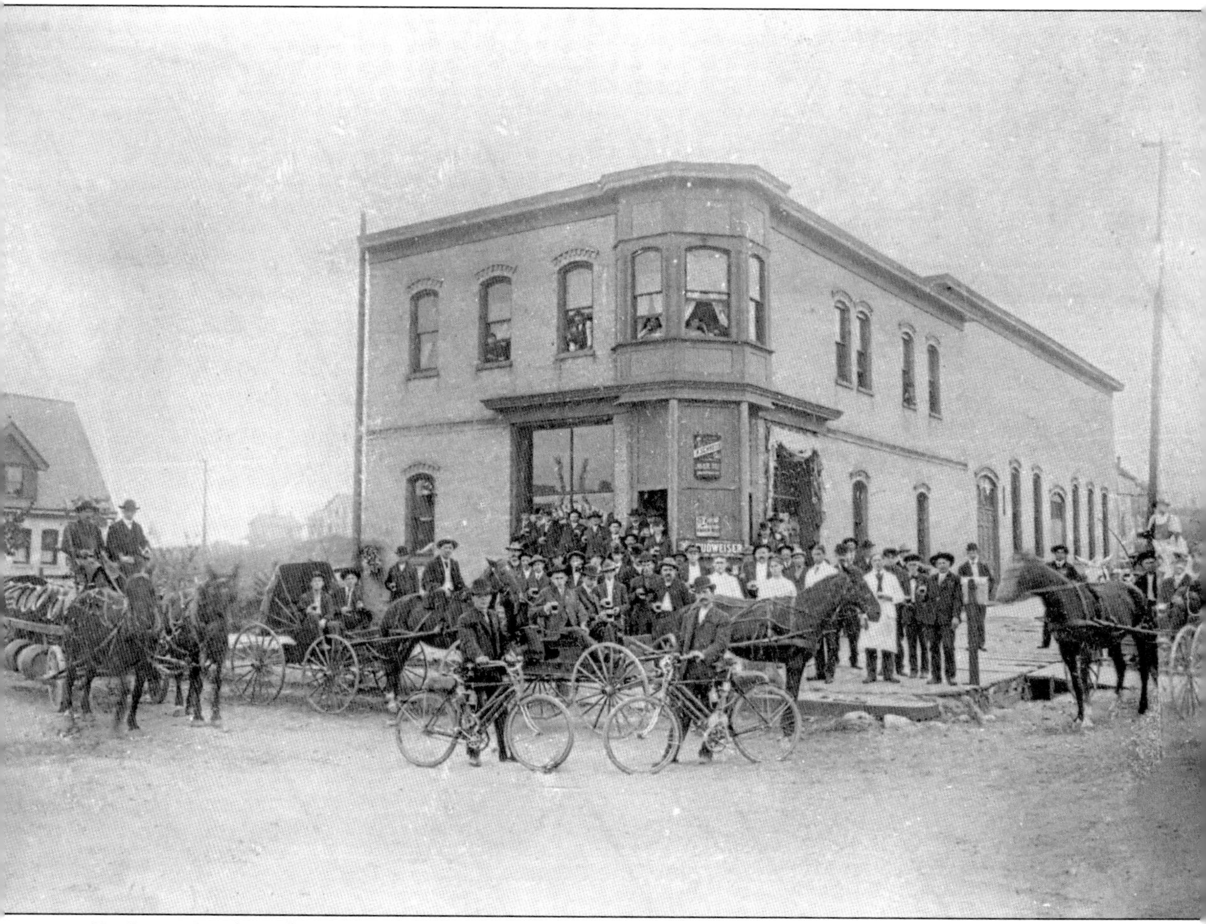

Built in 1890 by Julius Froelich, this bar was not named Standard Hall until 1902. Anton Gerber, Julius Martell, Arthur Mallmann, and Harry Quast were the next owners in that order. Quast owned the bar during Prohibition, operating a soda parlor on the premises. Theresa Zagozen, a native of Yugoslavia, owned the bar for 22 years after that. In the late 1940s and 1950s, the International Fur and Leather Workers of America Local 325 had its headquarters here. In 1950, Joseph Germ, another native Yugoslavian, took over the bar, owning it until 1967. In 1995, the bar was called Cadillac Ranch, and for the first time in 93 years, it was named something other than Standard Hall. Four years later, it was rechristened the Hillside Inn. Today, it is known as K&D Standard Hall.

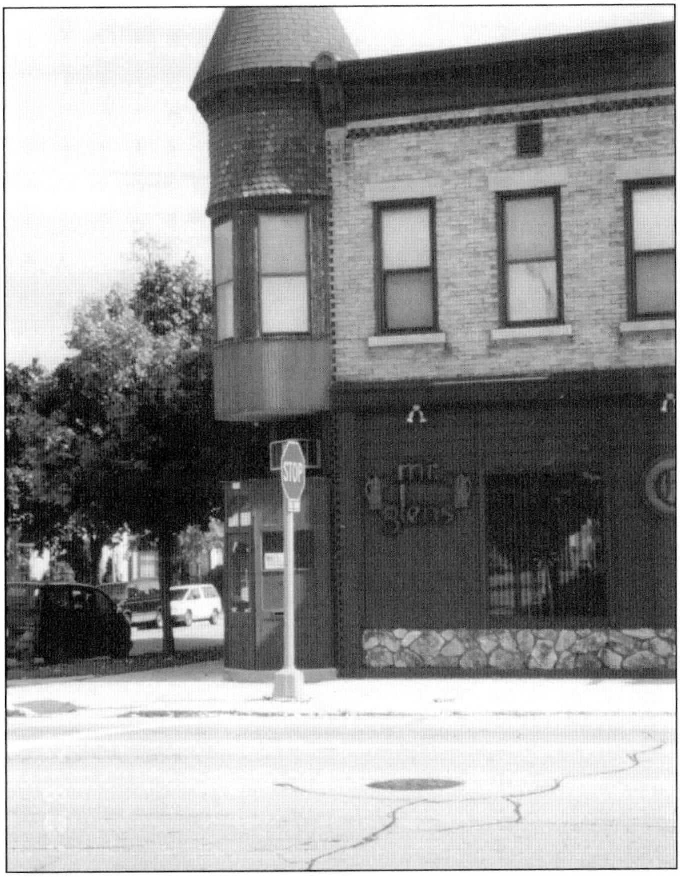

The bar currently known as Urbane at 1231 North Eighth Street is one of Sheboygan's first smoke-free bars. The current owners have done extensive remodeling, returning the bar to its former glory, even adding accordion windows, allowing the front of the bar to open. In contrast, Grube's Tavern, the original bar, was probably filled with men and their cigars and pipes. Members of the Grube family ran the establishment until 1965. Glen Usadel enjoyed a lengthy run of 35 years until his daughter Mary took over. Long before the popularity of Chinese buffets, the building was also home to Yep Chong's Restaurant in 1943 or 1944. Its specialty was chop suey.

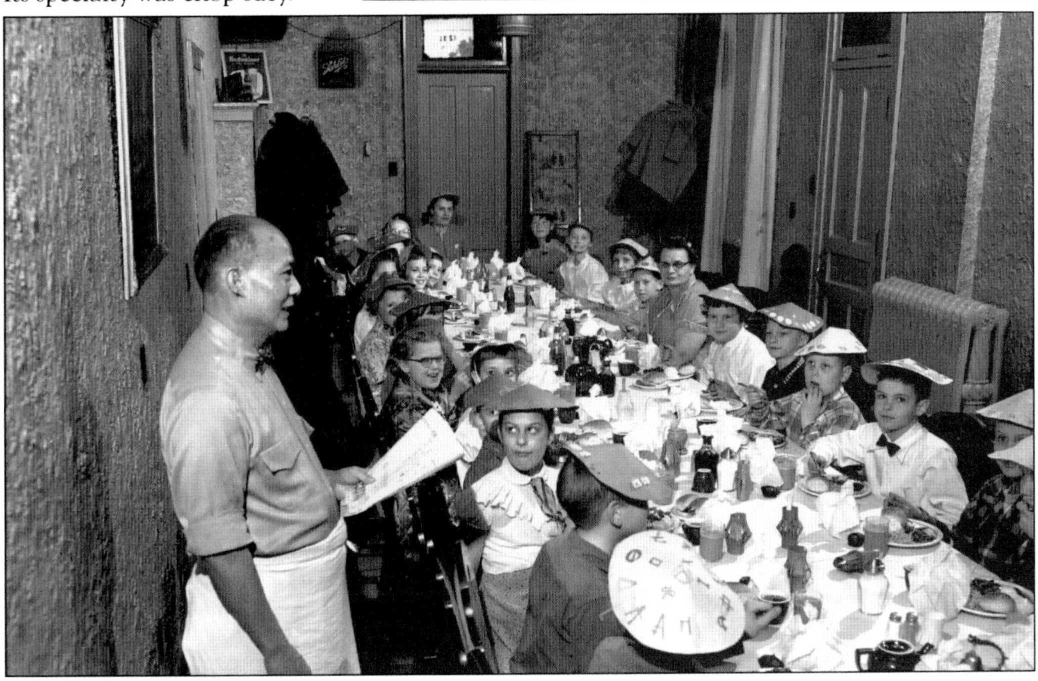

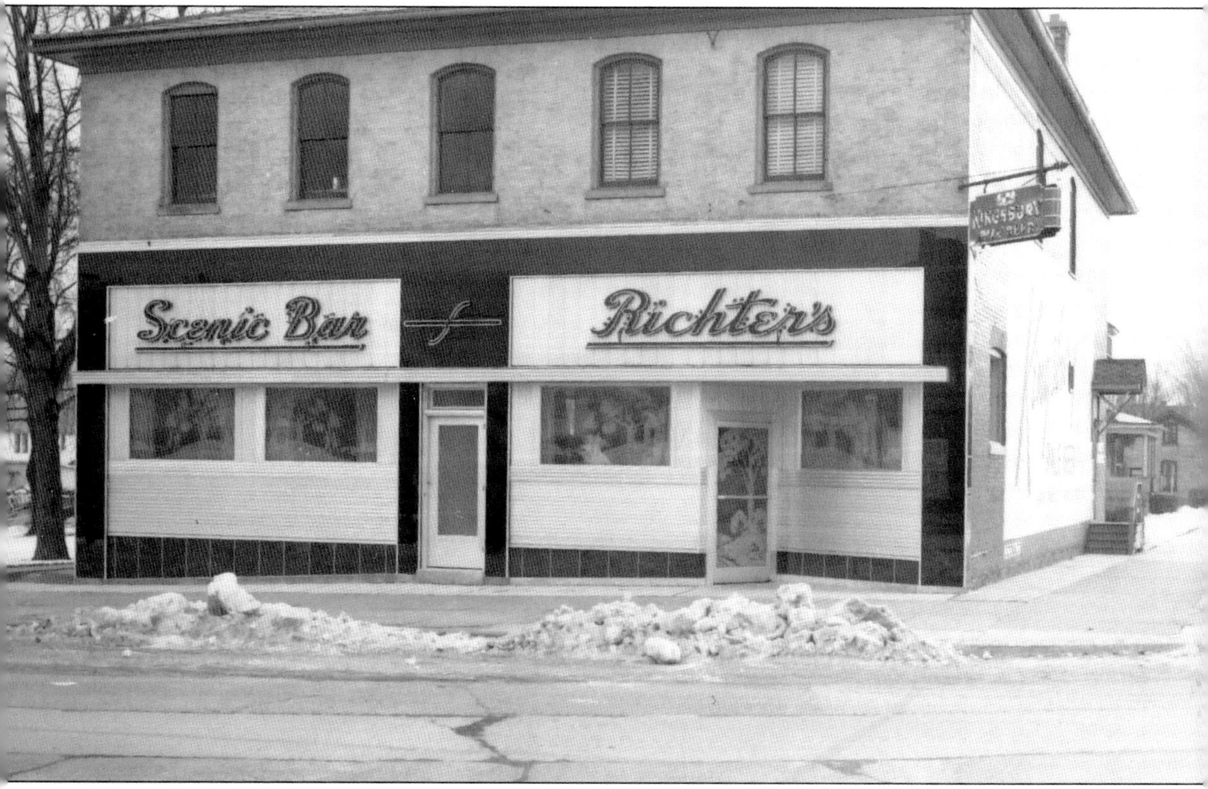

While the Scenic Bar at 1635 Indiana Avenue is a good place to go for a chicken dinner today, that was not always the case. In 1875, Henry Friedrichs, a German immigrant and harness maker and blacksmith by trade, owned a general store in the building. Albert Rust and Charles Hinze operated a grocery store there for a number of years. The first bar in the building was a soda parlor operated by Edward Friedrichs, but Herman Stubbe was the first man to own the bar after Prohibition. John Richter, a Russian immigrant, owned the bar for 24 years. John was a proud server of Kingsbury, as illustrated by the sign at the front of the bar and the mural on the west side of the building, pictured here in 1948. The bar may or may not have been named for the four scenic windows on the front of the building, which show a man, woman, and small dog walking past a big tree. William Meyer owned the bar for 29 years after Richter, and Jeff Gahagan is the current owner.

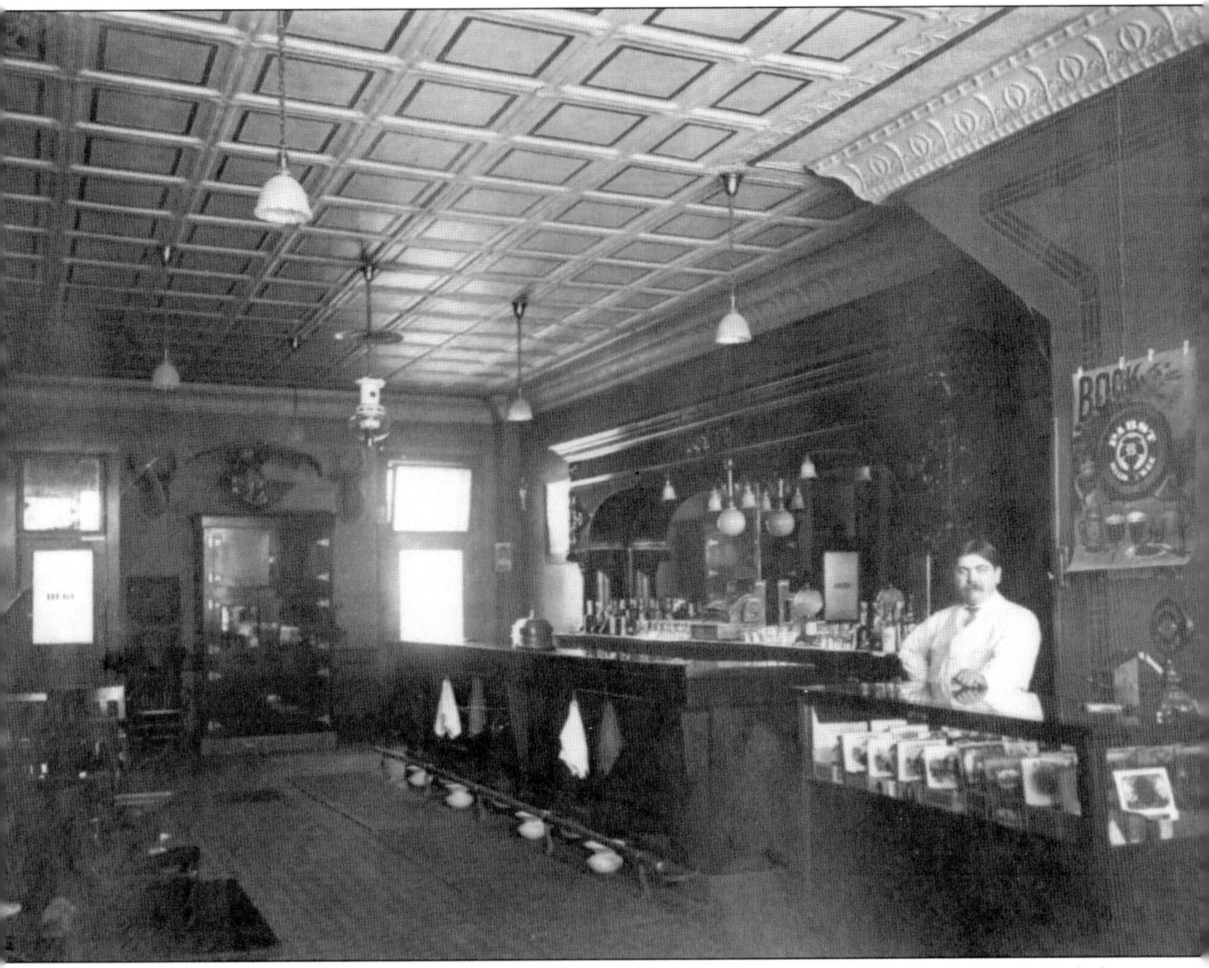

When this photograph was taken in 1908, Charles Weinert operated a tavern at 828 North Eighth Street that served Pabst Bock Beer and cigars and had spittoons at the ready. Toward the end of his run, Weinert operated a soft-drink parlor during Prohibition. Long before that, in 1884, Charles Schmidt owned a shoe store in the building. Within five years, a bar was opened at that address for the first time. The structure returned to its roots in 1922 when Samuel Solkovitz sold shoes there. Next, it was known as the Royal Lunch, Theo-Roy Lunch, and the Old Home Tavern and Restaurant. In 1936, the building housed the Bismark Café. Edgar Voss, who would later die while on duty, was the proprietor. Later versions of the Bismark were owned by Henry Hoffman of Riverdale fame and Raymond Rackow, one-time manager of the Rex, Majestic, and Wisconsin Theaters. The final tavern at the site was the Joker Club. After that, Katherine K. Foundations was a long-term tenant. Currently, the building is home to the Weill Center business office.

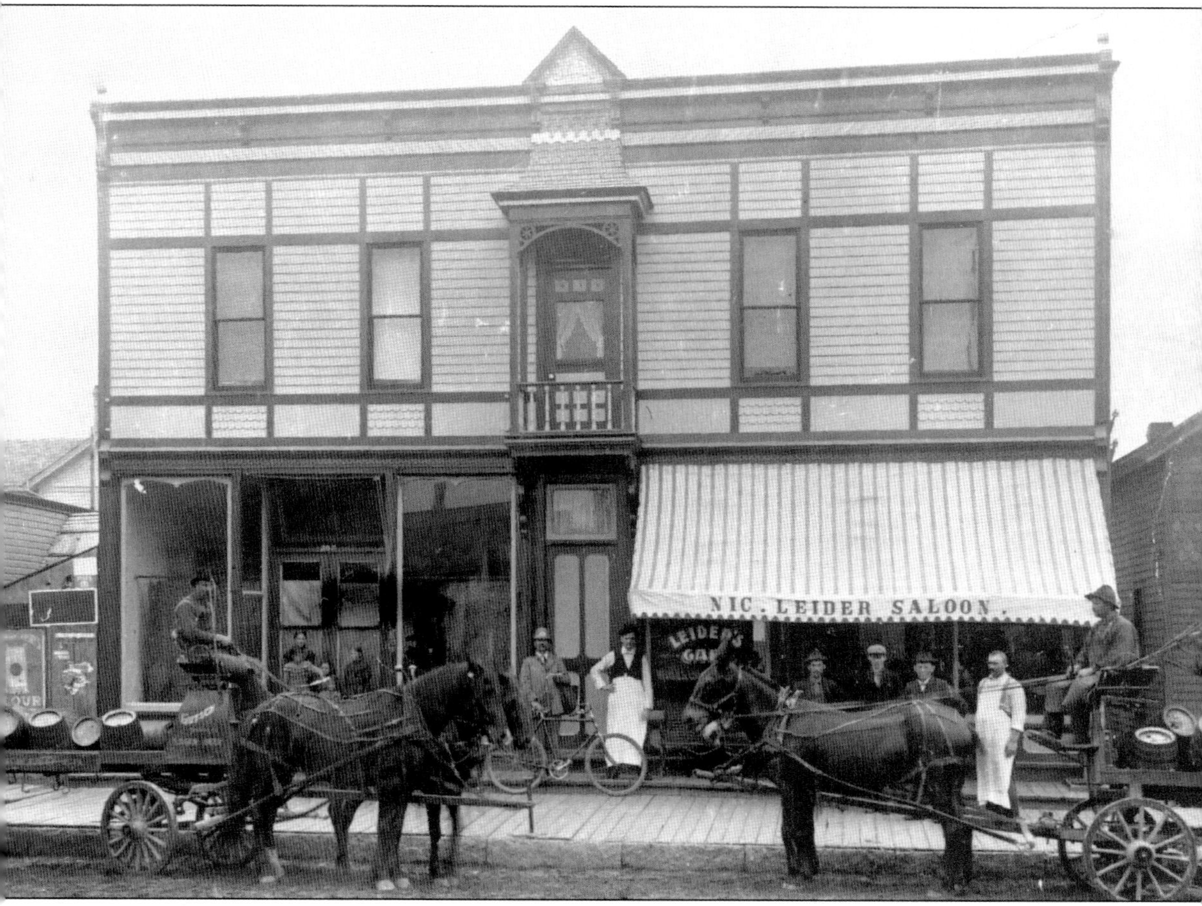

Currently the site of Ma Bell's Tavern, 1509 South Twelfth Street, it was home to the Nicholas Leider Saloon when this picture was taken in the early 1900s. John P. Weyker operated a saloon and gentlemen's furnishing store here, beginning in 1883. A number of men, including Peter Folz and Joseph Noreika, operated saloons until Prohibition. William Schroeter ran a drugstore at the address before and during Prohibition. Brothers Marvin and Milton Schroeter operated a bakery in 1920 and 1921. The Atlantic and Pacific Tea Company opened in 1926. After Prohibition, the site was shared by the Variety Beer Store (later Zarling Inc.) and a series of taverns. There was the Maple Leaf Tavern, Tex's Tavern, and Baier's Inn, which lasted for 25 years. Lavonne's Beauty Salon enjoyed a 23-year run. Sam's Ethnic Pantry, Room To Bloom Maternity Store, Sheboygan Bingo Supplies and Gifts, and Totally Aquariums all followed. Ma Bell's has been at this address for over 20 years.

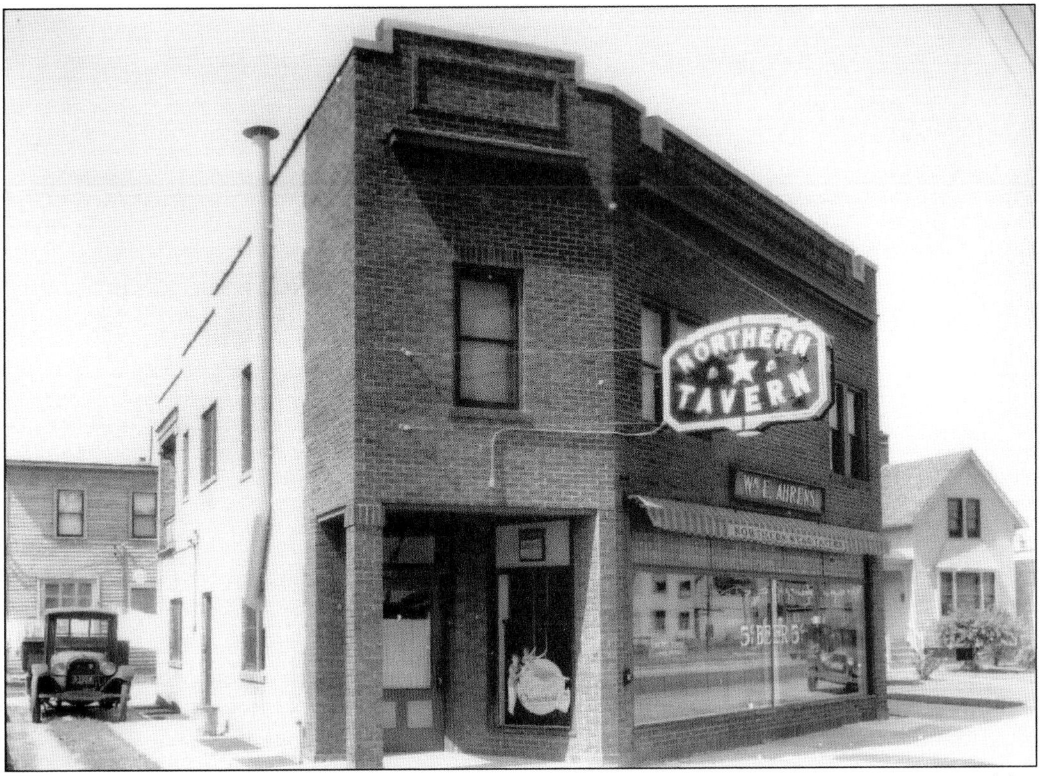

In the early 1920s, William and Elsie Ahrens owned the City Upholstering Company on Sibley Court. Perhaps searching for a higher traffic location, they moved the business to 1914 Calumet Drive. In 1935, the Ahrens combined the furniture business with the tavern business and opened the Northern Star Tavern. By the picture, one can tell that the Northern Star was a good place to get a cheap beer (5¢) and a Chesterfield cigarette. The interior was decorated for a time in the very popular Art Deco style, sporting clean lines, stainless steel, and etched glass. When William died in 1944, Elsie rechristened the bar the Golden Lantern Tavern. In 1949, brothers Arthur and Erving Lutz took over the space and opened Lutz's Bar. In 1974, the building, now renumbered 1910 Calumet Drive, became home to Mark's Fine Food. Today, it is Faye's Pizza.

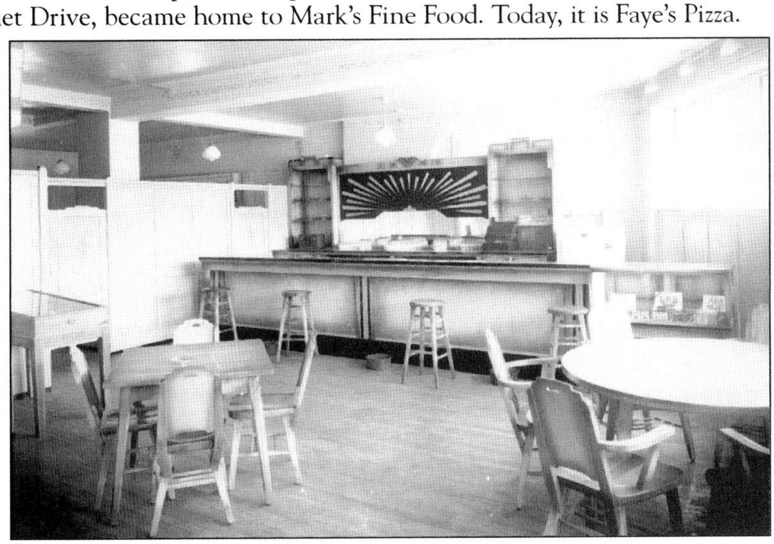

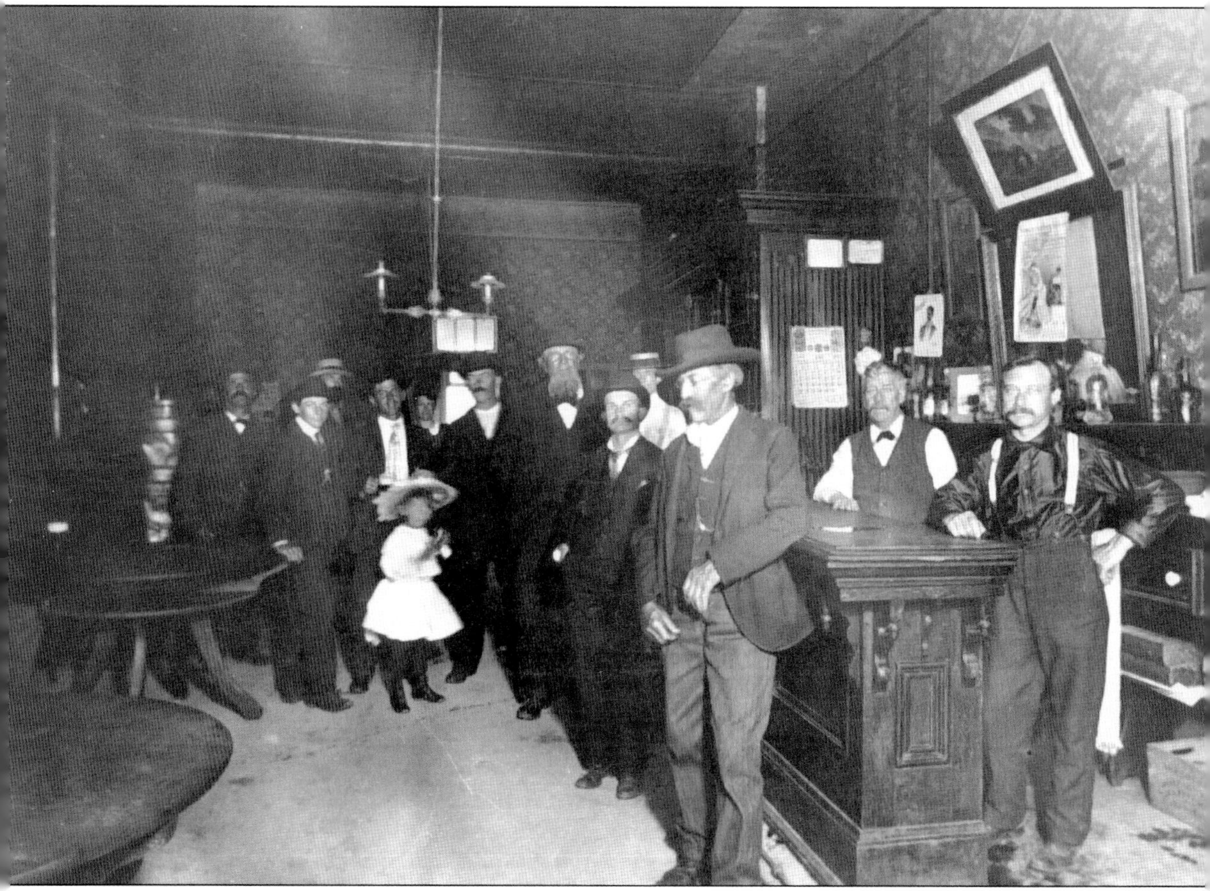

Christ Kampmann, pictured here at right in the vest with a tie, operated a saloon at 609 North Eighth Street for 28 years. Otto Rowe and Norman Rosenthal ran the Snyder and Rosie Saloon at the turn of the 20th century, and brothers Peter and Fred Stokdyk opened the Cadillac Café in 1915. It would be the last saloon to operate at this address. In 1920, the Oakdale Realty and the Local Exchange Glassware took over the building. They shared the space until 1926 when John Vekkos opened Secura Lunch. Morrow's Flowers then began a 16-year run in 1930. Scottish native John Murrow operated it for the first 3 years, and his widow ran it for the other 13. Dewey Maechtle followed up with Maechtle's Flowers. The Raatz Insurance Agency occupied the building for two years. In 1955, Don Caan's Flowers became the last occupant of the building. Eventually, 609 North Eighth Street and adjacent buildings were demolished so that an annex could be added to the Security Bank Building.

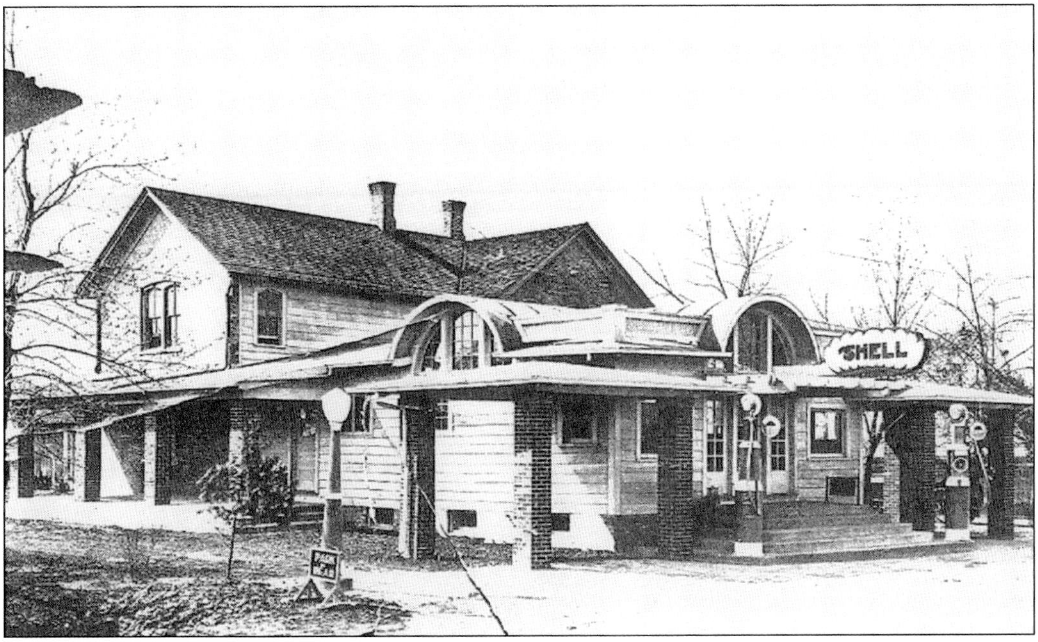

Ed Sohre, the bartender in the photograph below, was a telegraph operator for the Chicago & North Western Railroad (C&NW); however, in 1927, he built and ran the Big Apple Tavern, pictured here, from 1928 to 1939. While it was a good place for a shot, a beer, and a fill-up of Shell gas, it was also a place with a questionable reputation. The next owners, Peter and Emma Jesky, formed a partnership with their daughter Joyce and their son-in-law Frank Kummer. The final owner of the bar was James Richardson, who rechristened the business as JR's Big Apple. The bar was razed in 1988, and American Auto Sales on South Fourteenth Street now occupies the property.

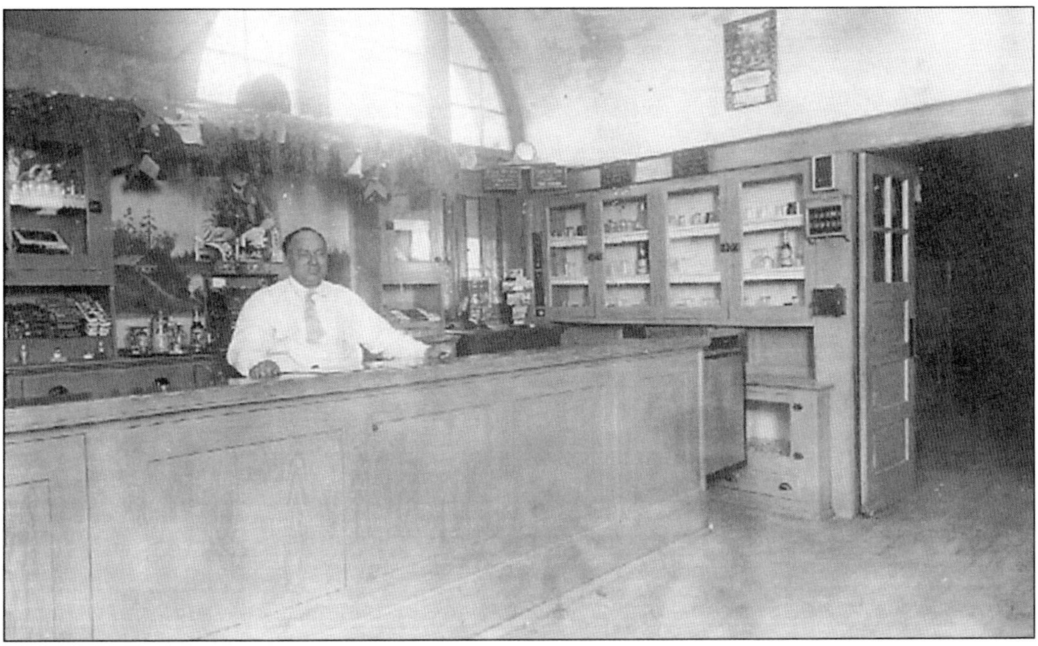

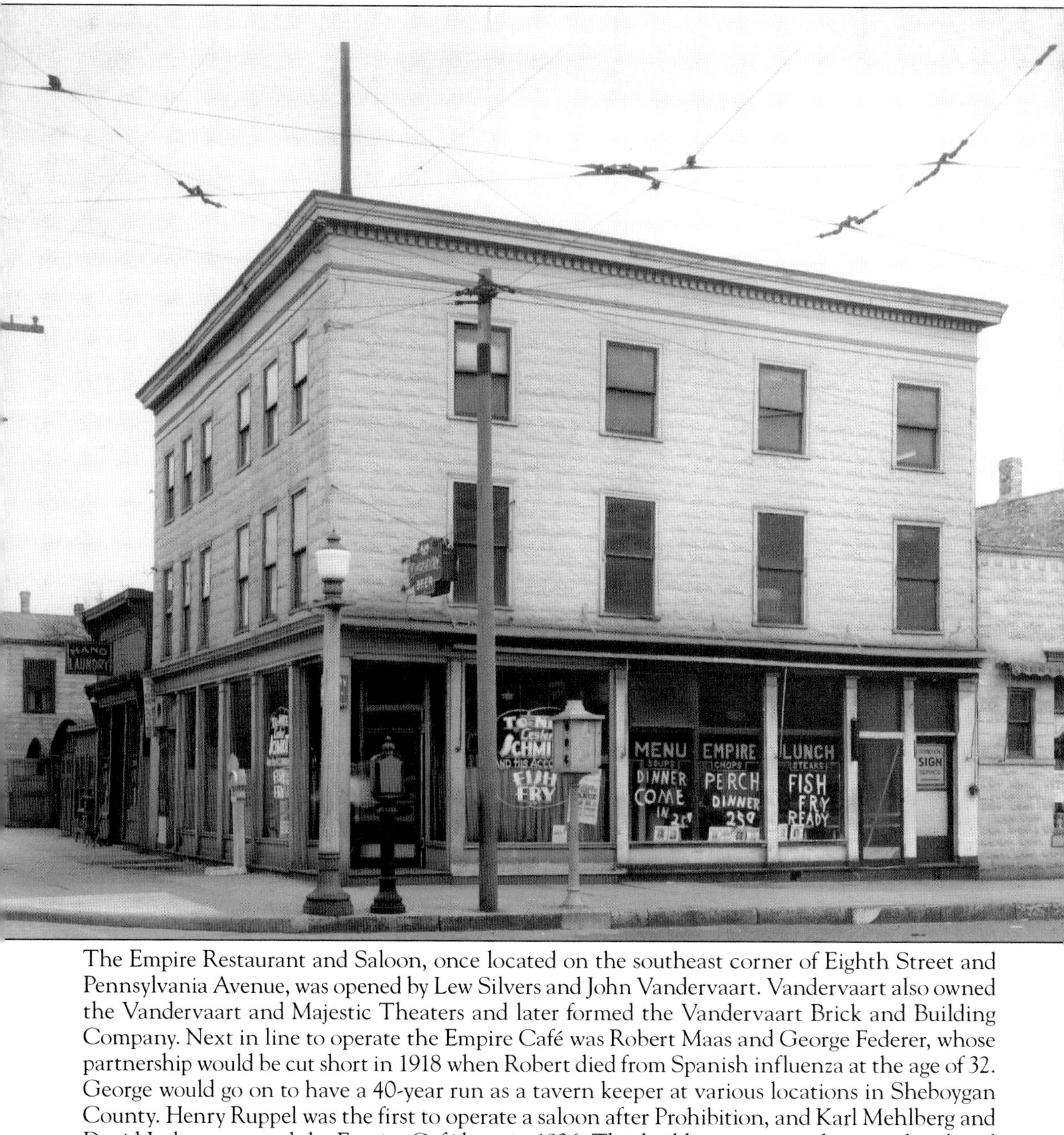

The Empire Restaurant and Saloon, once located on the southeast corner of Eighth Street and Pennsylvania Avenue, was opened by Lew Silvers and John Vandervaart. Vandervaart also owned the Vandervaart and Majestic Theaters and later formed the Vandervaart Brick and Building Company. Next in line to operate the Empire Café was Robert Maas and George Federer, whose partnership would be cut short in 1918 when Robert died from Spanish influenza at the age of 32. George would go on to have a 40-year run as a tavern keeper at various locations in Sheboygan County. Henry Ruppel was the first to operate a saloon after Prohibition, and Karl Mehlberg and David Jurk resurrected the Empire Café here in 1936. This building was torn down and replaced by a new one that Carl Weichmann opened as the Inn in 1940. The Inn later became Ye Olde Inn and then Sherlock's Home in the 1980s. It is now Legend Larry's.

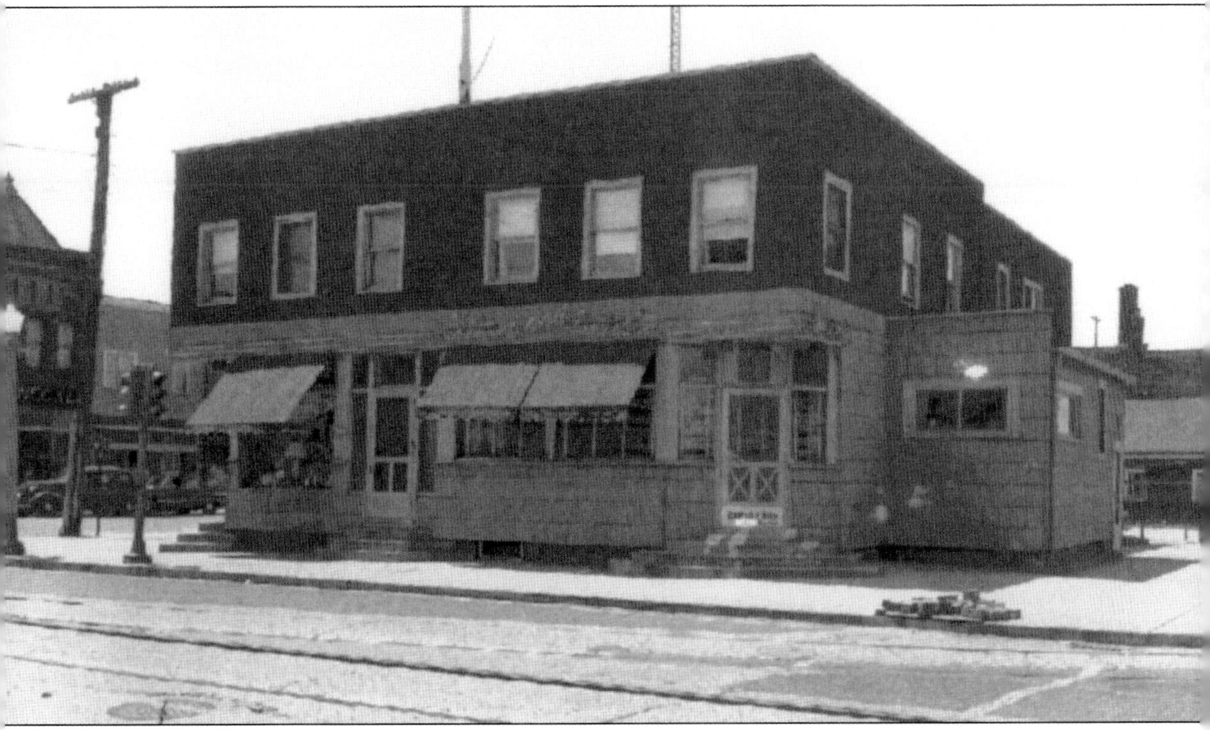

Back in 1875, when Eighth Street was still Griffith Avenue, F. Oetking was serving beer in his saloon at the northwest corner of Griffith and Indiana. A few years later, Charles Boehme branched out, running a saloon, a boardinghouse, and an ice-making business at 1026 South Eighth Street. In 1897, Louis Menking had a saloon on that corner. Three years later, either his brother or son took over. Julius Janke, Charles Schwartz, and Fred Retzlaff all operated saloons at that address before Prohibition. Mike Skok operated a soft-drink parlor and later a tavern in the location for a total of 18 years. Mike's son-in-law Louis Francis and his daughter Stanza operated Stan and Lou's, seen here, for 25 of the next 27 years until the building's demolition in the mid-1960s. The couple's only break came for two years in the late 1950s when Chris Weinberger operated the Top Hat Tavern.

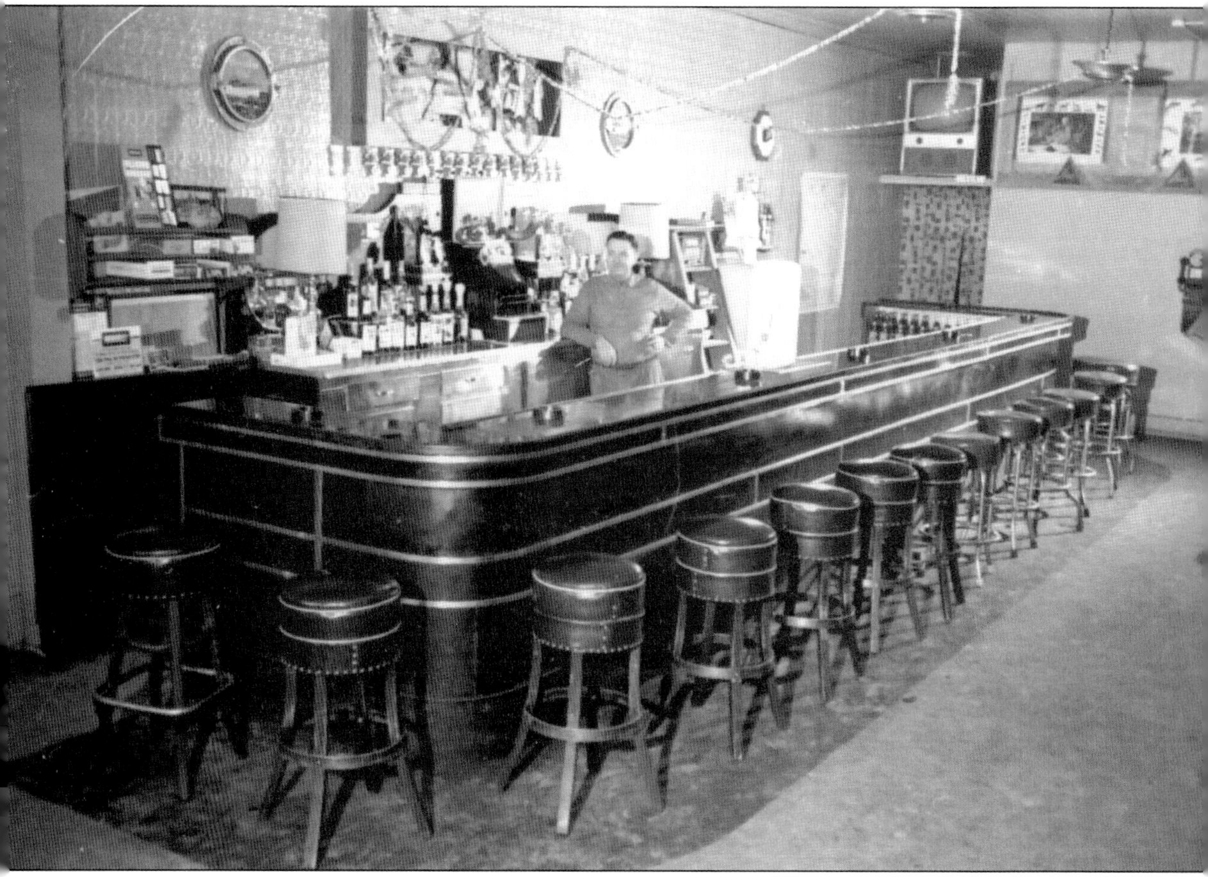

Very early in Sheboygan's history, brothers William J. and Anton J. Mallmann operated a grocery store at the corner of Seventh and Center Avenue. In the late 1890s, William ran a real estate, insurance, and loan business in the building. Before Anton was involved in real estate, he owned a copper mine, mined gold in California during the Gold Rush, and operated a coal and wood business. In 1906, Herman Stahl operated a saloon and a boardinghouse for farmers at the site. In 1910, the building was home to the *Sheboygan Daily Journal*. The editor was L.E. Reed. For a short time, the *Sheboygan Press* also operated there. At that time, brothers Timothy and Edward Bowler and Charles Broughton owned it. In 1946, former sheriff Joe Dreps opened his saloon on this site. This interior image of the bar was captured in August 1961. Joe Dreps is the bartender. The final business in this space was the Rush Inn, operated by Richard Weinberger. Later, that building and others on the same block were torn down to make way for Security Bank's drive-thru terminals.

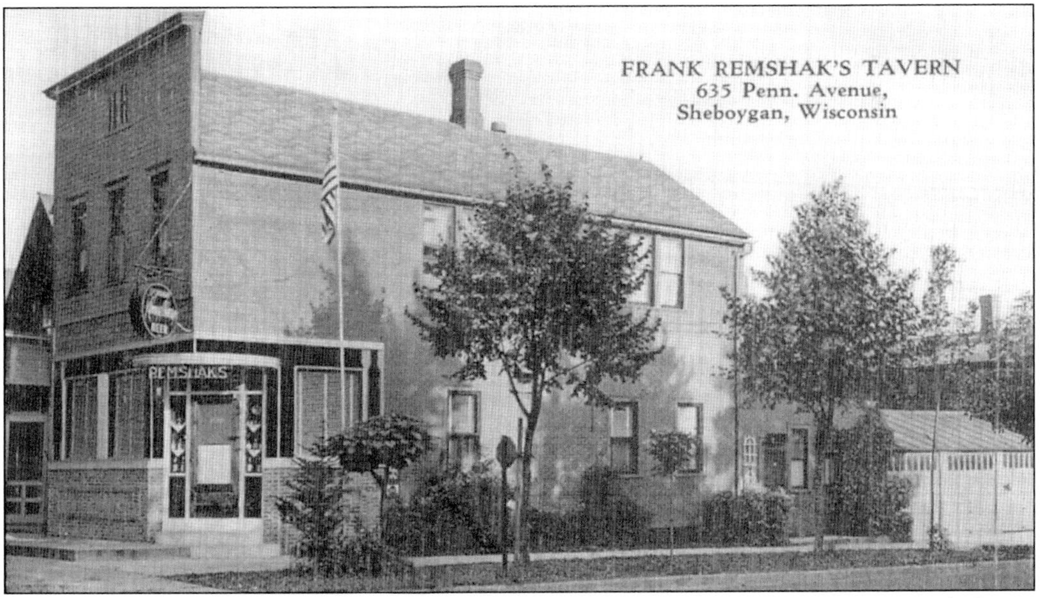

In the 1930s, Frank Remshak operated a soft-drink parlor and then a tavern at Seventh Street and Pennsylvania Avenue. Over time, it was Roy's, Mitzke's and then Chuvy's Bar. Dave Repinski Sr. opened Who's Inn in 1974. In the late 1980s, it was razed to make way for an office building. Who's Inn eventually moved to the former Cappy's Bar at Ninth and Indiana Avenues, where it remains to this day.

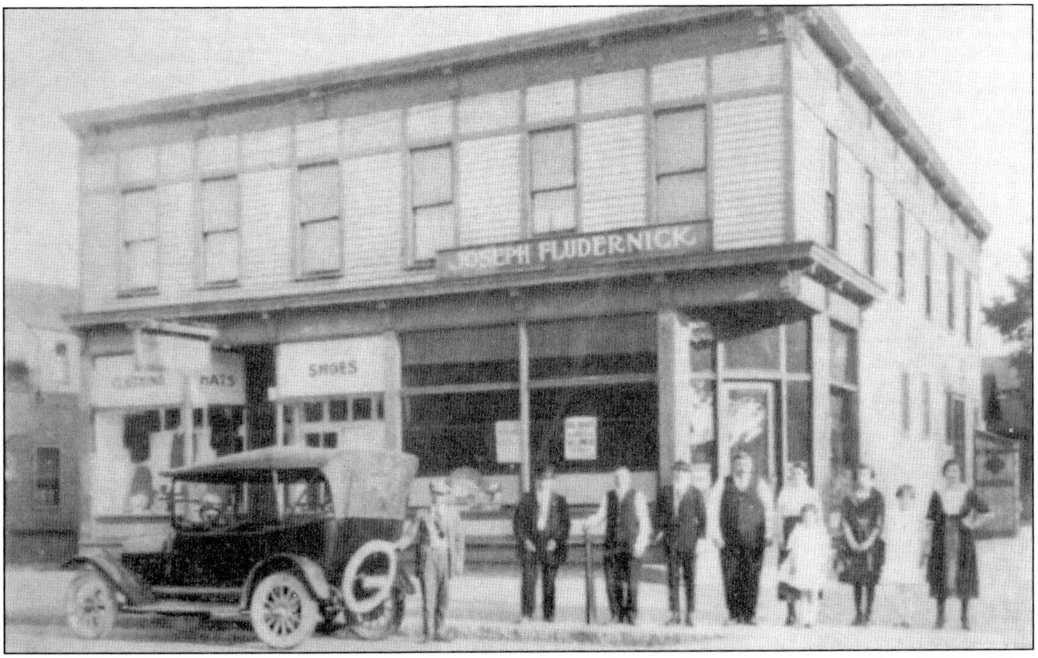

Joseph and Mary Fludernick opened a soda parlor at 835 Indiana Avenue in the 1920s. The Slovenian National Benefit Society and the Amalgamated Clothing Workers Local 197 had their headquarters upstairs. The next owner, Lawrence J. Casper, kept the Fludernick's name for more than 40 years into the 1950s. After that, it became Cappy's Bar. Who's Inn opened in 1991 and has been there ever since.

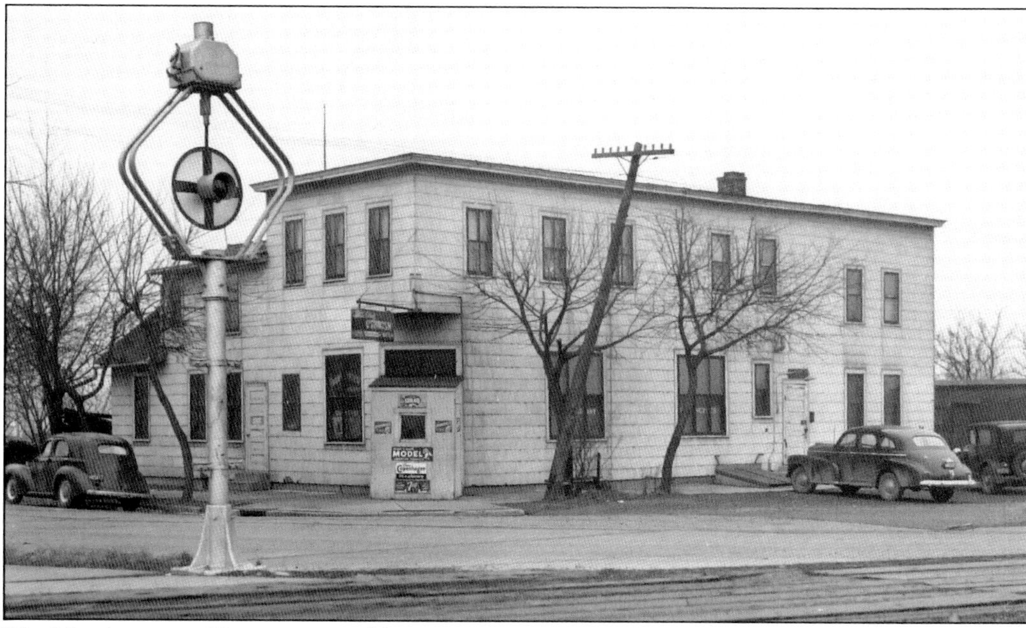

The Northwestern House, pictured here in 1949, was one of a series of taverns and restaurants in this building located at Union Avenue and Sauk Trail Road. Originally Herman Polste's Meat Market, it was converted to a saloon in 1908. Frank and Christina Kolenc ran the establishment for the next 30 years. The Kath family did extensive remodeling in 1995 and operated the Northwestern House until Gosse's restaurant opened in 2001.

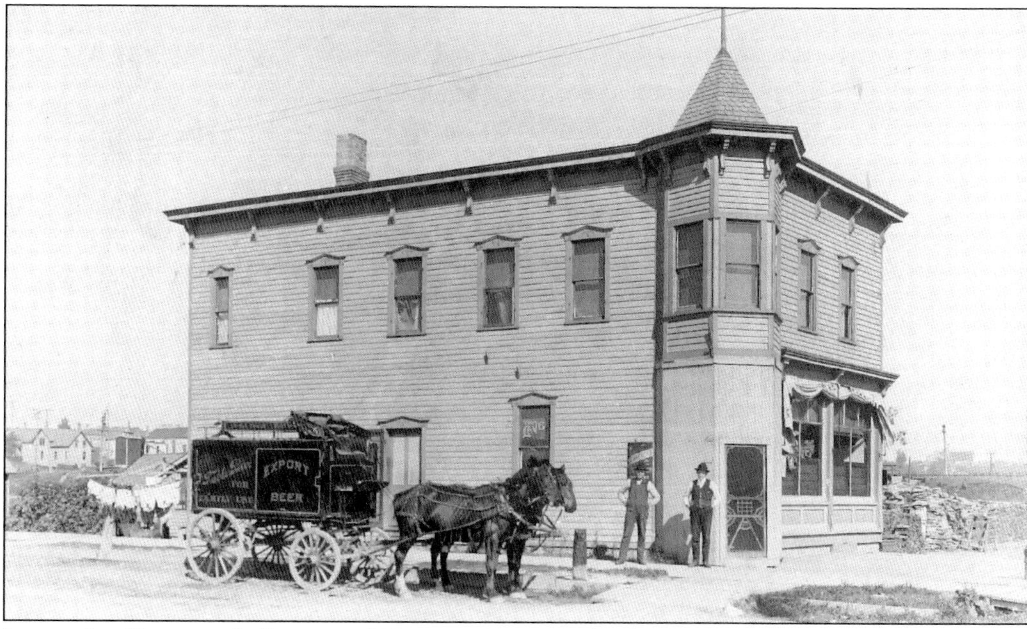

Located at Fourteenth Street and Niagara Avenue, this building was once home to a saloon called the Cave, during the 1880s. In 1903, Gutsch Brewing purchased the property. In 1922, John Planinshek took over the property and opened a soda parlor. After Prohibition, it became the Harmony Bar. The business stayed with the Planinshek family until 1992, when John's son Stanley sold it to Reuben Mertz. Currently, Mertz's daughter Ruby Brock owns the bar.

Four

Railroads Bring Prosperity

Sheboygan's earliest claim to fame was its harbor. It was one of the best on the west shore of Lake Michigan. In 1850, just three years after Sheboygan was incorporated as a village of 800 citizens, more than 17,800 passengers landed here. A year later, more than 800 ships called at the harbor, delivering nearly 242,000 tons of merchandise and hauling away more than a million feet of lumber, tons of fish, animal hides, wool, shingles and potatoes, and barrels full of beer. All that traffic posed a serious problem, as there was no good way to move people and imports away from the harbor and, even more serious, no good way to move produce and products from farms and factories to the harbor for shipping. Plank roads proved to be too fragile under heavy loads, but railroads provided the most practical solution. This is their story.

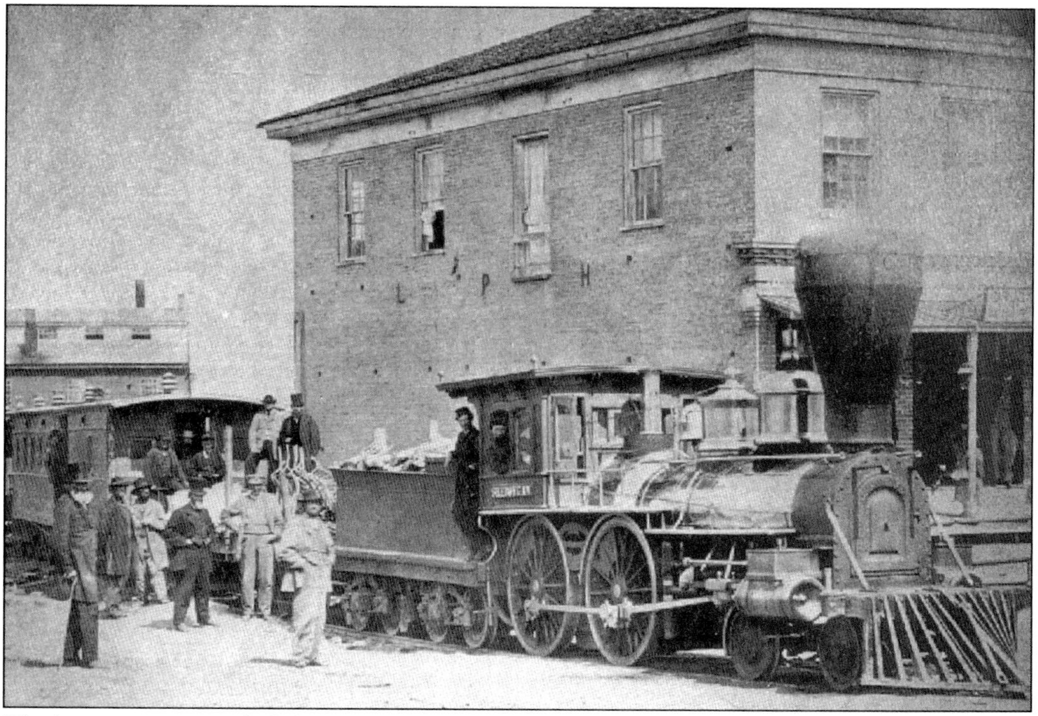

The locomotive named *Sheboygan* pulled the first Sheboygan & Mississippi Railroad train out of its namesake city on January 17, 1859. The railroad line initially ran from the Sheboygan harbor five miles west to Sheboygan Falls. There, it connected with Wisconsin Stage Company coaches for Milwaukee, Fond du Lac, Manitowoc, and Two Rivers.

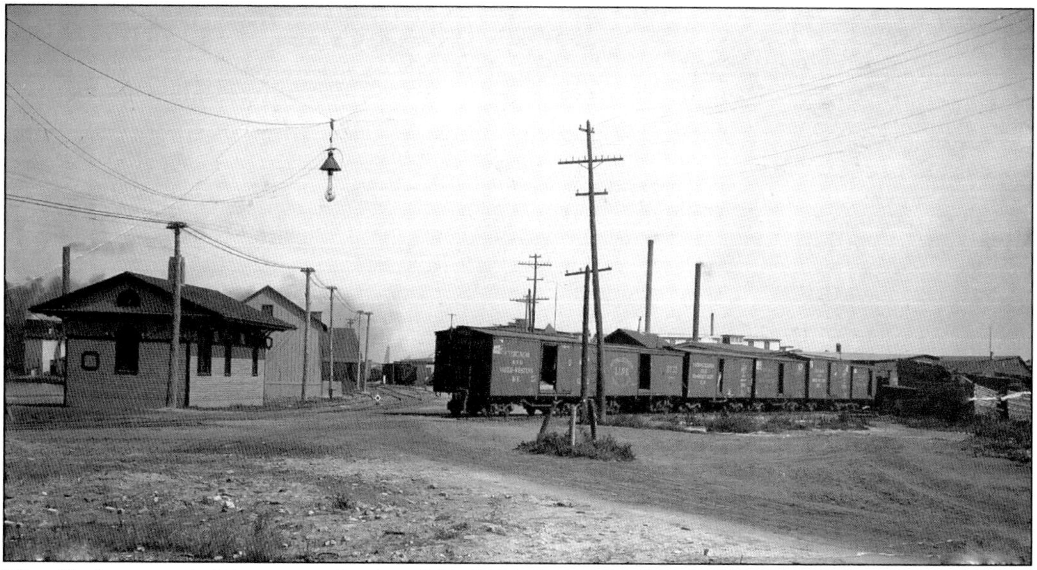

The Sheboygan & Mississippi Railroad built Sheboygan's first railroad depot in 1859 just east of South Eighth Street and Indiana Avenue. The roof of the 20-foot-by-45-foot depot had an unusual 10-foot overhang to protect passengers from the weather. The building still stands today as a private residence about five blocks south of its original site on Clara Avenue. (Courtesy Mark Fredrick.)

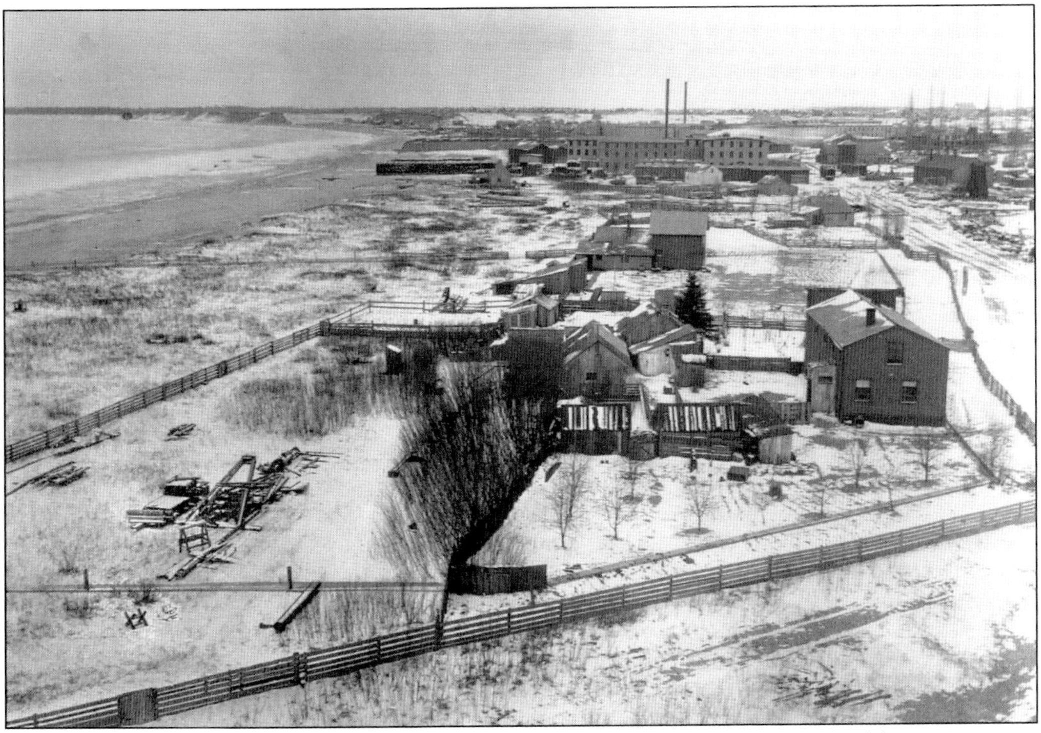

East of the first depot, the railroad company constructed an engine house, turntable, water tower, and machine shop, all visible in the upper right of this image. Frost Veneer Seating Company is seen left of the railroad's facilities. Sidings ran along the river and onto the south pier. The road's initial motive power consisted of two 22-ton locomotives named *Sheboygan* and *Cape Cod.* Rolling stock included 22 freight cars and two passenger coaches.

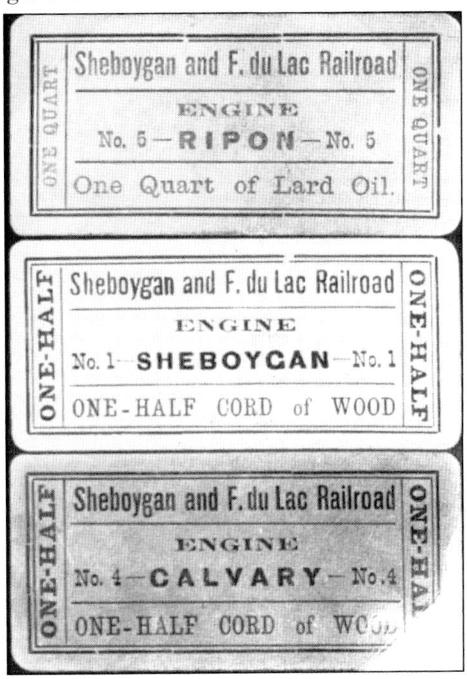

The Sheboygan & Fond du Lac Railroad succeeded the Sheboygan & Mississippi Railroad in 1861. It opened the rail line from Glenbeulah to Fond du Lac in January 1869 and was sold to the C&NW Railroad in 1880. The Sheboygan & Fond du Lac Railroad used tickets to purchase wood and lubricating oil for its engines and reimbursed the sellers when they turned in their tickets.

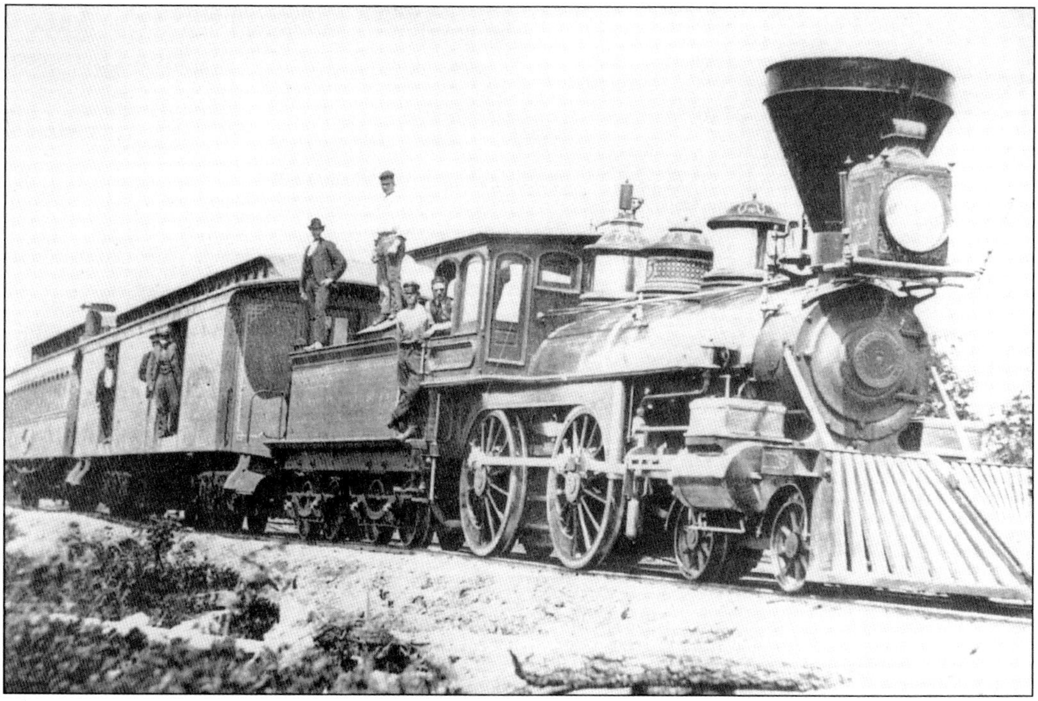

The steam engine *Ripon* was typical of Sheboygan & Fond du Lac Railroad engines in the 1870s. It was built by the Baldwin Locomotive Works in Philadelphia in 1871 and was No. 5 on the Sheboygan & Fond du Lac roster. It was known as a 4-4-0 engine because of its wheel arrangement. The Sheboygan & Fond du Lac Railroad reached Ripon in January 1872 and Princeton in May of that year.

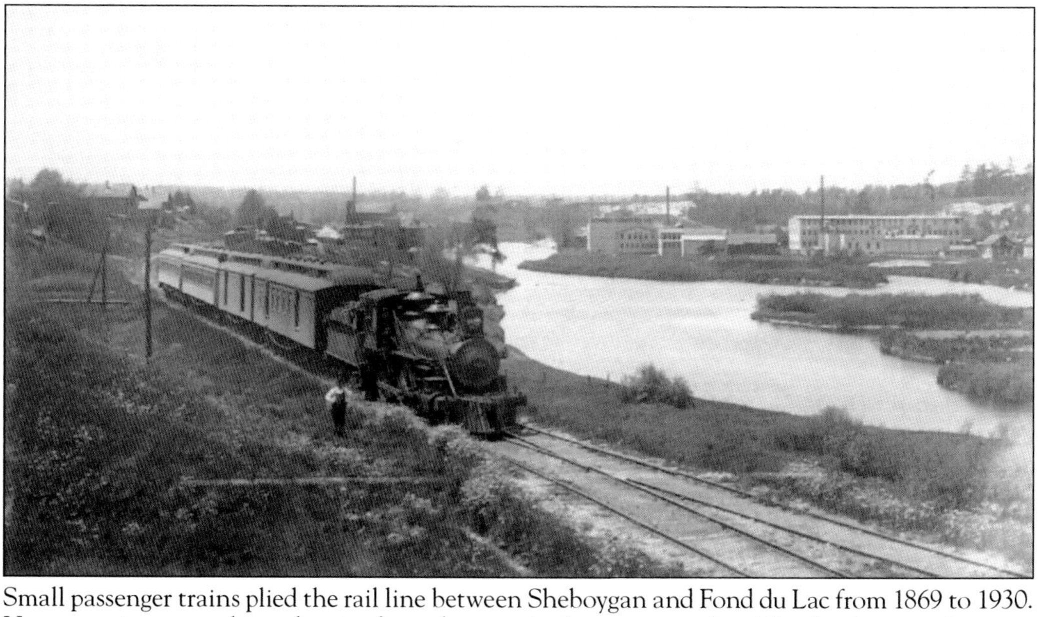

Small passenger trains plied the rail line between Sheboygan and Fond du Lac from 1869 to 1930. Here, a train approaching the city from the west is about to pass the siding leading northeast to the Schreier Malting Co. It has just passed the Aladdin Soap factory (left of center) on the south side of the Sheboygan River and the Art and Advance Furniture factories across the river.

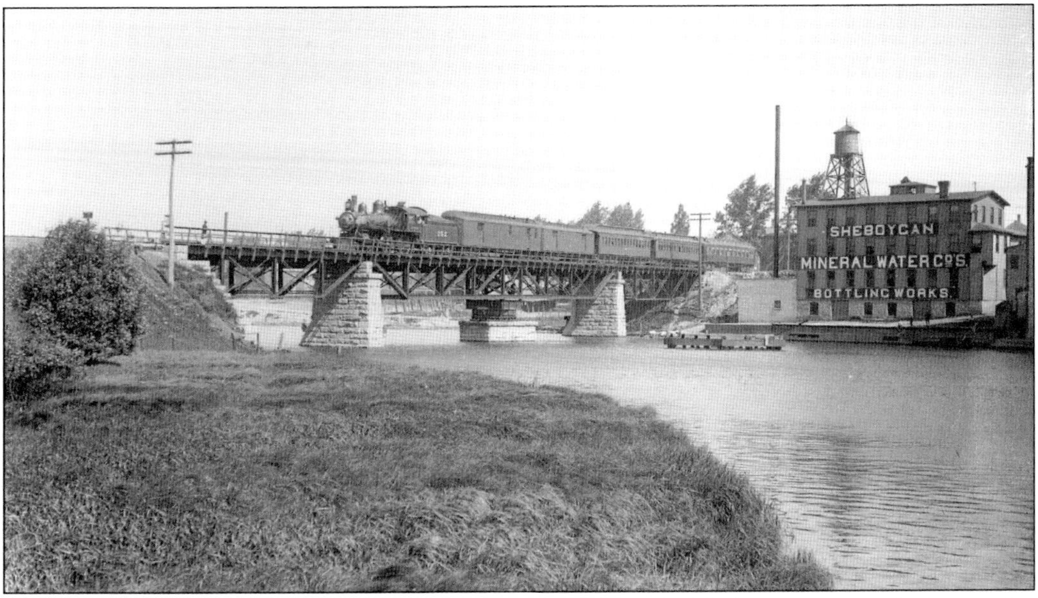

Engine No. 252 leads a southbound passenger train across the Sheboygan River Bridge on the C&NW Railroad's main line through the city. The next stop was the depot on Pennsylvania Avenue. The Sheboygan Mineral Water Company's bottling works near Thirteenth Street and Erie Avenue shipped carloads of mineral water in wooden kegs and glass bottles. The water was piped from a spring near Eighth Street and Erie Avenue in Fountain Park.

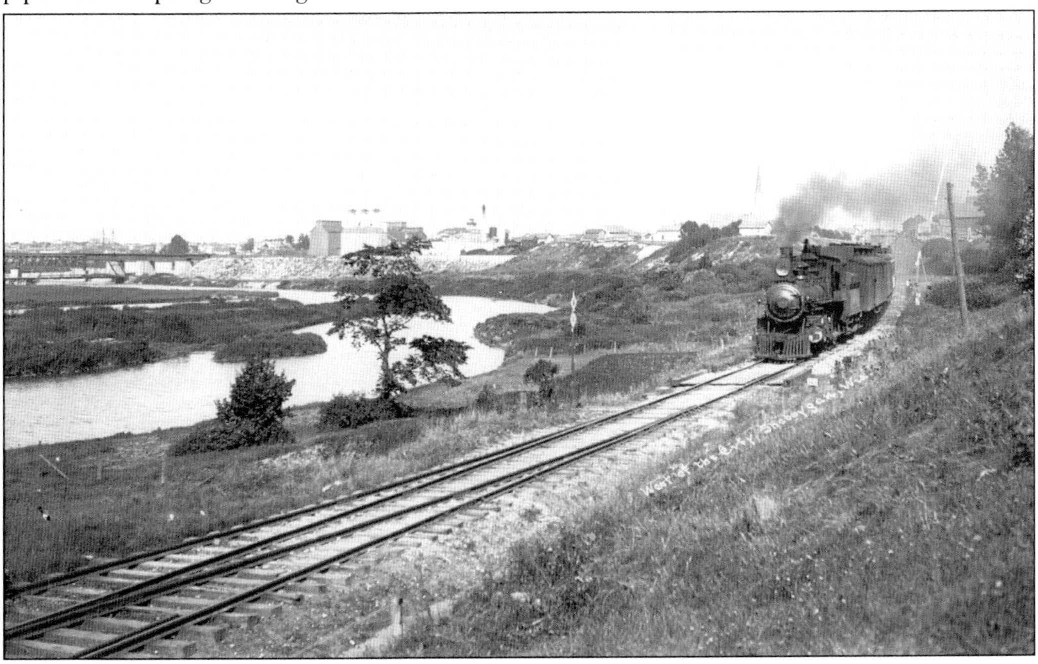

A small passenger train heading west approaches the siding to the Aladdin Soap Company. Visible in the background are the New Jersey Avenue Bridge over the Sheboygan River, fill for the new Sheboygan Cutoff rail line (which opened in 1907), the Schreier Malting Company, and the steeple of Emmanuel Evangelical Lutheran Church. Early on, passenger fares from Sheboygan were 20¢ to Sheboygan Falls and 60¢ to Plymouth.

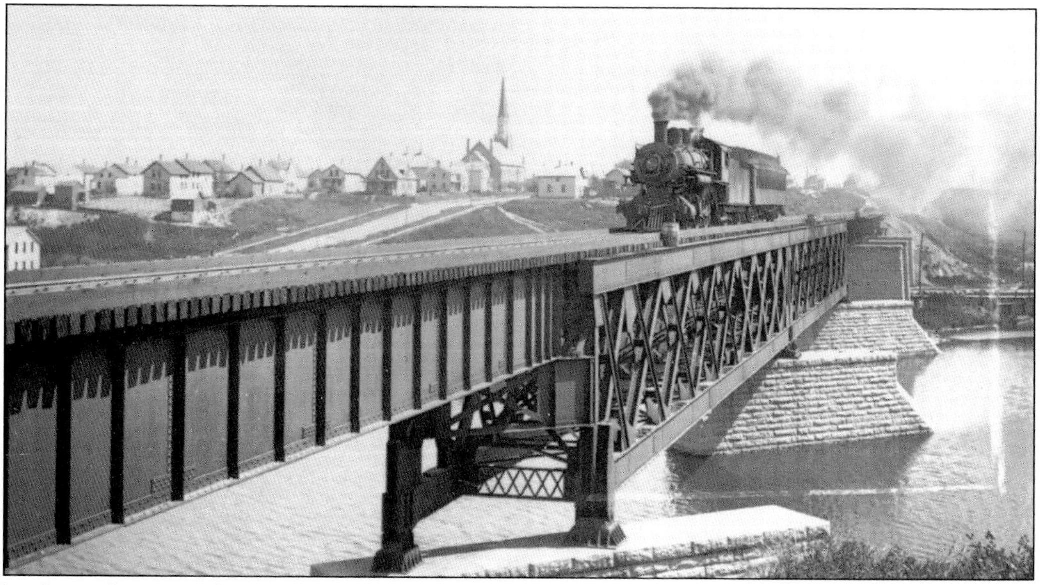

In the early 1900s, the C&NW Railroad invested more than $1 million to improve Sheboygan's rail-related facilities. A cutoff line on the western edge of the city included a massive bridge over the Sheboygan River. Dynamite used to blast foundations for the stone piers of the bridge knocked plaster off the walls of Emmanuel Evangelical Lutheran Church, seen in the background.

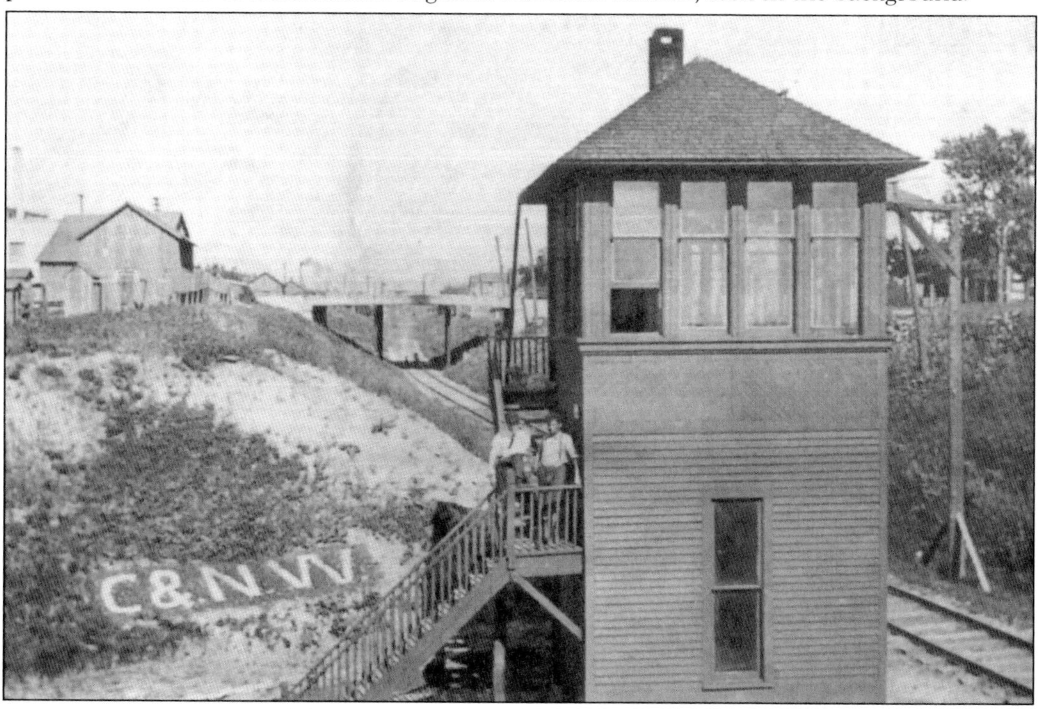

A two-story tower guarded the crossing where the east-west Fond du Lac line intersected with the 1907 cutoff that ran north-south along the then western edge of Sheboygan. In 1917, tower operator William Behring narrowly escaped death when a derailment sent a car crashing toward the tower. Fortunately, it just missed the building. The Seventeenth Street Bridge over the tracks is visible to the east. (Courtesy Dale Kuhn.)

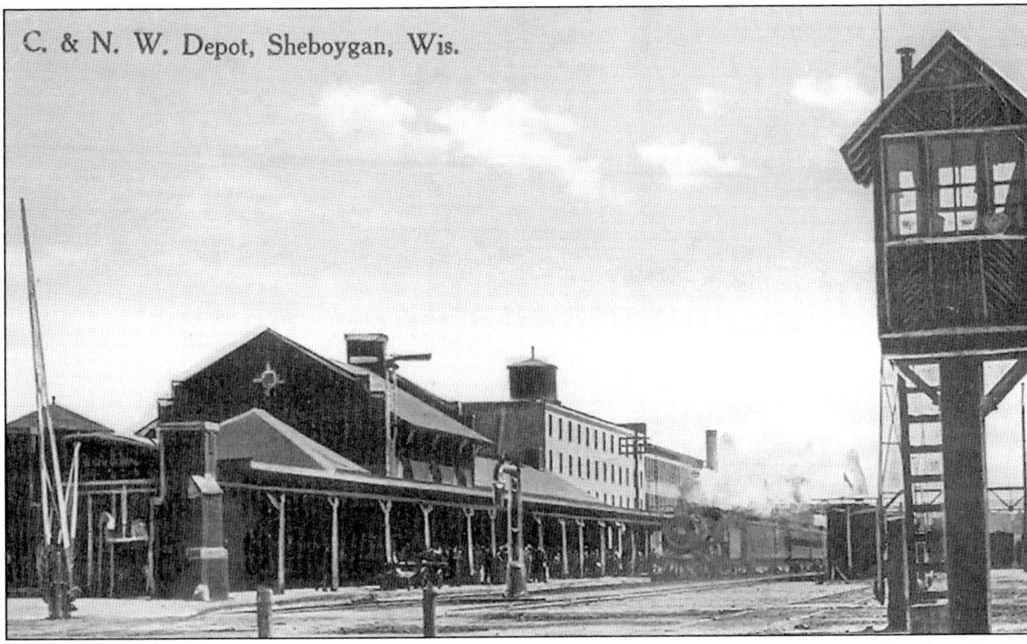

No railroad project engendered more civic pride than the new 100-foot-long redbrick C&NW depot, which opened in 1906 and still stands today. A crossing tower and gates guarded the railroad's Pennsylvania Avenue crossing. As many as 18 passenger trains arrived at or departed from the depot each day when service was at its peak. The Phoenix Chair Company factory stood behind the depot.

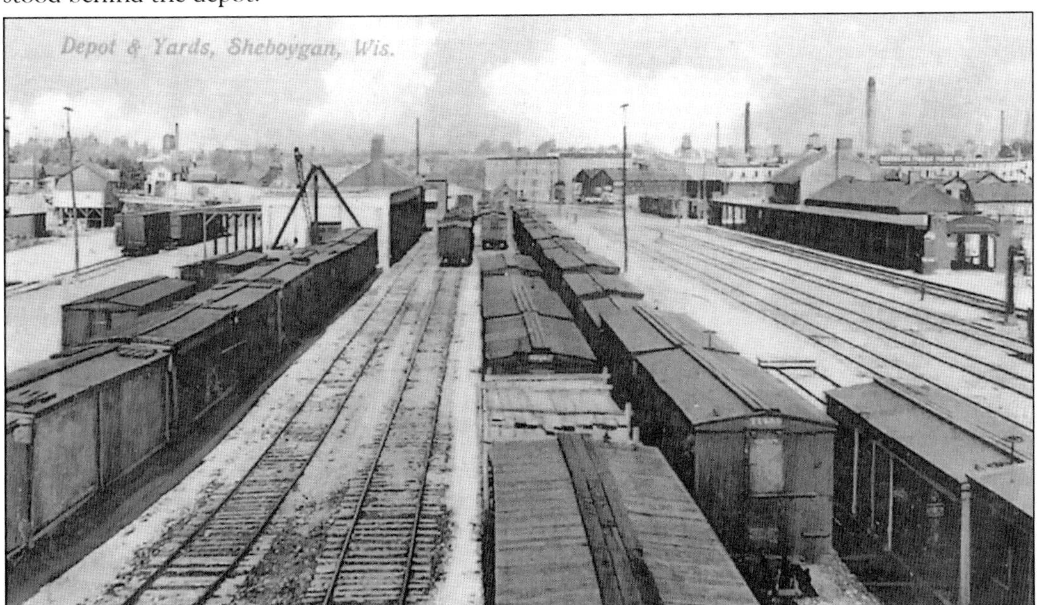

When the Milwaukee, Lakeshore & Western Railroad came to Sheboygan in 1872, it established a depot and rail yards along South Twelfth Street south of Pennsylvania Avenue. This view looks north toward Pennsylvania Avenue from a 500-foot-long pedestrian viaduct built in 1906, allowing residents employed at area factories to cross the yard safely. The passenger depot is on the right, and the freight house is on the left.

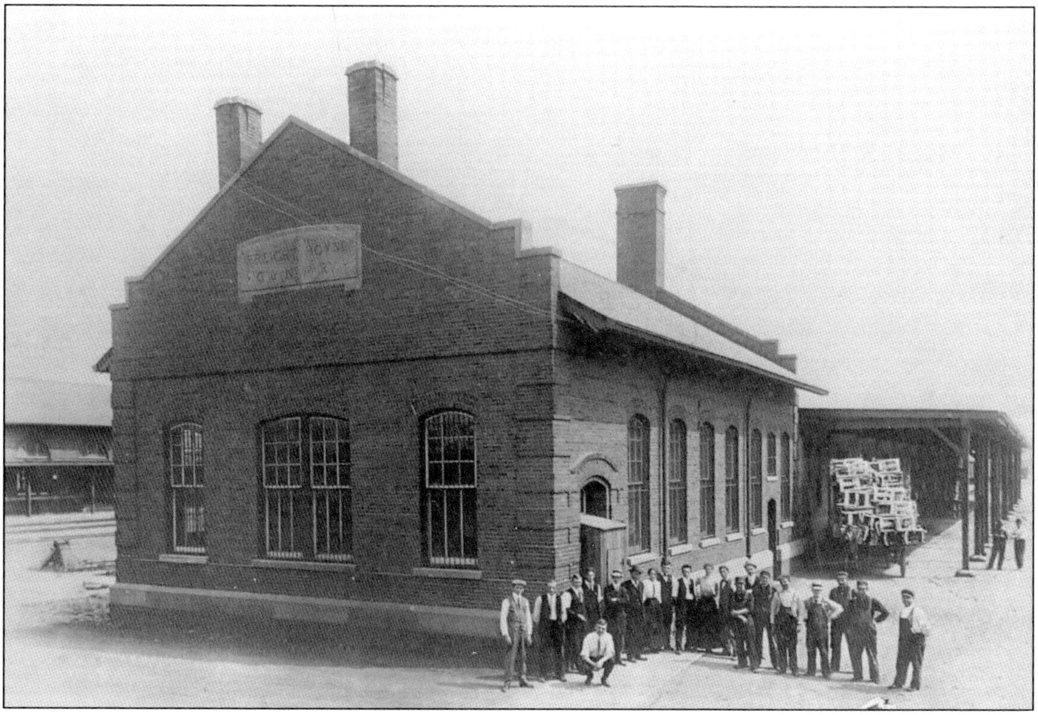

The Chicago and North Western Railroad Company opened a large freight house on the west side of the rail yard across from the depot in 1906. The brick building measured 296 feet by 36 feet with a two-story office on its north end. In 1911, the freight house employees posed for a photograph. Note the baggage cart in the background piled high with locally made chairs ready for shipment.

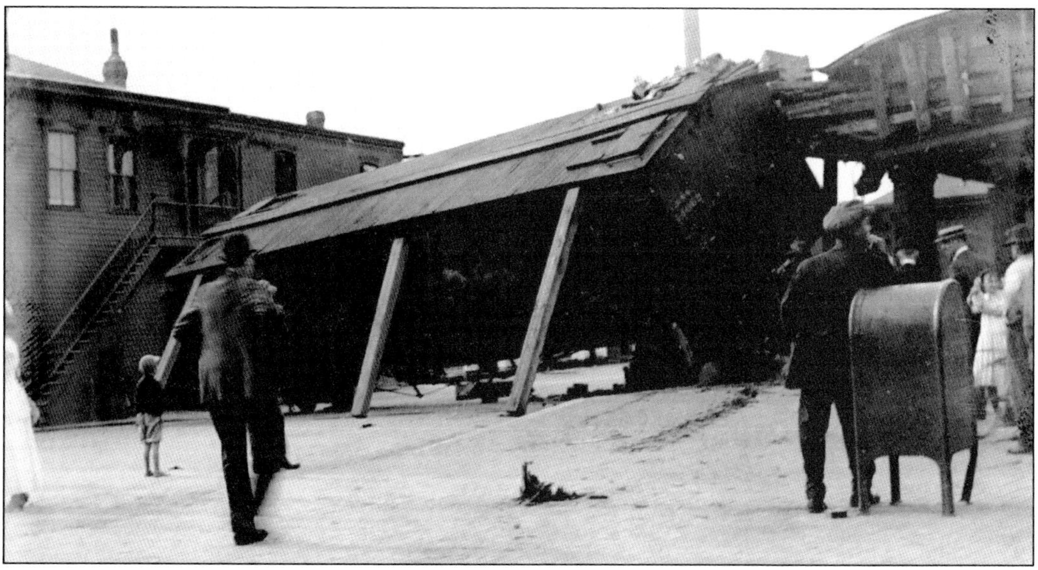

Fifteen boxcars broke away from a switch engine in 1913 and shot down a siding serving the freight house on the north side of Pennsylvania Avenue. The first car smashed through the bumper at the end of the siding, careened across Pennsylvania Avenue, and damaged the passenger station's covered platform (seen in the upper right). When the car finally stopped just short of another building, it was leaning precariously.

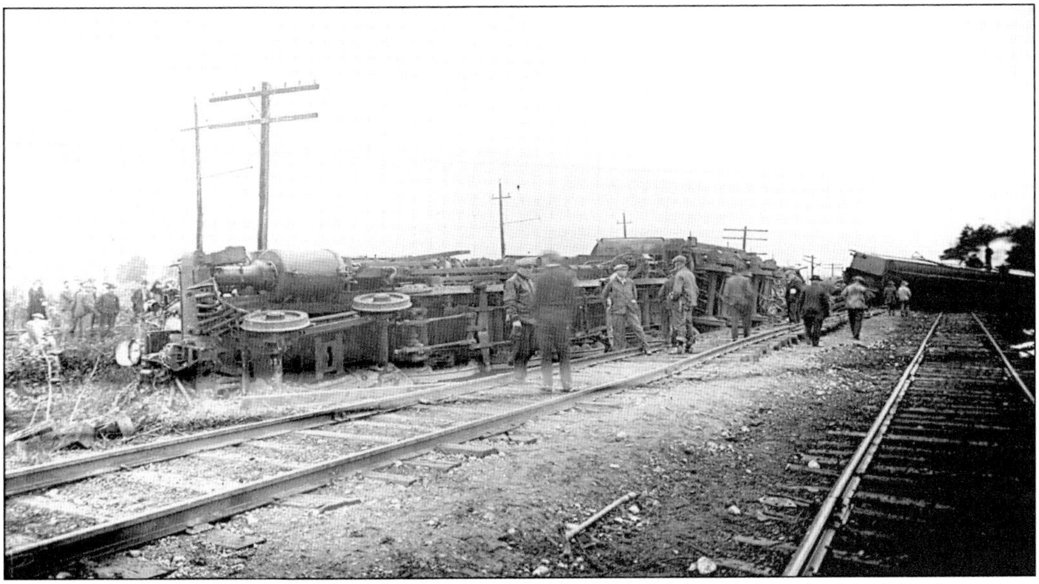

"Dashing through the night in an effort to make up time, the Ashland Limited of the Northwestern, train Number 111, struck a spread rail about 9:00 pm last night south of Weeden Station, sending Engineer James Gallagher to his death, severely injuring 10 passengers and endangering the lives of hundreds," reported the *Sheboygan Press* on September 20, 1923. Gallagher was pinned under his overturned engine, while most of the 150 passengers on the northbound train were thrown about as the cars tipped over and ploughed along the right-of-way. A relief train from Sheboygan, along with ambulances and taxicabs from the city, rushed to the wreck to assist the injured. The next morning, spectators examined the scene along the Milwaukee Northern interurban tracks, as seen in the photograph below.

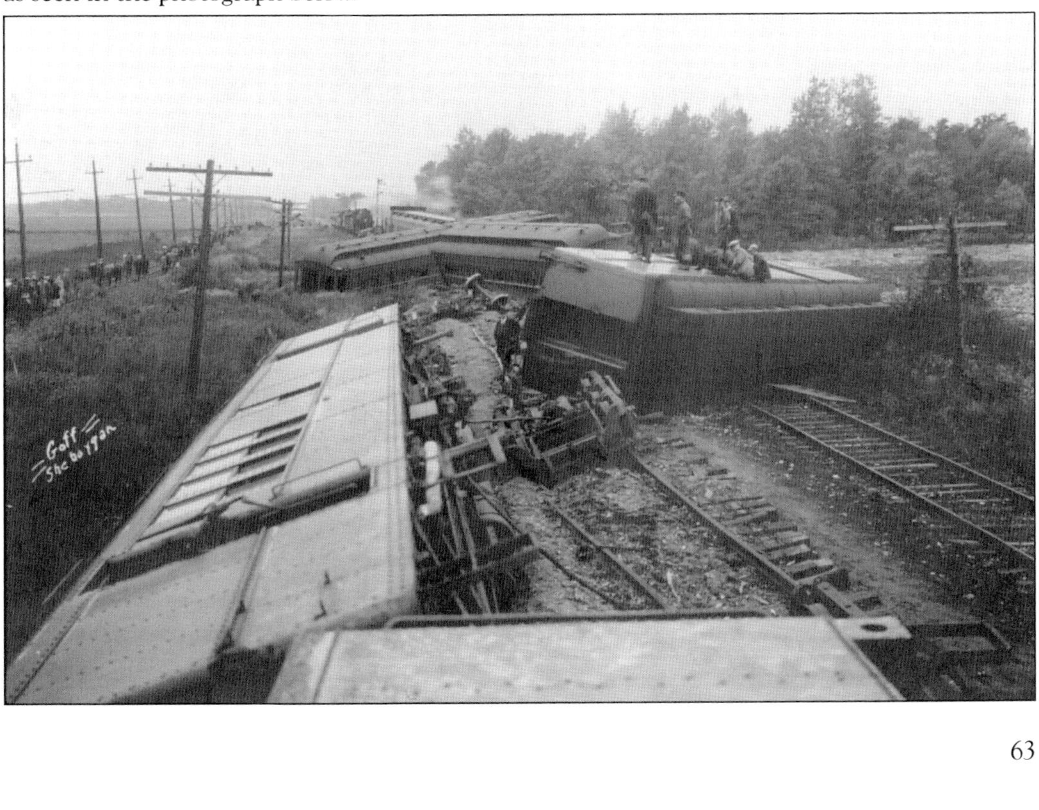

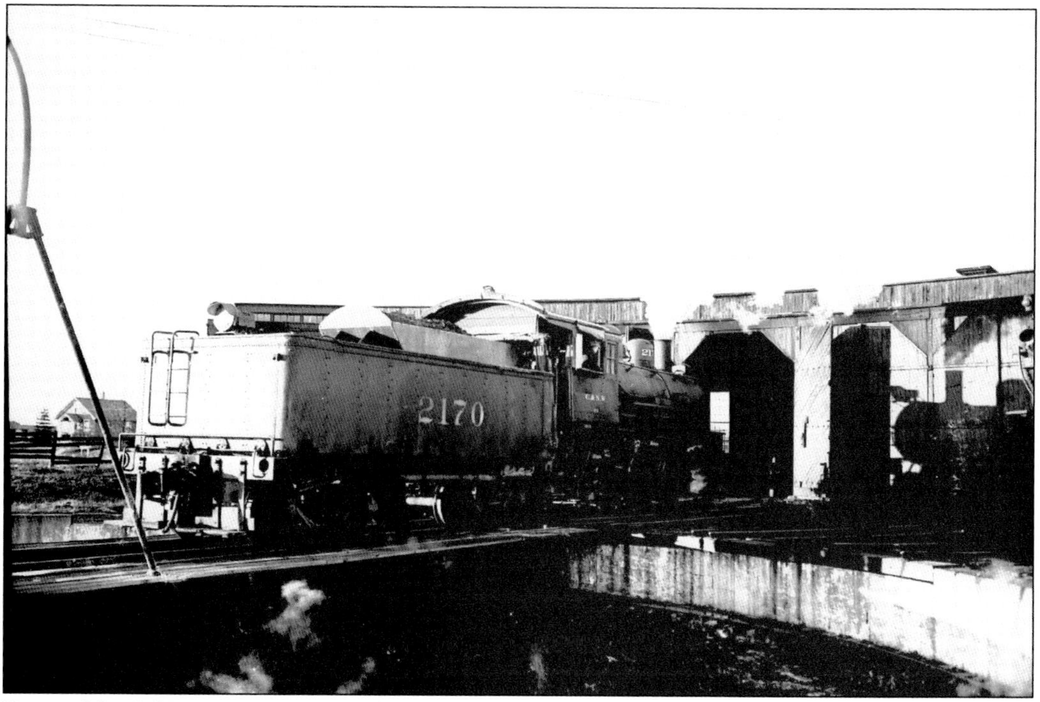

Engine No. 2170, a 0-6-0 M-2 switch engine, glides off the turntable and into the roundhouse at South Yard, the C&NW's rail yard and engine service facility south of Union Avenue. The six-stall roundhouse opened in 1907. The railroad added two longer stalls in 1927 to accommodate larger engines. Those stalls were removed in 1952, and most of the remaining roundhouse was gone by 1972.

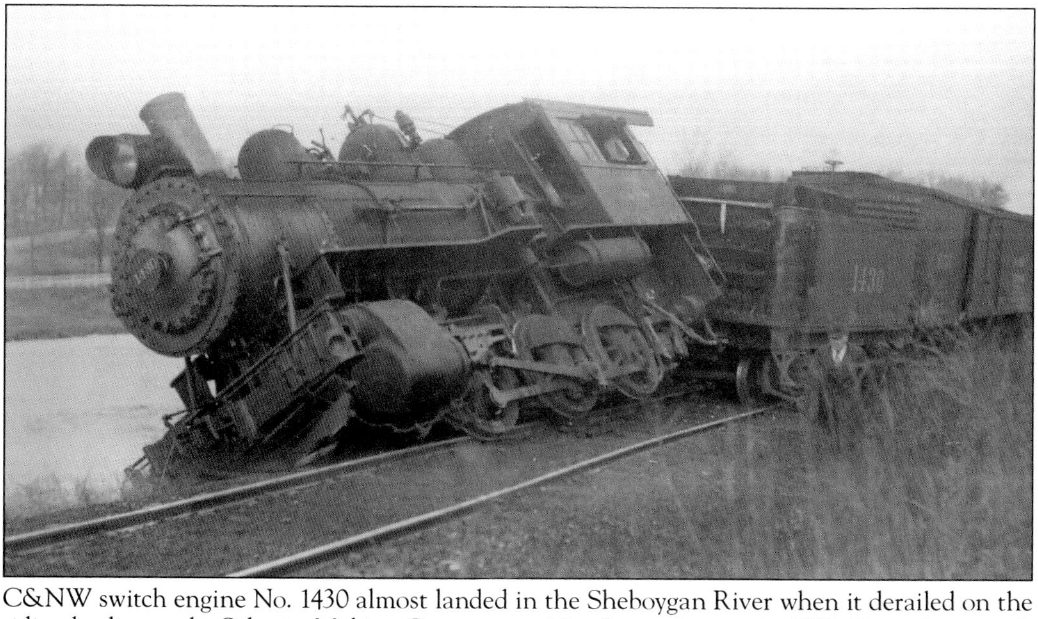

C&NW switch engine No. 1430 almost landed in the Sheboygan River when it derailed on the siding leading to the Schreier Malting Company on New Jersey Avenue in 1928. Two other switch engines narrowly missed falling in the river during earlier derailments at the same spot. The siding, laid before the turn of the 20th century, is one of the few still active in Sheboygan.

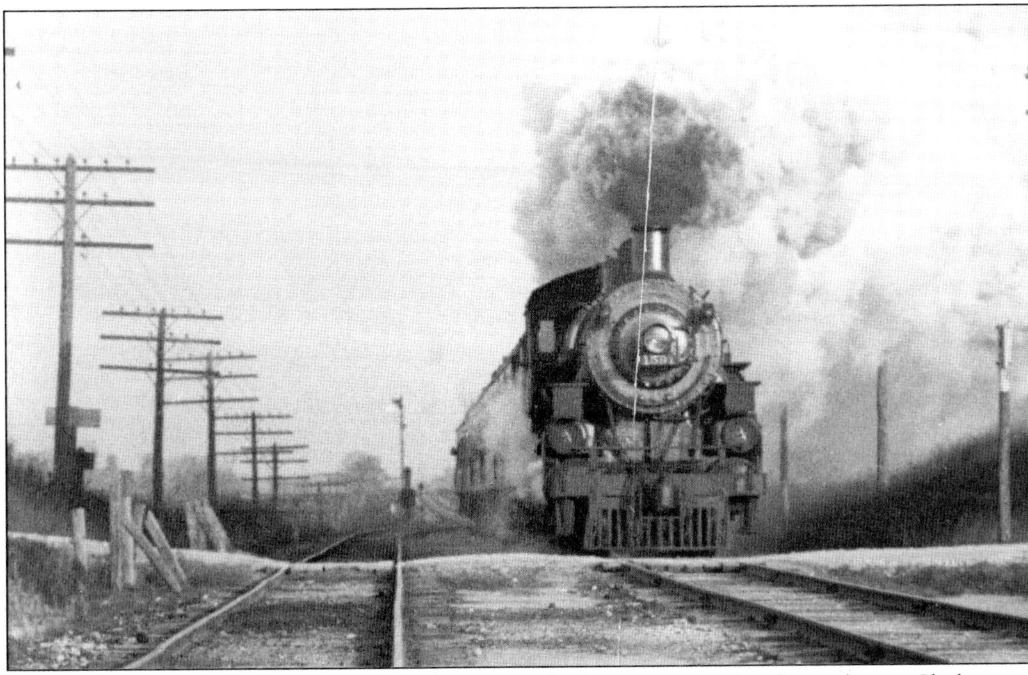

Engine No. 1591 charges across Eisner Avenue with three cars as it heads south into Sheboygan. The 4-6-0 Class-E Pacific engine is pulling train No. 306 on its daily (except Sunday) Manitowoc-to-Milwaukee morning run. Popular with travelers, the train was scheduled to arrive in Sheboygan at 7:36 a.m. and pull into the North Western Depot on the end of Wisconsin Avenue in Milwaukee at 8:50 a.m.

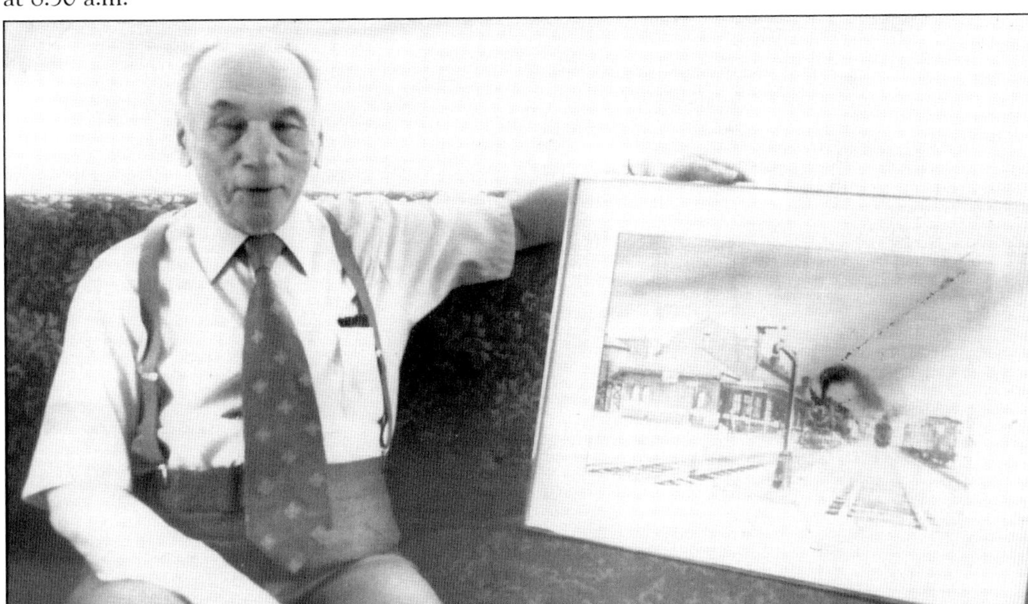

Andrew Driedric Sr., a longtime depot agent in Sheboygan, held the record for years of service with a railroad in Wisconsin when he retired in 1980 at age 82. He joined the Chicago & North Western Railroad Company as telegrapher in Belgium in 1916. He worked in Two Rivers, Port Washington, and Mequon, then spent his final 29 years at the Sheboygan depot. He retired with 64 years of service.

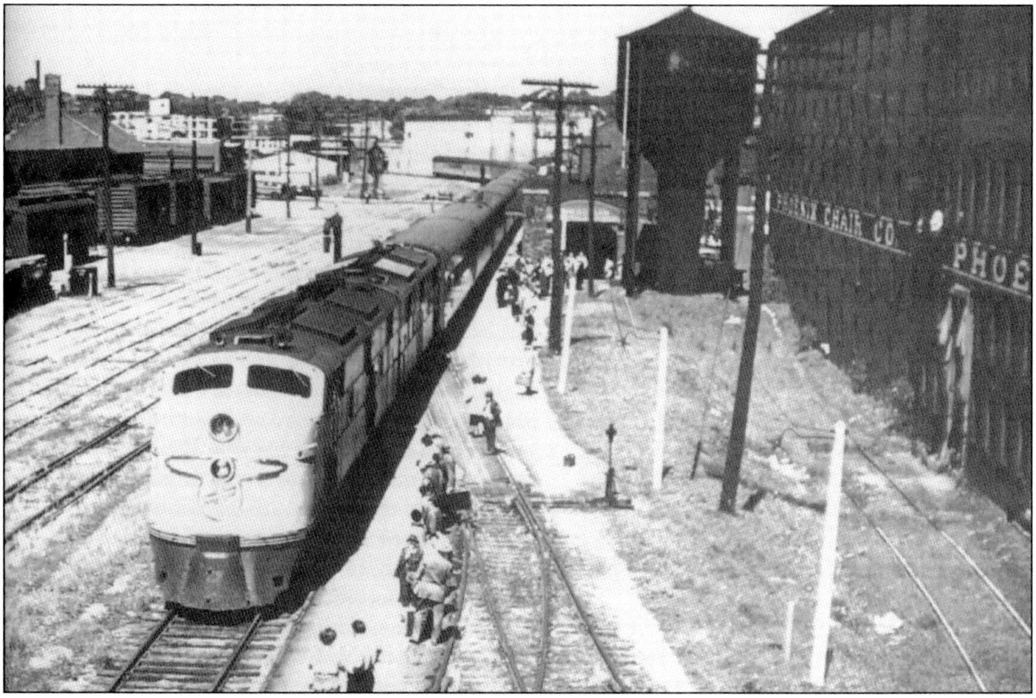

Train No. 214, the southbound Peninsula 400, arrives at the busy Sheboygan depot in the 1940s. A May 31, 1942 timetable shows the crack streamliner leaving Green Bay at 11:00 a.m., stopping in Sheboygan at 12:10 p.m. and arriving in Milwaukee at 1:15 p.m. The railroad's water tower and the Phoenix Chair Company are seen at right. The freight house is visible in the upper left. (Courtesy John Sachse.)

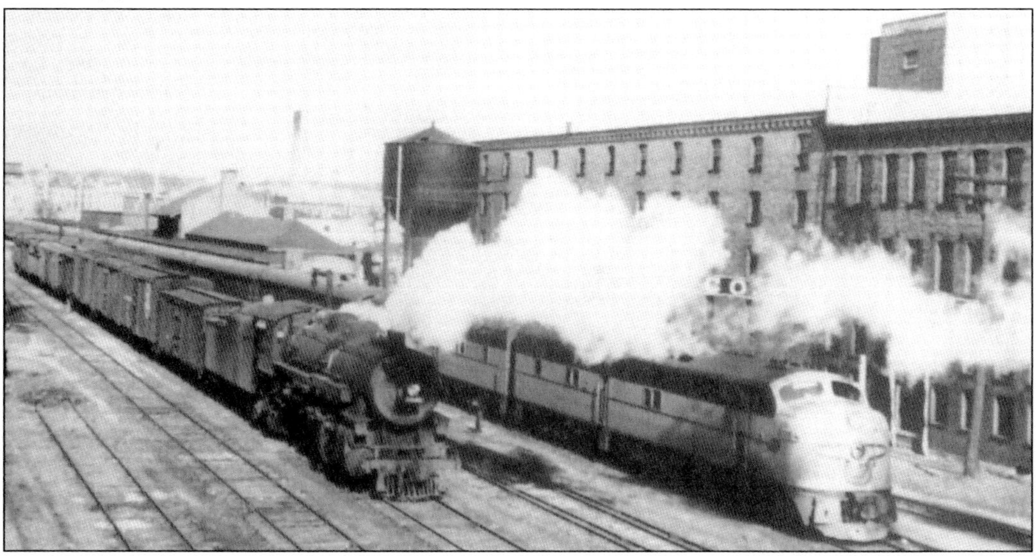

The morning way freight led by C&NW 2-8-2 engine No. 2591 has pulled into the rail yard south of Pennsylvania Avenue to make way for the southbound Peninsula 400 passenger train on its way to Milwaukee. The depot, water tower, and Phoenix Chair Company are seen behind the two trains. Way freights served the railroad's customers located between larger cities. (Courtesy Charles McCreary.)

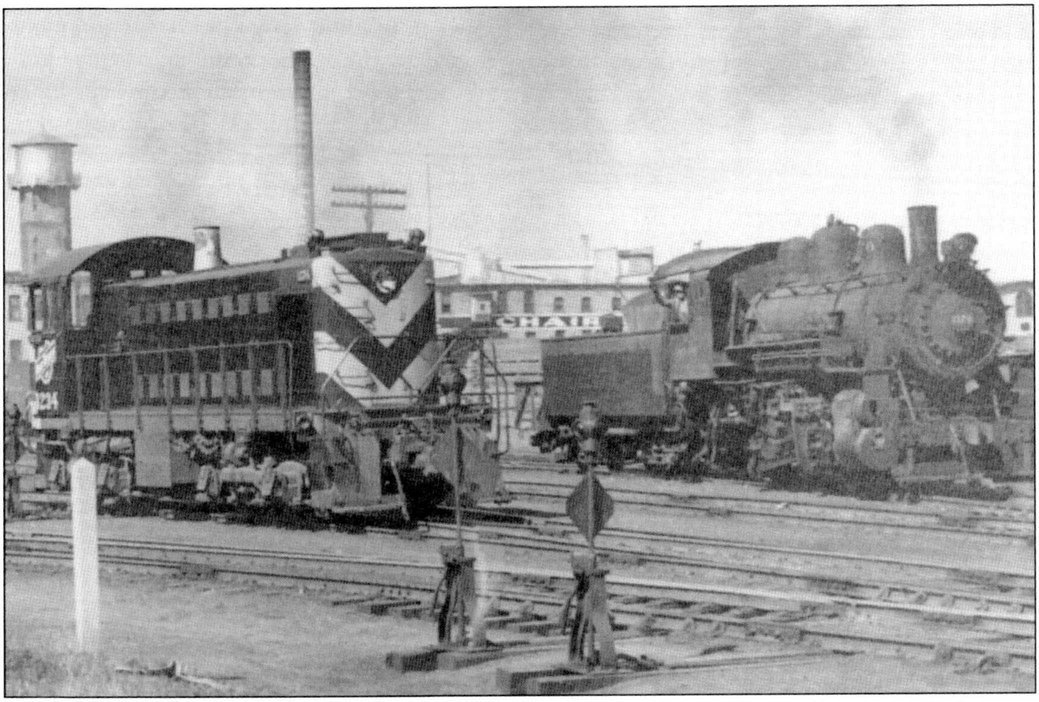

C&NW steam and diesel engines shared switching duties in the freight yard near the Sheboygan depot in the late 1940s as the railroad transitioned from steam to diesel power. At left is Alco S-1 No. 1234. The steamer at right is 0-6-0 M-2 No. 2177. (Courtesy John Sachse.)

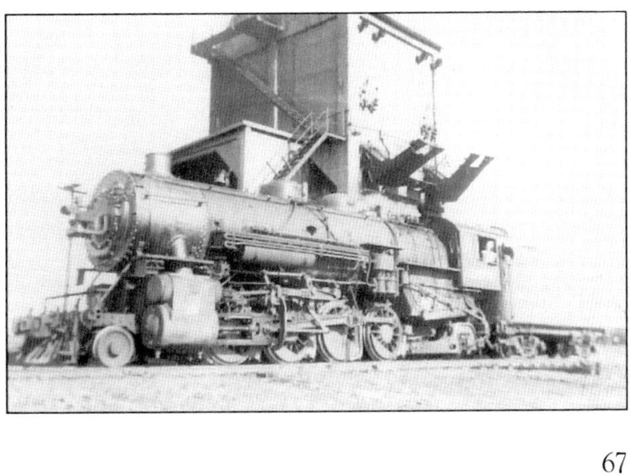

The Chicago & North Western Railroad Company erected a wooden coaling tower when it built its South Yard and engine service facilities south of Union Avenue. The tower burned to the ground in a spectacular fire in 1928. The railroad replaced it with a 100-ton concrete tower that was torn down in 1955. Engine No. 2553, a 2-8-2 Mikado, is pictured taking on coal from the latter tower. (Courtesy Dale Kuhn.)

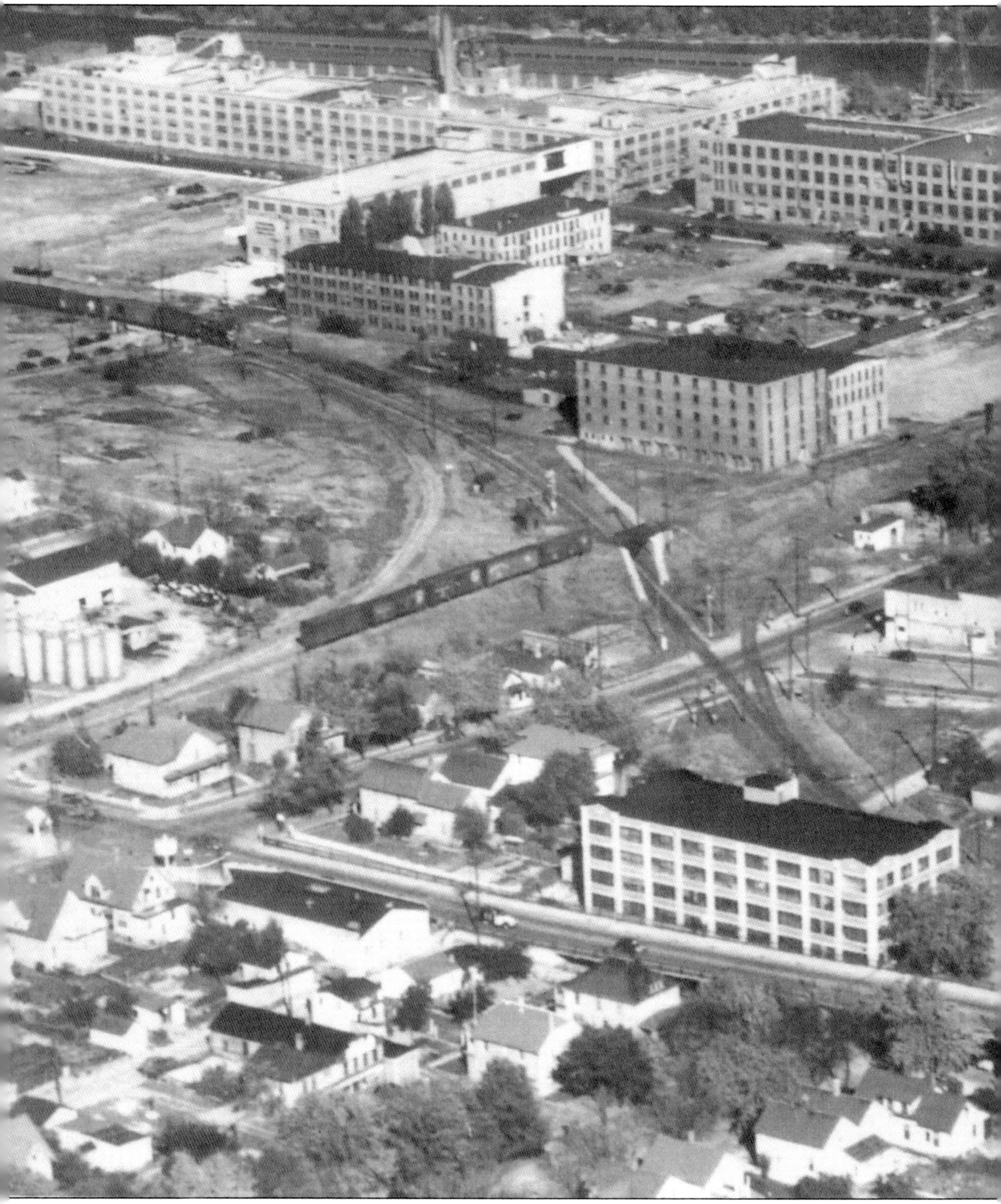

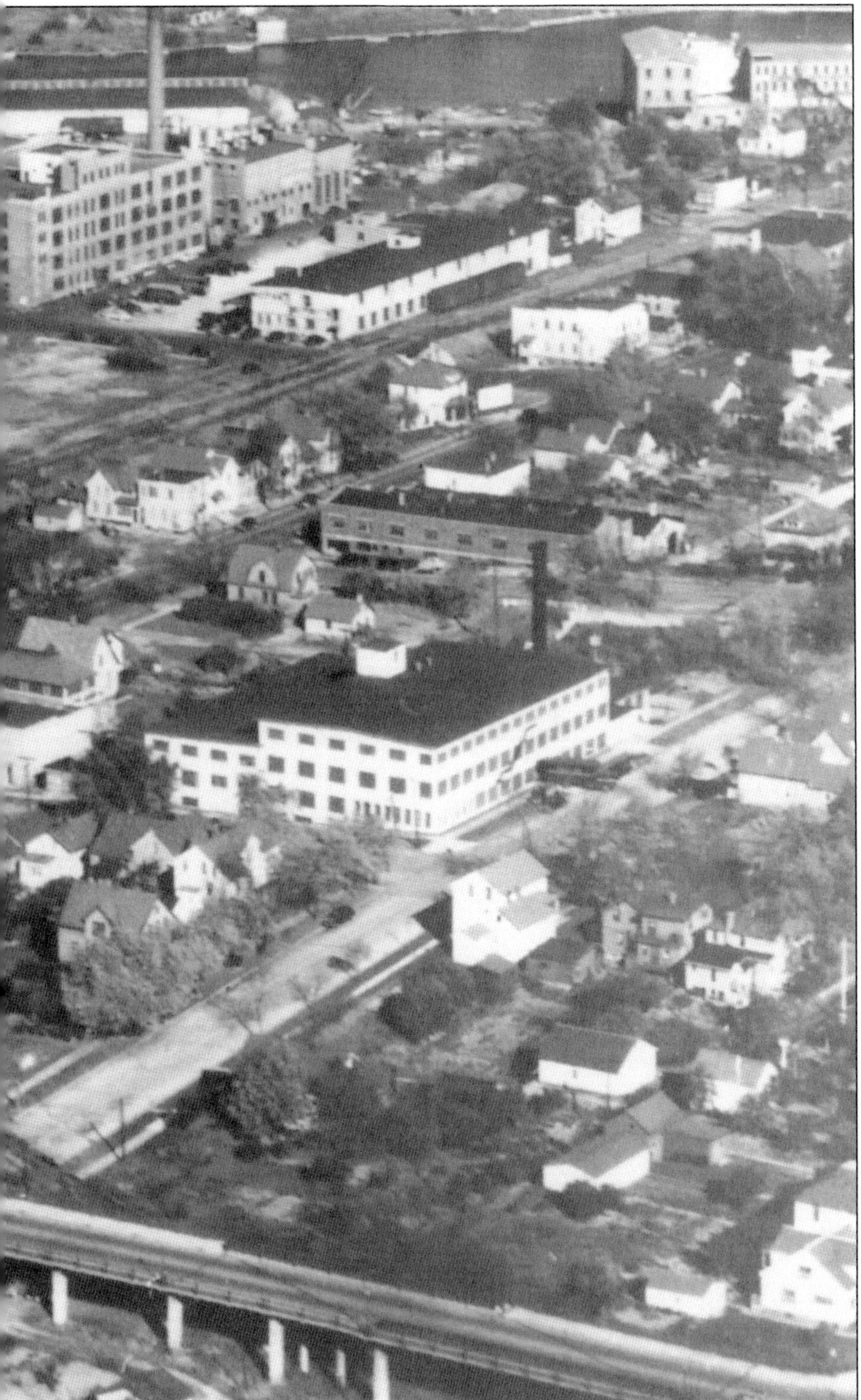

The railroad yard between Pennsylvania and Indiana Avenues was called the "bullpen" by those who worked there. The maze of tracks included an overpass seen in the center of the picture at left. It carried the old east-west line of the Sheboygan & Fond du Lac Railroad across the north-south line of the early Milwaukee, Lake Shore & Western Railroad. The view looks northeast over the city's industrial district.

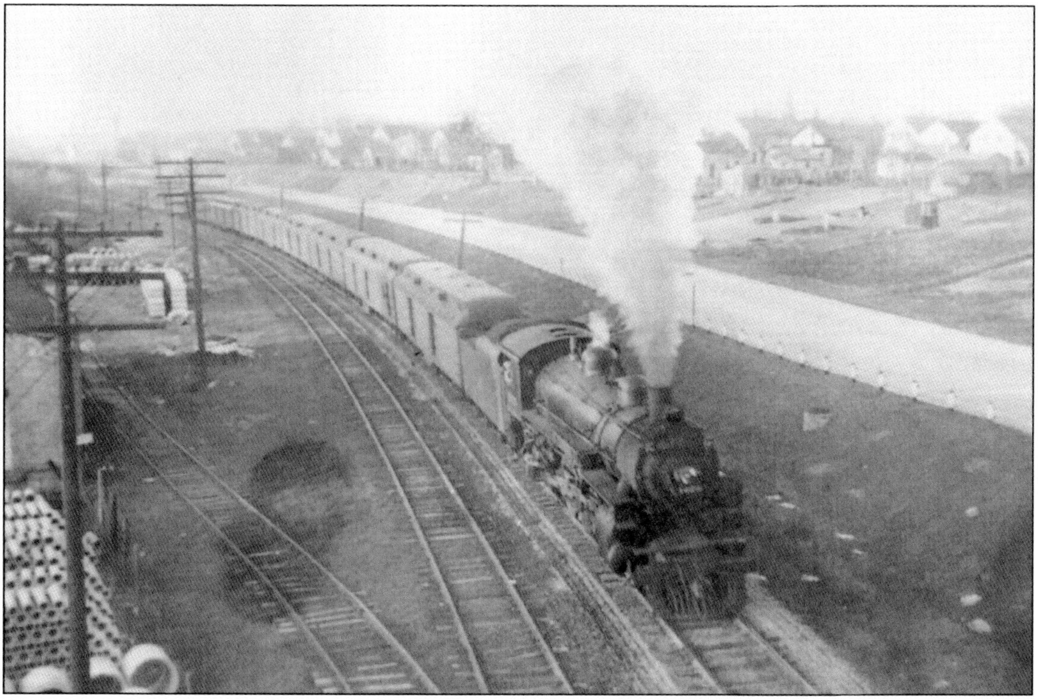

Passenger train No. 120, known as the *Evening Mail*, heads south out of Sheboygan in the late 1940s or early 1950s. Behind the 4-6-2 Class-E Pacific engine are cars full of mail followed by cars full of passengers. The train was scheduled to arrive in Sheboygan at 6:06 p.m. The railroad siding at left served the Van der Vaart Brick and Building Supply Company. (Courtesy John Sachse.)

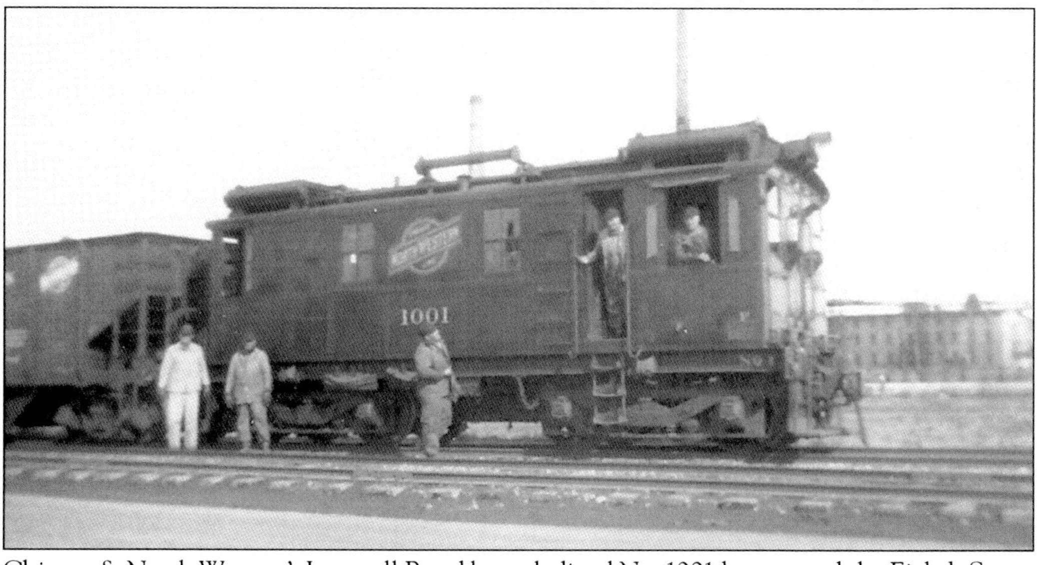

Chicago & North Western's Ingersoll-Rand boxcab diesel No. 1001 has crossed the Eighth Street Bridge over the Sheboygan River to switch cars at Sheboygan Coal Company in 1941. The railroad used streetcar and interurban tracks abandoned by Wisconsin Power and Light and the Milwaukee Electric Railway and Transportation Company to serve industries north of the river, including Upholstery Spring (later Spiller Spring), Superior Parlor Frame, Fashioned Furniture, and the coal company. (Courtesy Dale Kuhn.)

Five

Riding the Trolley

At one time, a person could board an interurban railroad car in Elkhart Lake and ride it more than 1,000 miles on interconnecting trolley lines almost all the way to New York City. The trolley era in Sheboygan began in 1886. With tickets initially priced at 3¢ per ride, residents took the streetcar company's advertising slogan, "Cheaper than Walking," to heart. By 1892, more than 11,000 passengers were riding the cars each month. Trolley lines in the city gradually expanded until they reached west to Kohler, Sheboygan Falls, Plymouth and Elkhart Lake and south to Oostburg, Cedar Grove, Belgium, and on into Milwaukee. Improved streets and highways and the popularity of the automobile brought the trolley era to an end. City cars were taken off the streets of Sheboygan in 1935. Service to Plymouth ended in 1938, and the interurban line south was abandoned in 1940.

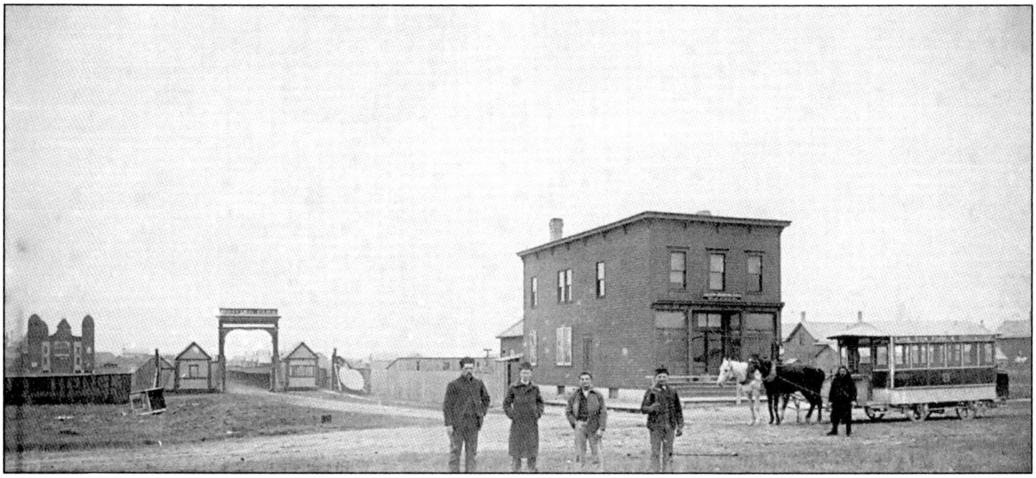

Sheboygan's first streetcars, pulled by horses or mules, began service on September 22, 1886. Tracks initially ran from Eighth Street and Kentucky Avenue to Fifteenth Street and Michigan Avenue. The line was extended to the railroad depot at Twelfth Street and Pennsylvania Avenue and later to the fairgrounds and horse racetrack on Saemann Avenue just west of the Calumet Road. The little four-wheel streetcars were hard riding and unheated, but they were also inexpensive, convenient, and popular.

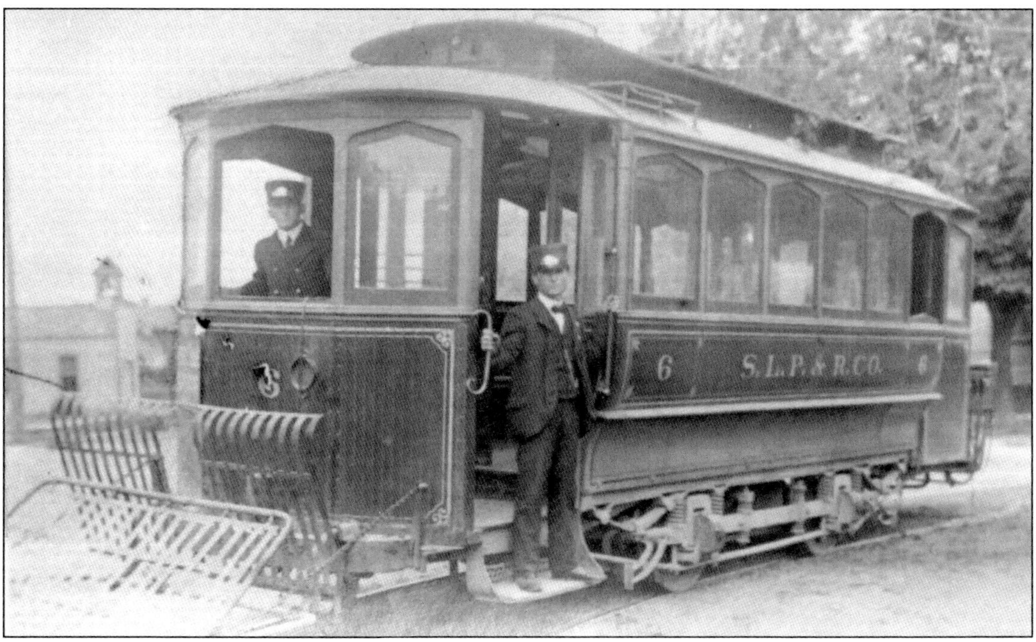

The first electric streetcars to run in local service were often small single truck cars like No. 6. The cars were not as smooth riding as the bigger cars, which had sets of wheels on both ends. The fender at the front of the car was designed to scoop pedestrians, animals, and bicycles off the tracks and then hold them in the basket until the car stopped.

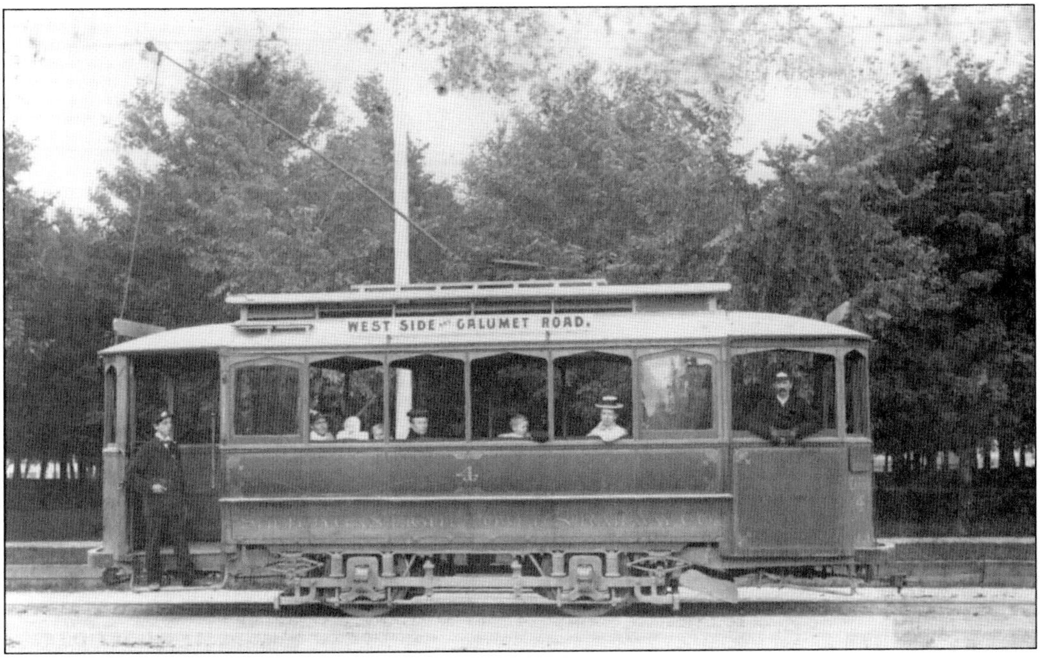

The Sheboygan Light, Power and Railway Company introduced electric streetcars to local residents on November 27, 1895. West Side cars eventually served the Calumet Road area and ran as far north as the Polar Ware Company, located north of North Avenue. East Side cars traveled north on Eighth Street to Bluff Avenue, and followed Fourth and Fifth Streets south to Pennsylvania Avenue, where there was a siding to the Goodrich steamship docks. The cars then returned to Eighth Street and Pennsylvania Avenue.

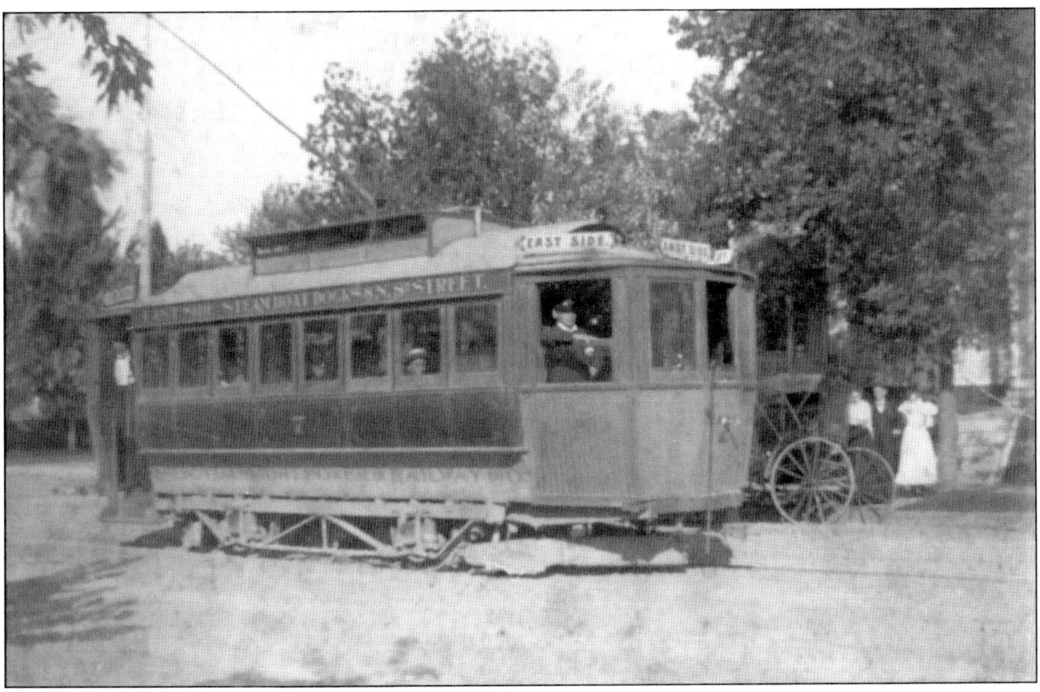

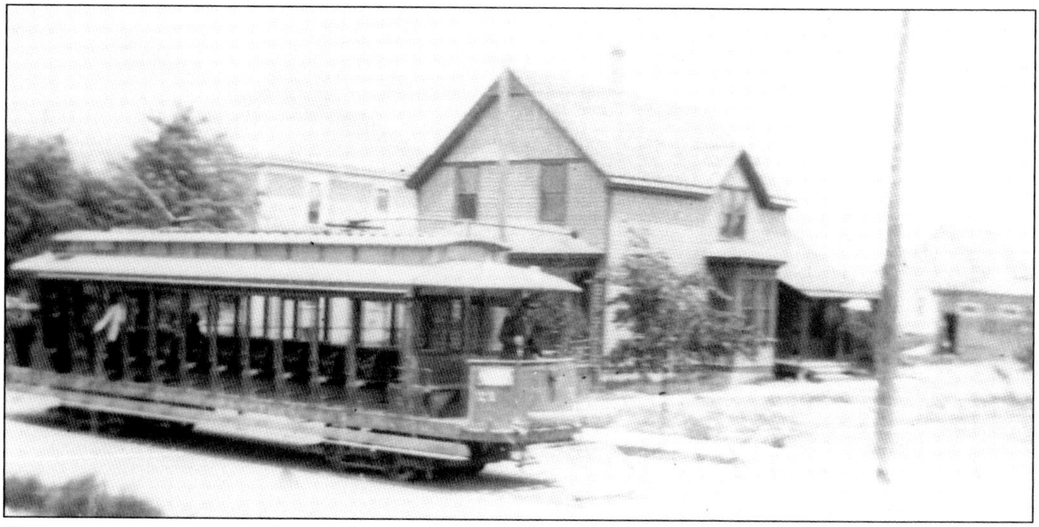

Open streetcars, ones with no sides, were the preferred cars for summer excursions to Lake View Park on Sheboygan's far south side and to Crystal Lake and Elkhart Lake after the interurban line opened in 1909. They featured bench-type seats that ran the width of the car and running boards for quick and easy access. Pictured appears to be car No. 21 at Eighth and National Streets prior to 1916.

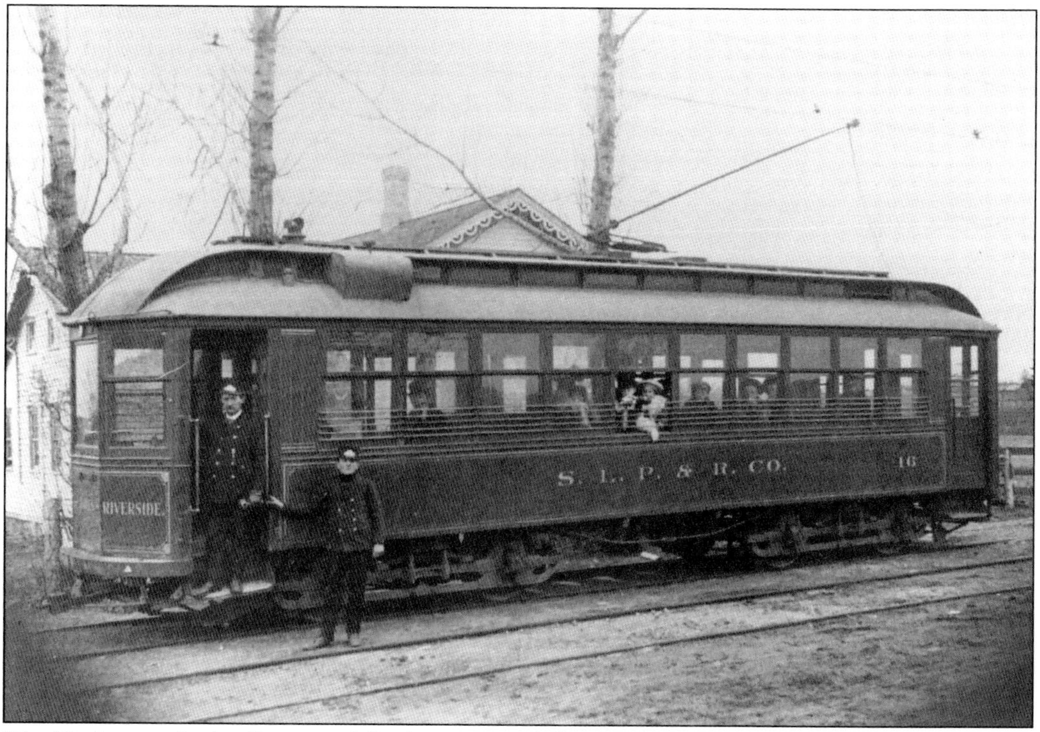

The Sheboygan Light, Power and Railway opened the first leg of its interurban line to the west on November 26, 1899. Some 460 patrons took advantage of 10 round trips between Sheboygan and Riverside, now Kohler, that day. Interurban cars traveled north on Eighth Street, west on Michigan Avenue, traveled over to Erie Avenue on Seventeenth Street, and then followed Erie Avenue west to Riverside.

As ridership increased, the old horse-drawn streetcars were pressed into service as trailers attached to the new electric cars. The combination of trolleys is shown here at Fountain Park during a stop to pick up passengers. The horse car is distinguished by its small size and large wheels.

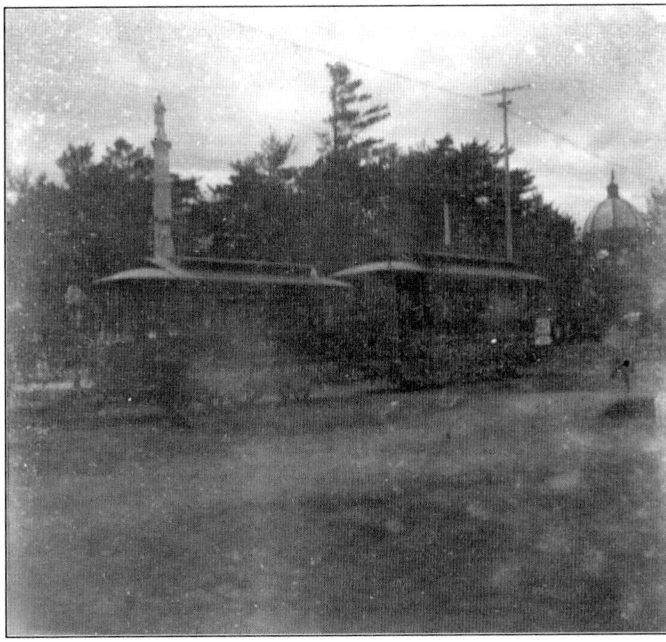

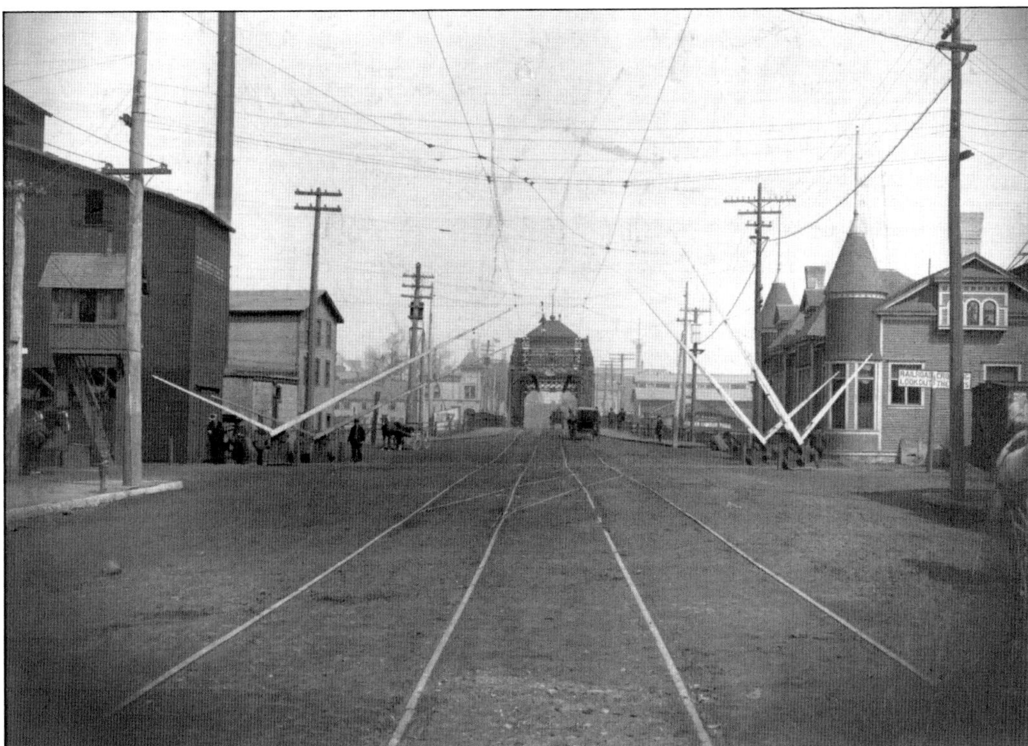

Streetcar and railroad tracks crossed just north of the intersection of Eighth Street and Indiana Avenue. A crossing tower (pictured left) and long white railroad gates keep pedestrians, streetcars, and other vehicles away from the tracks when trains approach. The bridge over the Sheboygan River is seen to the north of the crossing, and the offices of the C. Reiss Coal Company are on the right.

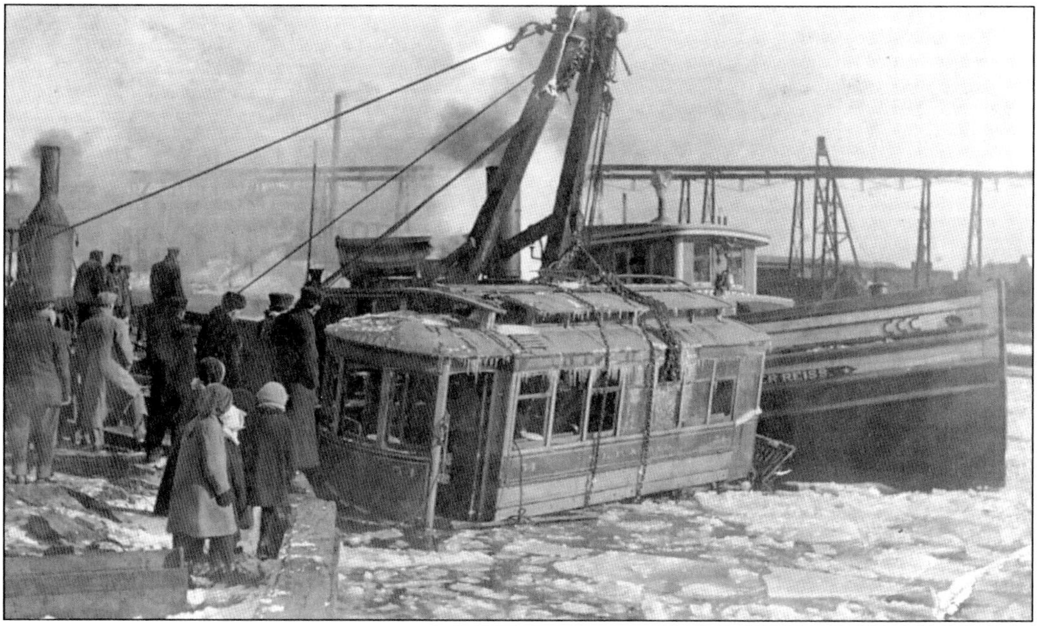

The most tragic streetcar accident in Sheboygan occurred on February 9, 1911. Southbound car No. 54 slid down the Eighth Street hill on icy rails and plunged into the river at the open drawbridge. Three women passengers died, despite rescue efforts by the crew of the tugboat *Peter Reiss*. Car No. 54 was never returned to passenger service.

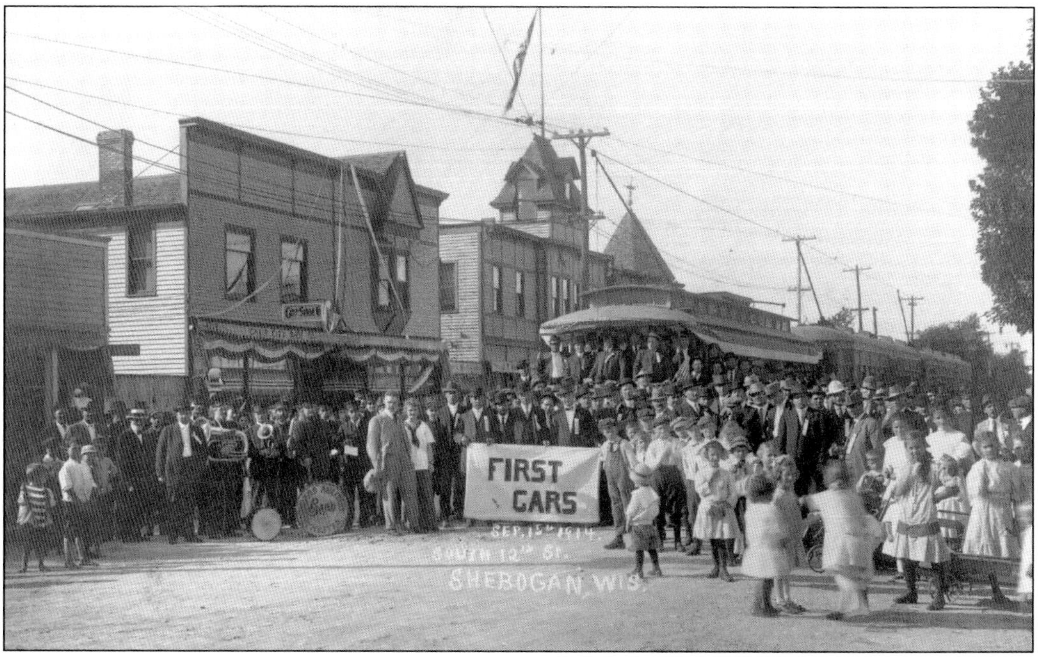

The Sheboygan Railway and Electric Company, which succeeded the Sheboygan Light, Power and Railway Company in 1910, extended service to the southwest side of Sheboygan in 1914. The first streetcars arrived in the business district of South Twelfth Street on September 15 and were welcomed by large crowds. The southwest line ran from Seventeenth Street and Indiana Avenue to Georgia Avenue and then east to South Twelfth Street.

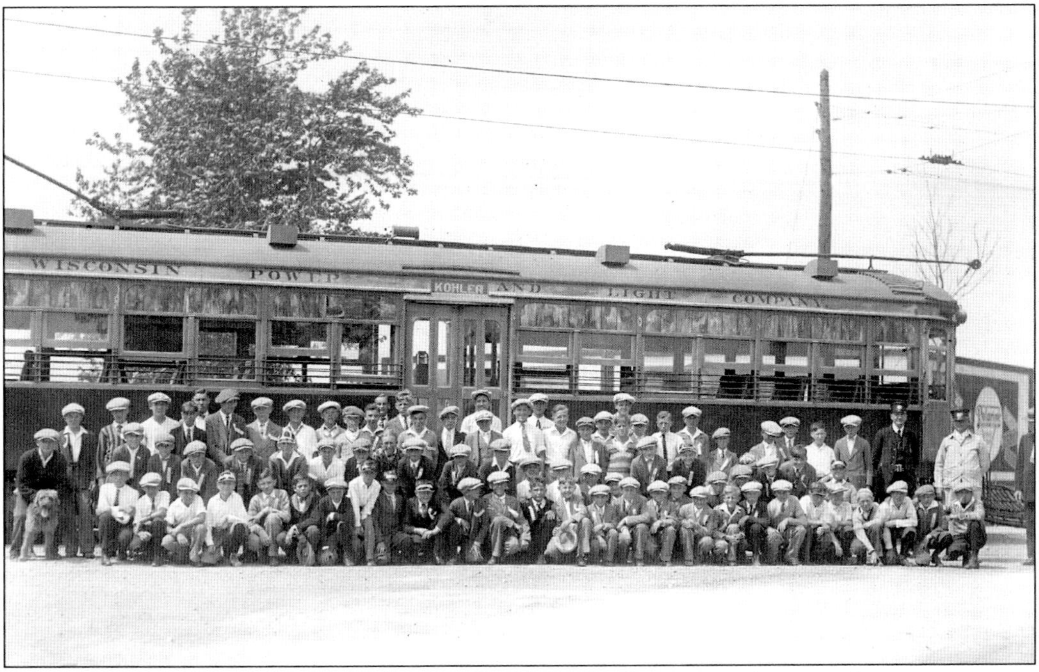

Riding the trolley lines was a special treat. The *Sheboygan Press* treated its paperboys to an outing at Shooting Park in 1926 that included a ride on car No. 31, a center-door steel interurban car. Cars No. 31 and No. 32 were built by the St. Louis Car Company in 1914 to provide limited service to Elkhart Lake. They were remodeled into freight motors in 1929.

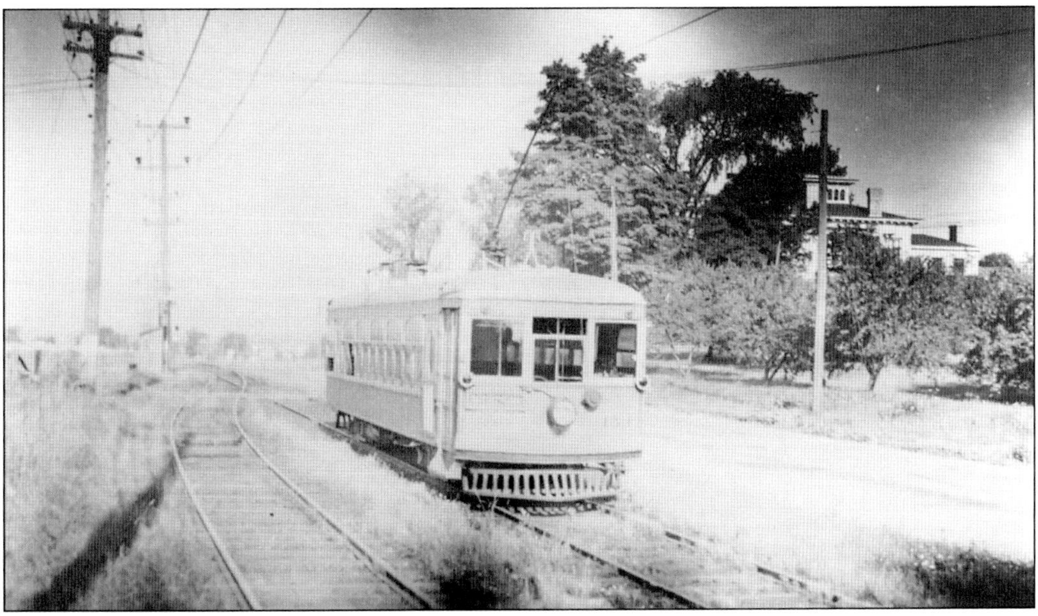

Car No. 153 passes Taylor Siding on its left and Taylor House on its right as it travels west on the interurban line to Plymouth and Elkhart Lake. Taylor House is now part of the Sheboygan County Historical Society Museum complex at the intersection of Erie Avenue and Taylor Drive. No. 153 was one of five cars that came to Sheboygan when the Fond du Lac–Neenah line closed in 1930.

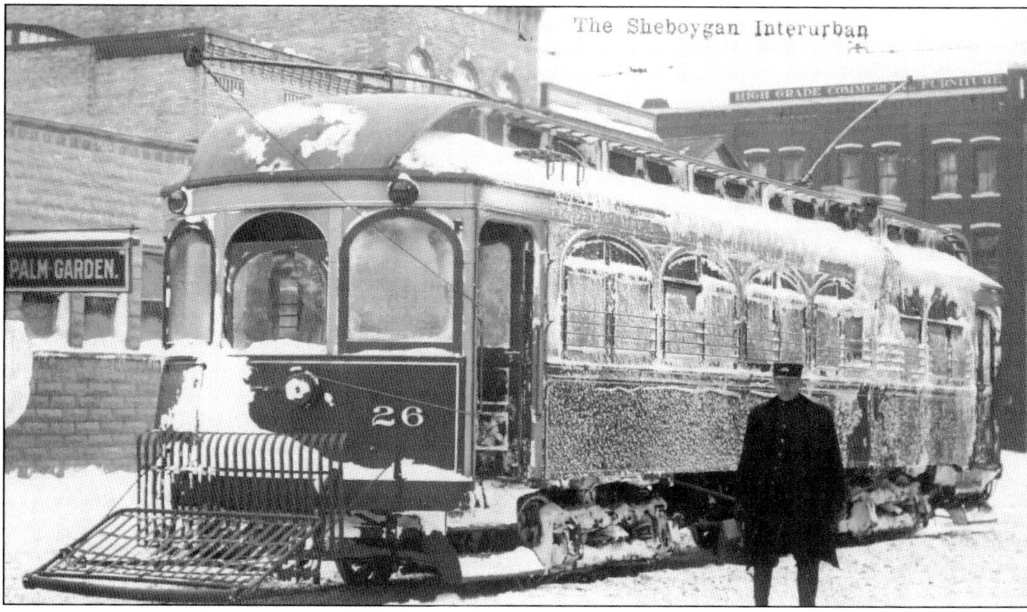

Local interurban railroads usually fared better than steam-powered rail cars during winter storms. Interurban cars ran on more frequent schedules than trains, and interurban companies had powerful snowplows designed to keep their lines open no matter how deep the snow. During the summer, these same cars (minus their plows) hauled packaged freight between Sheboygan and Elkhart Lake. Car No. 26, shown above covered in snow and ice in downtown Sheboygan, has the longest history of any local car. After 30 years on the rails and more than 40 years as a summer cottage on the shores of Lake Michigan, it was carefully restored to its original grandeur and is now on display at the East Troy Electric Railroad Museum, located west of Milwaukee.

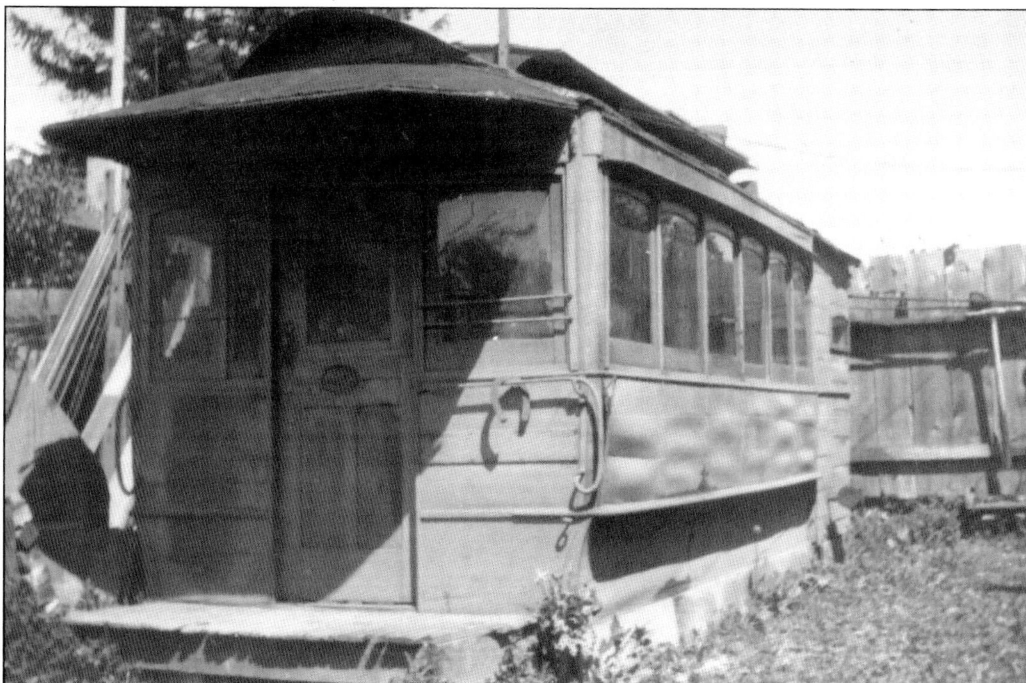

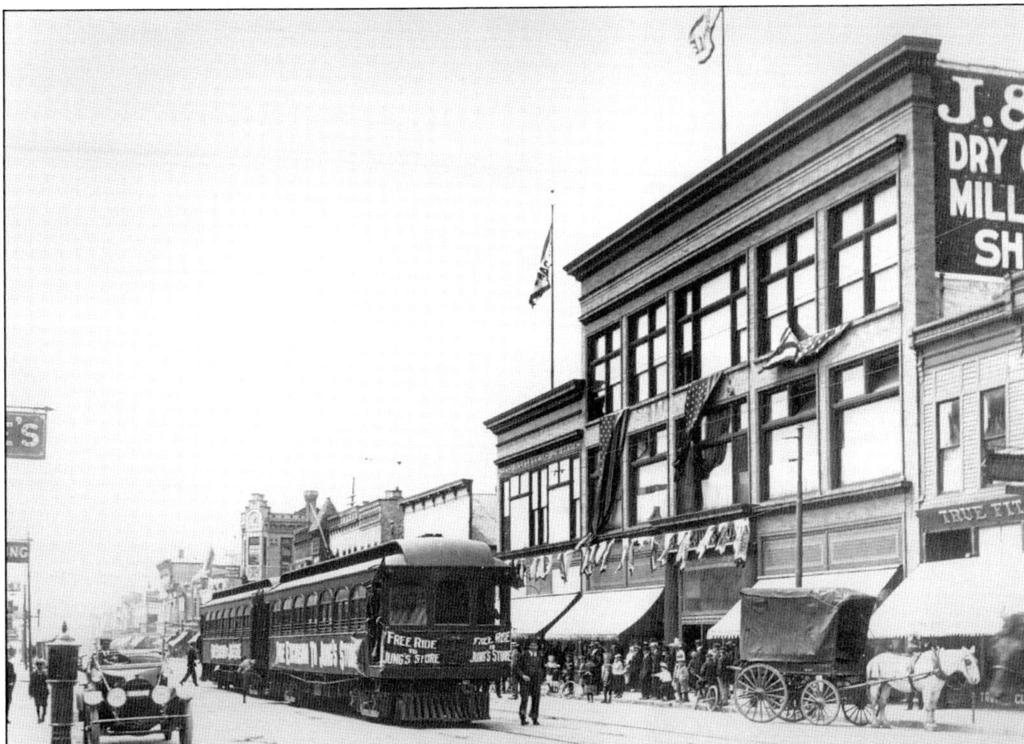

To lure patrons into downtown Sheboygan, large department stores occasionally offered customers free rides on the interurban cars. Here, two trolleys have just delivered shoppers to the front of the J&W Jung store on Eighth Street. Banners on the cars promoted the free rides. Note the contrast of the automobile parked on one side of the street and a horse-drawn wagon on the other.

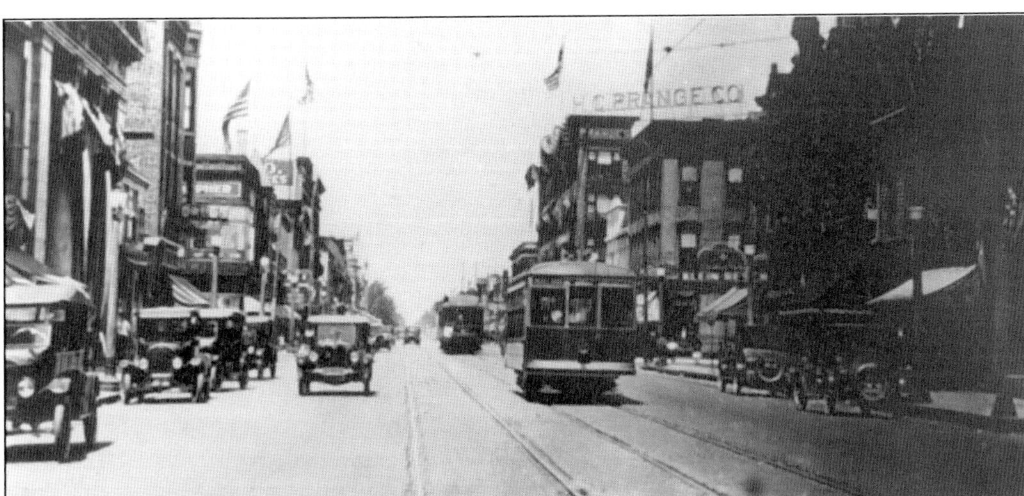

By the mid-1920s, streetcars and interurbans were losing out in popularity to the automobile. Here, a small city car follows a large interurban car north on Eighth Street through the downtown business district where the trolley lines were double-tracked. The H.C. Prange Company department store is seen on the right, and the Bank of Sheboygan is decked out in bunting on the left.

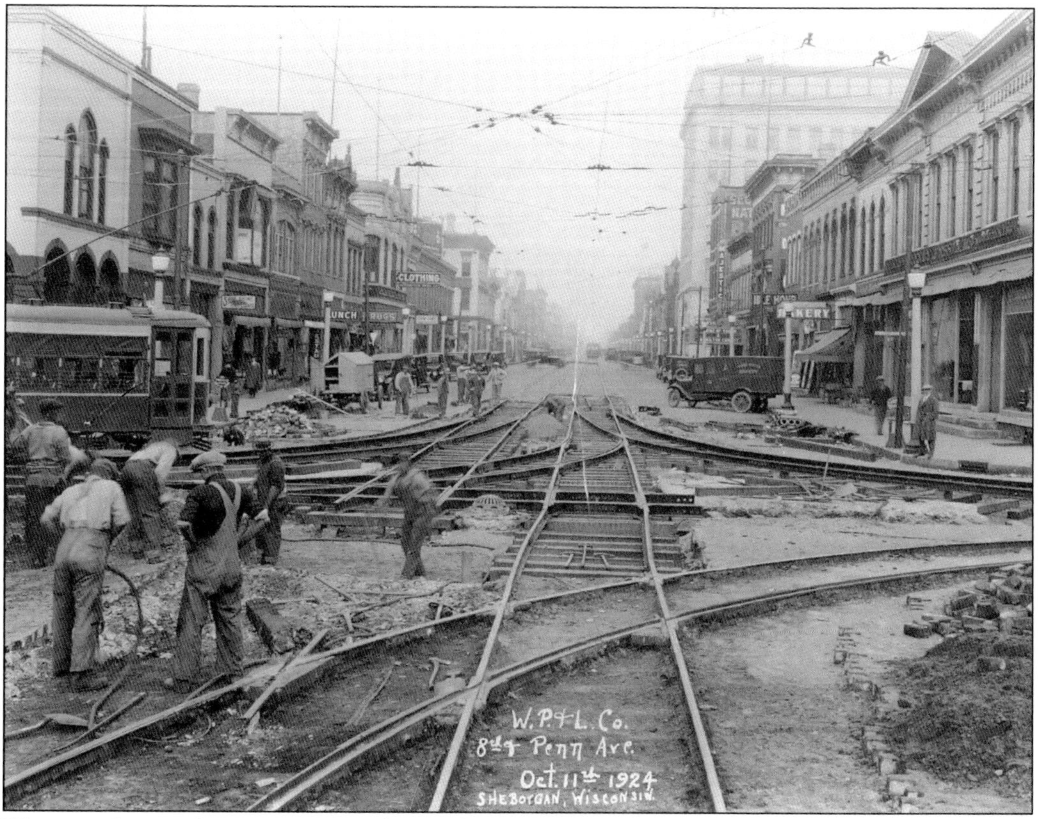

The complexity of intersecting tracks on the corner of Eighth Street and Pennsylvania Avenue boggles the mind. Wisconsin Power and Light Company (WP&L) took ownership of Sheboygan's streetcar and interurban lines in 1924. That same year, the company began a $122,000 improvement project that included laying new tracks through downtown and installing noiseless switches at both Eighth Street and Pennsylvania Avenue and Eighth Street and Michigan Avenue. These switches could be operated electrically by motormen from their cars. Before new tracks could be laid, WP&L hired a local demolition expert known as "Dynamite Bill" to blast out the old tracks and 18 inches of concrete under them without breaking nearby store windows around the Pennsylvania Avenue intersection. Complicated track work was also installed at the WP&L carbarn on the northeast corner of South Eighth Street and Clara Avenue.

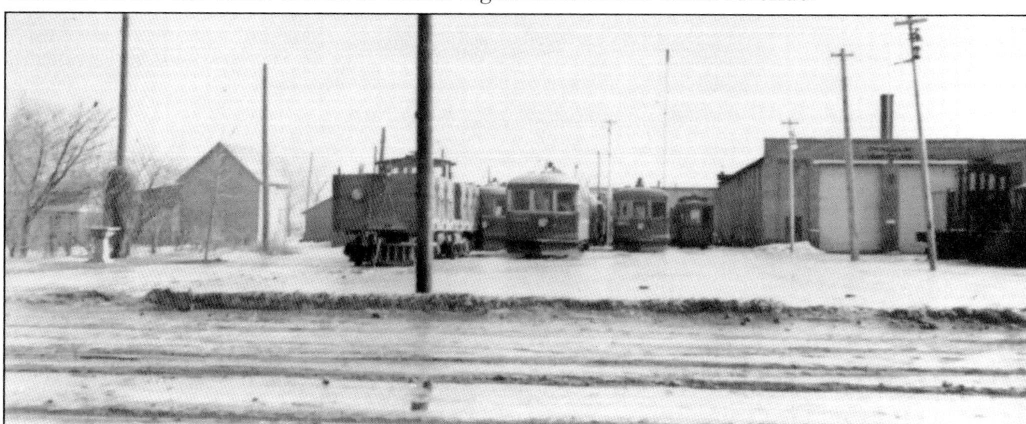

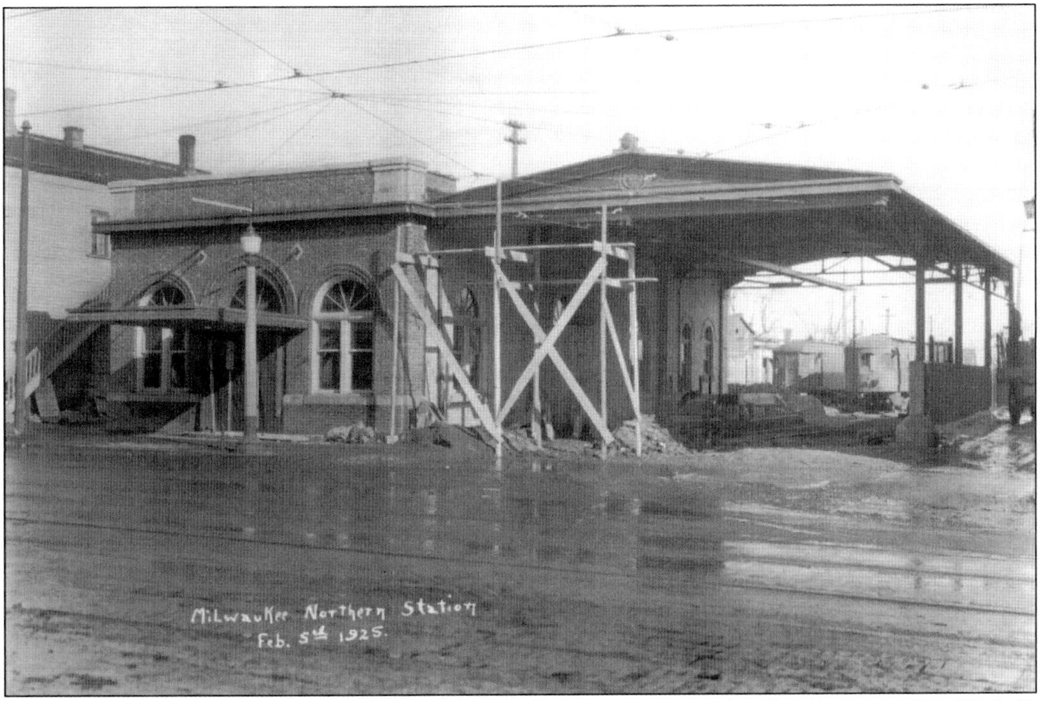

Wisconsin Power and Light and the Milwaukee Electric Railway and Light Company (TMER&L) opened a union terminal on the east side of Eighth Street south of Pennsylvania Avenue in 1925.

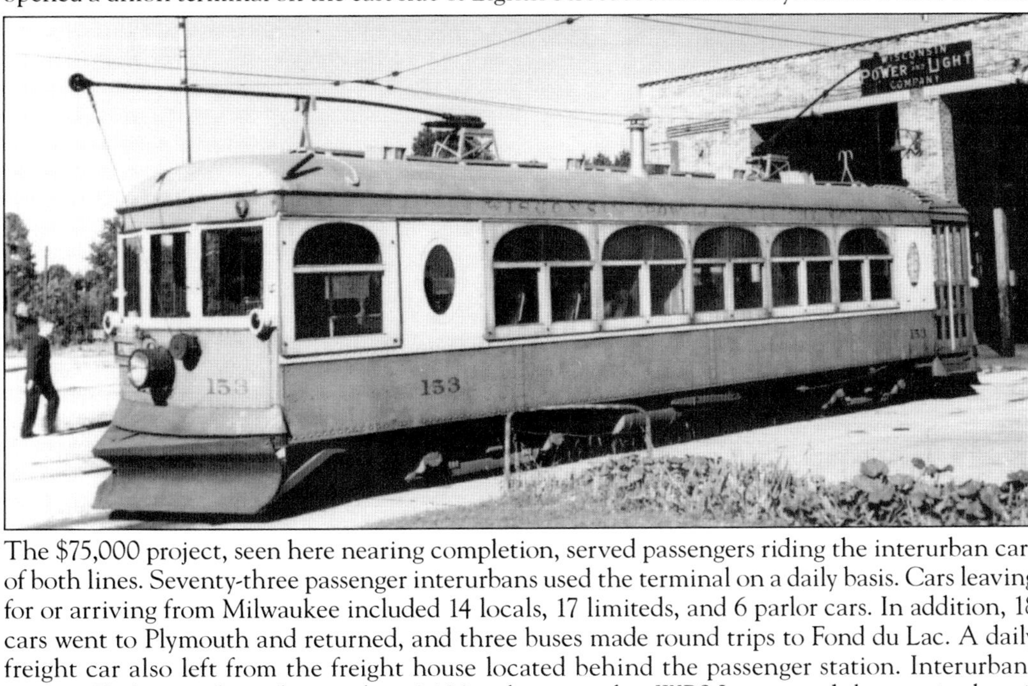

The $75,000 project, seen here nearing completion, served passengers riding the interurban cars of both lines. Seventy-three passenger interurbans used the terminal on a daily basis. Cars leaving for or arriving from Milwaukee included 14 locals, 17 limiteds, and 6 parlor cars. In addition, 18 cars went to Plymouth and returned, and three buses made round trips to Fond du Lac. A daily freight car also left from the freight house located behind the passenger station. Interurbans serving Sheboygan logged more than 2,100 miles every day. WP&L cars used the terminal until December 10, 1938, and Milwaukee Electric Railway and Light cars until September 22, 1940. The Victorian Chocolate Shoppe at 519 South Eighth Street is listed in the 2010 Yellow Pages as occupying the old union terminal building.

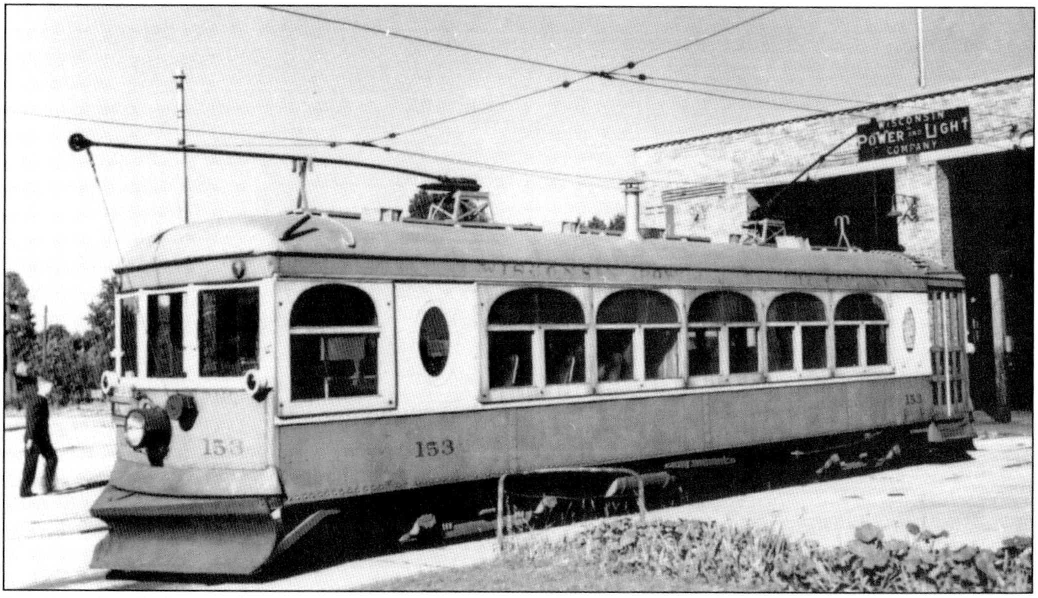

In 1930, five lightweight interurban cars from the abandoned WP&L line in Oshkosh arrived in Sheboygan. These 43-foot cars built by the St. Louis Car Company were numbered 150 through 154. They provided most of the interurban service from 1930 until the line to Plymouth was abandoned on December 10, 1938. Car No. 153 is shown at the carbarn on South Eighth Street and Clara Avenue.

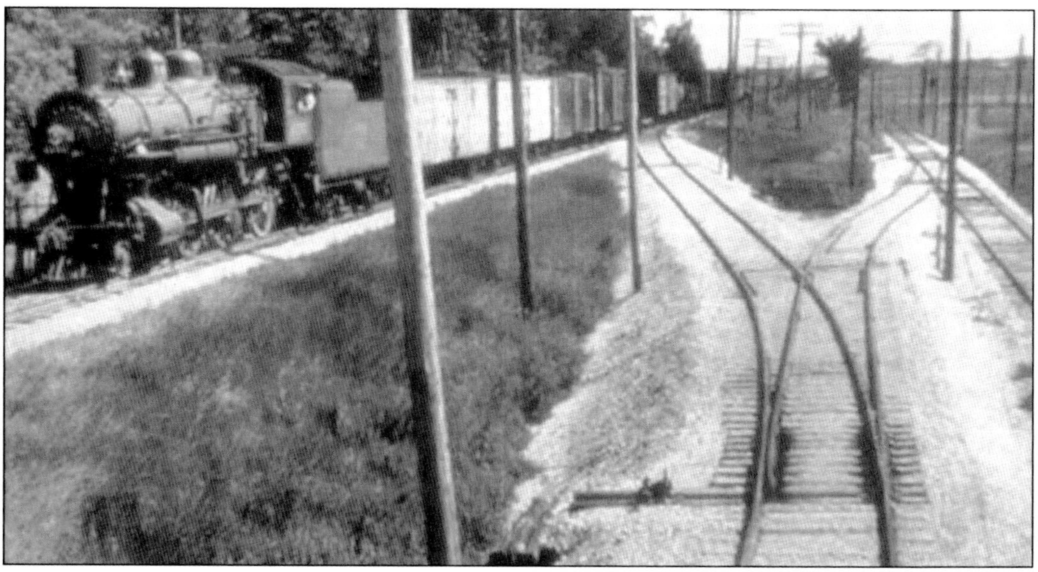

In 1930, Wisconsin Power and Light opened an interchange with the Milwaukee Road in Plymouth and began running interurban freight trains to and from Sheboygan. A Westinghouse electric locomotive powered trains like the one shown above near Eighteenth Street and Erie Avenue. The trains delivered coal to the Edgewater power plant. They rumbled down Erie and Michigan Avenues at night, then turned south onto Eighth Street to Edgewater.

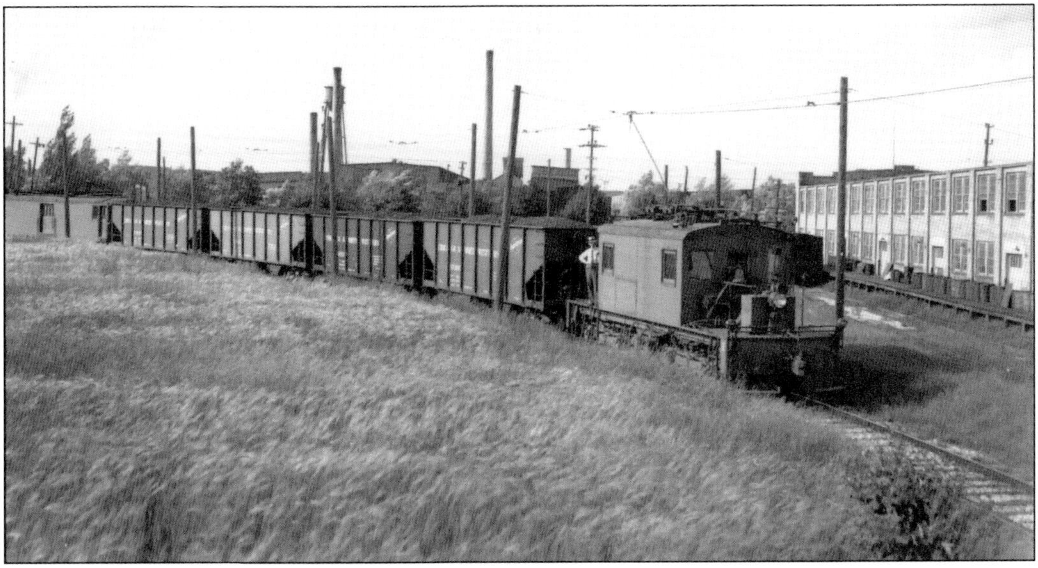

After more than four years of delays, C&NW finally built an interchange between its line and the Milwaukee Electric Railway & Light interurban line south of South Yard. The railroad delivered coal cars to the interchange, and interurban freight engines pulled the cars to the Edgewater power plant. On August 4, 1937, the last of the big rumbling coal cars rolled down city streets, ending seven years of annoying traffic.

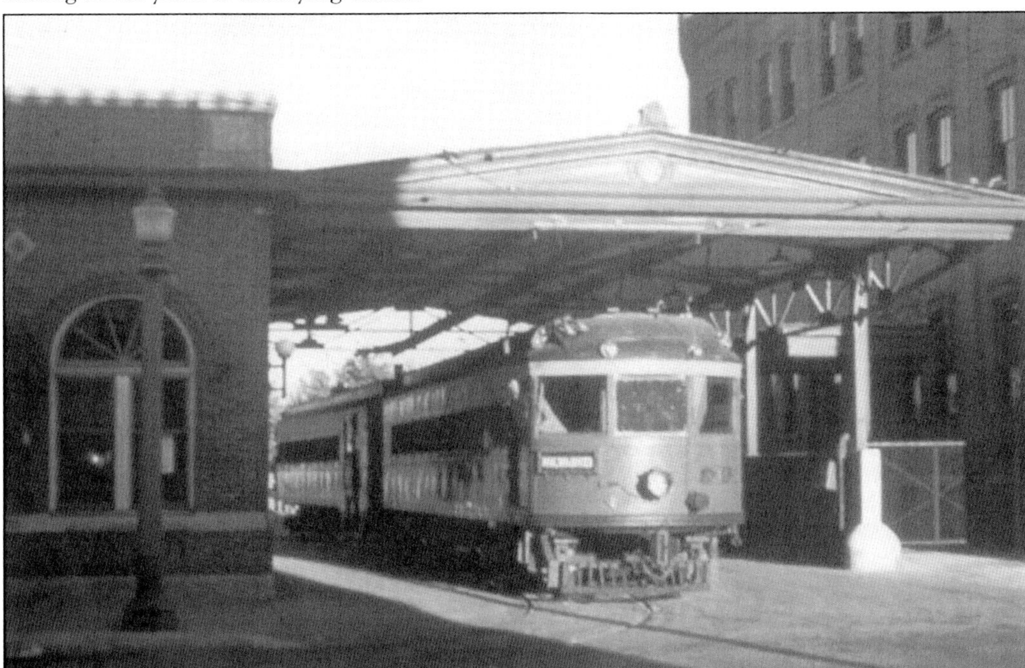

A TM interurban car and its trailer bask in the afternoon sun at the Sheboygan terminal awaiting the start of another trip to Milwaukee. The TMER&L purchased the Milwaukee Northern (MN) Railway for $6 million in 1922, but Sheboygan County residents considered the MN their line until the interurbans made their final run south on September 22, 1940.

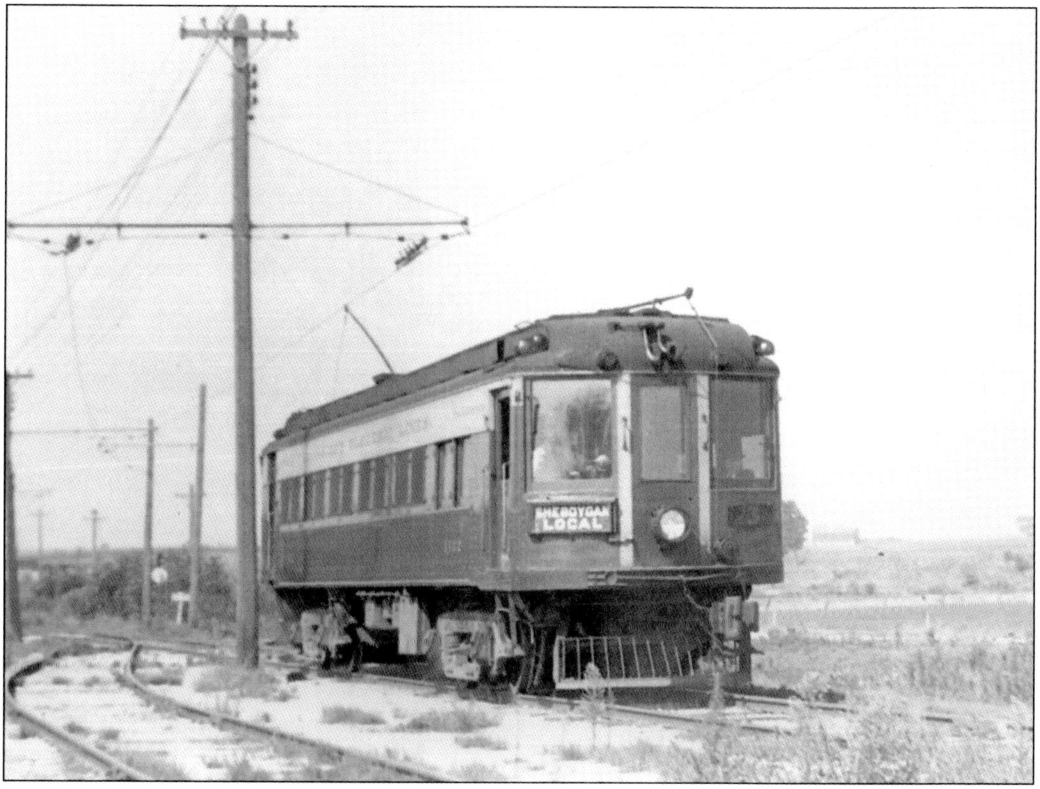

The MN Railway completed its interurban line into Sheboygan in 1908. The line paralleled the C&NW tracks from Port Washington north to near today's Washington Avenue. There, it turned east to connect with local streetcar tracks on South Eighth Street. This southbound MN car is passing the Lakeview siding west of the overpass on Highway 141, now Business Drive-South, as seen in the background.

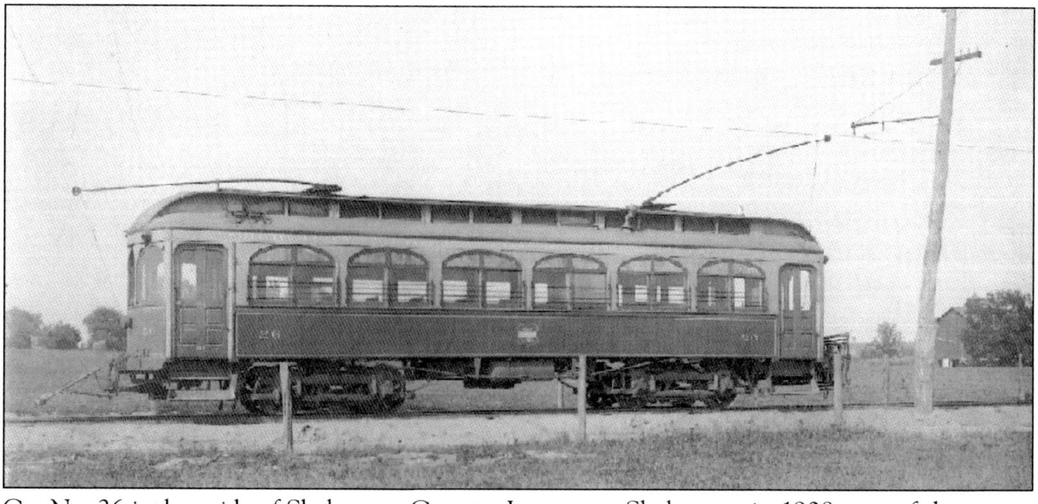

Car No. 26 is the pride of Sheboygan County. It came to Sheboygan in 1908, one of three new high-speed interurbans, and served until the line was abandoned in 1938. Sold and turned into a cottage on Lake Michigan, it was donated by the Doedens family, completely restored, and now, more than 100 years later, it rides the rails again at the East Troy Electric Railroad Museum.

Six

Eighth Street, the Heart of Sheboygan

Eighth Street has been the heart of the city for more than 100 years, but it was not always the commercial hub. In the early years, it was Center Avenue, the main route from the lakefront. When the railroad entered the picture in the late 1850s, the center of business shifted to Pennsylvania Avenue. Later, when the automobile reigned supreme, the business hub finally moved to Eighth Street.

In 1928, there were 115 businesses lining the six central blocks of Eighth Street. Old-timers remember the Palace of Sweets. Grandpa Skaff always wore an apron that he used to polish the apples. Sometimes he spit on them to make them shiny. Kalitt's Ice Cream shop had the best homemade candy. It became Keitel's in 1929. They made the best peach ice cream in the state, complete with hot fudge topping.

Eighth Street was the best place to find a job, whether you were the breadwinner of the family or a teen looking for a way to make a few dollars. In 1938, J.C. Penney cleaning boys were paid 22.5¢ an hour. Prange's grocery department paid 16¢ an hour.

Shoppers may remember the trolley money system that was used both at Prange's and Penney's. The ceiling in each store was a maze of wire for little trolley baskets that carried the money to the office on the upper floors. Women in the accounting offices would make the transactions and send the change back in the little basket. Each department had its own car. Prange's system was electric, and Penney's trolley was pulled by hand.

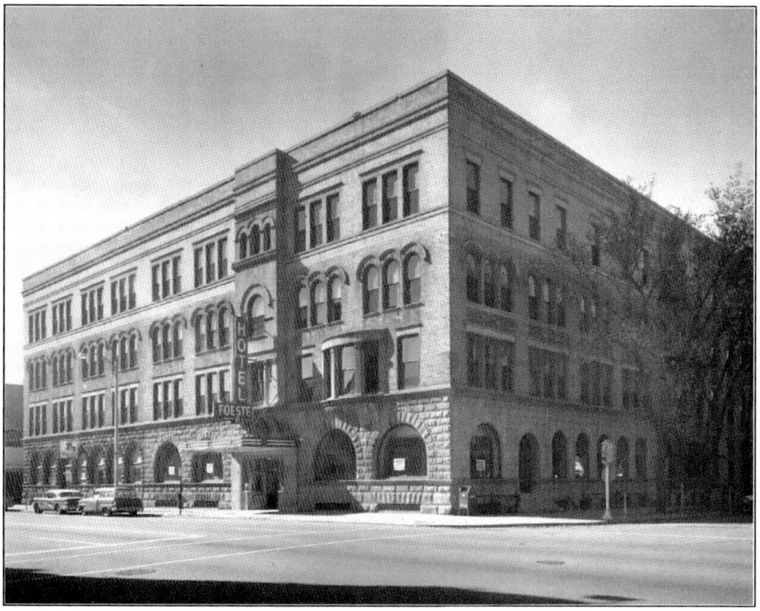

The Foeste Hotel, formally located on the southwest corner of Eighth Street and Ontario Avenue, was once described as the most popular and plush place for travelers and businessmen. Built in 1893 on the site of the old Commercial Hotel, it is seen here in the 1930s. The hotel had three major renovations over the course of its life before it was torn down at the end of 1960.

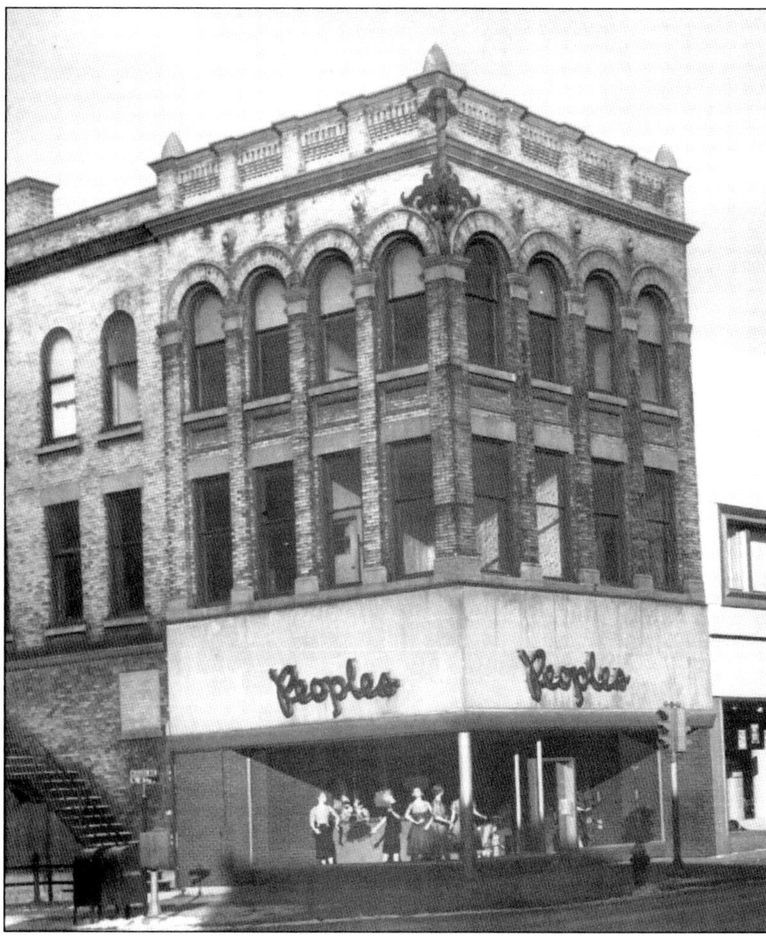

Peoples Clothing store was originally located at 524 North Eighth Street between Center and Pennsylvania Avenues. Opened in 1922 by the Meyer family, Peoples was a leading women's apparel store in the county for nearly 80 years. It moved in 1927 to the building in what is now the Above and Beyond Children's Museum on the northwest corner of Eighth Street and Niagara Avenue. The store closed in 1998.

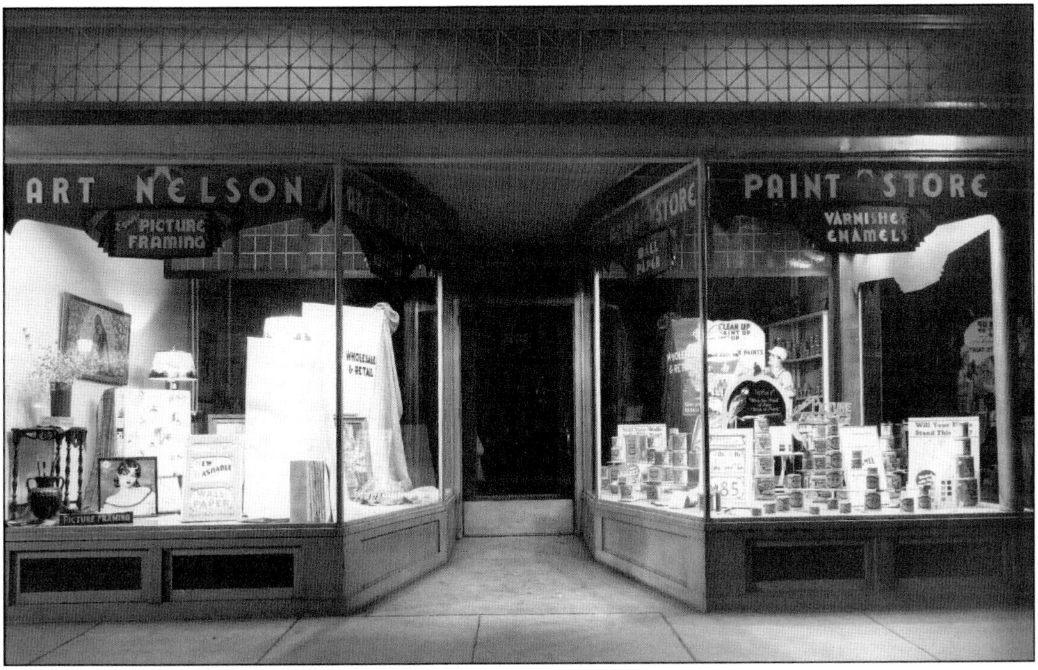

Art Nelson Paint Store, 830 North Eight Street, located just north of the Sheboygan Theater, sold paint and wallpaper. The company also did framing.

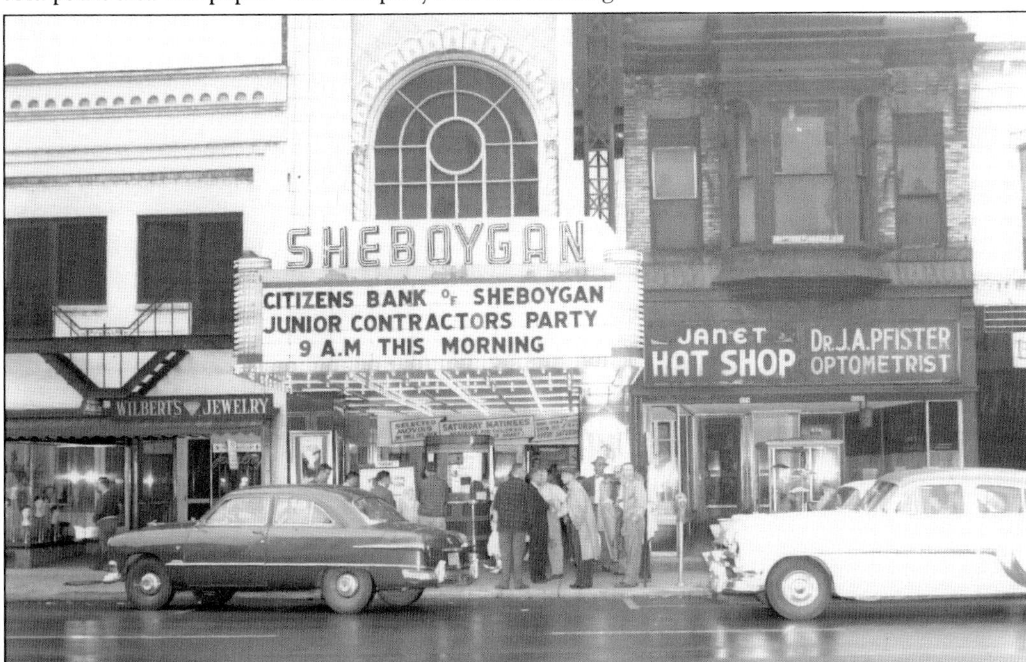

This image documents the west side of Eighth Street between Niagara and Wisconsin Avenues in the 1940s. From right is Dr. Pfister's optometry office, Janet Hats, the Sheboygan Theater and Wilbert's Jewelry. Opened in 1928, the Sheboygan Theater has always been the city's biggest and grandest theater. It had a vaulted ceiling with twinkling stars and architecture with a Spanish flair.

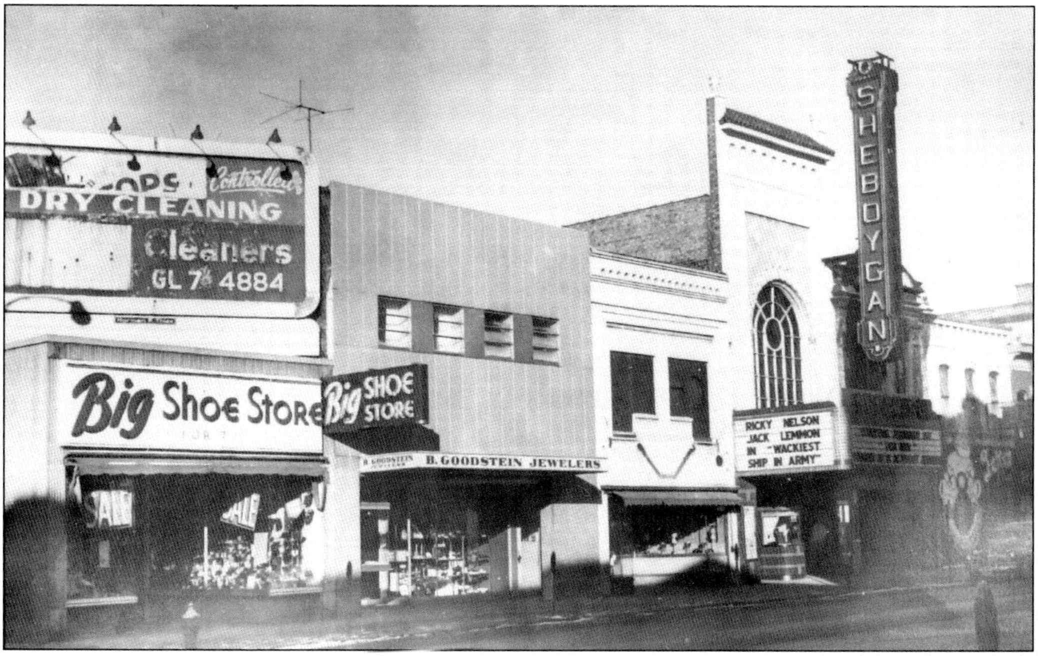

Seen here, in 1960, is another view of the west side of Eighth Street between Niagara and Wisconsin Avenues. The old Sheboygan Theater, at right, went through a major renovation in the late 1990s and opened for business in 2001 as the Stefanie H. Weill Center for the Performing Arts. Goodstein Jewelers, was started by Ben and Harry Goodstein in 1931 and closed in 1985. At left is the Big Shoe Store.

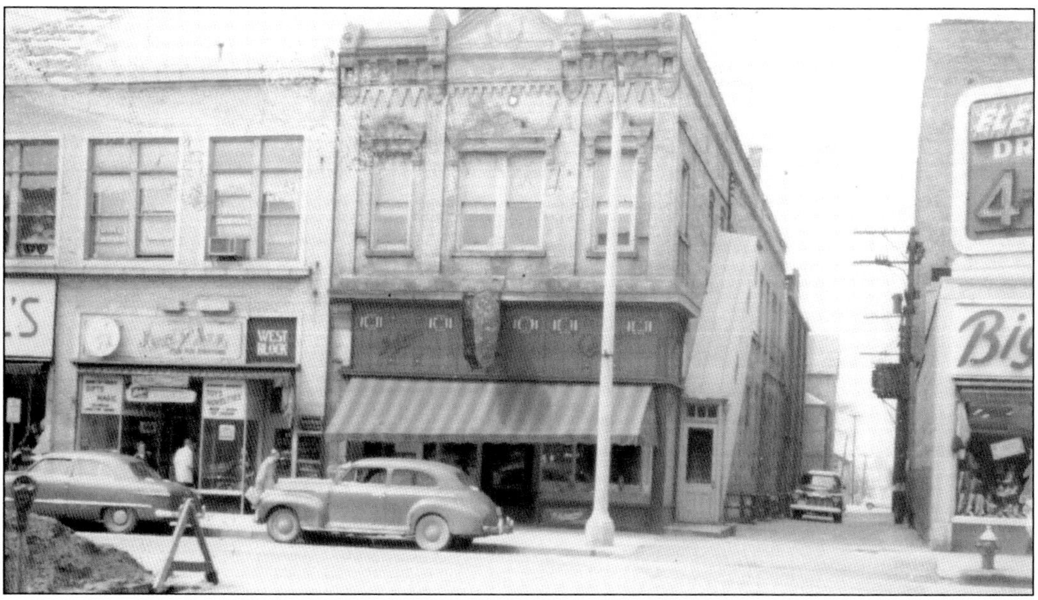

Keitel's Confectionary located at 816 North Eighth Street was formerly August Kalitt's Candy Shop. Kalitt's shop opened in 1892. Arthur G. Keitel bought the store in March 1929. The store specialized in homemade chocolates, pan candies, and ice cream. Keitel, a World War I veteran, had worked for Kalitt for 11 years, learning the candy-making trade. Keitel's was in business until 1959.

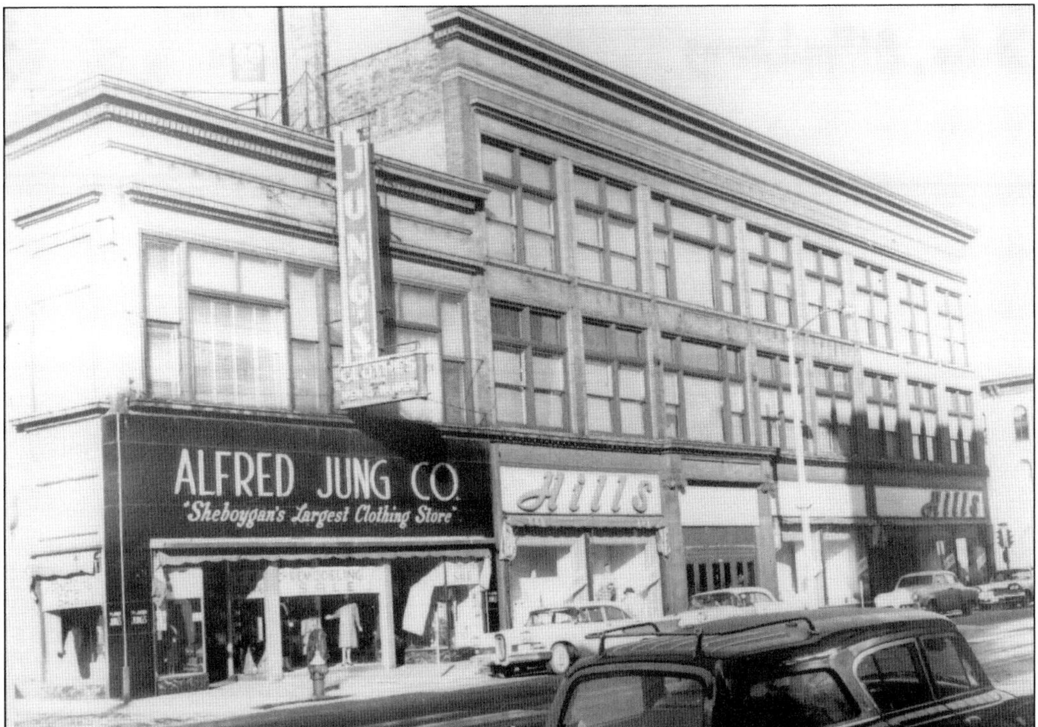

Located on the southwest corner of North Eighth Street and Wisconsin Avenue, this building housed the Jung Department Store beginning in 1901. The three-story building was built by Jacob and William Jung. It became Sheboygan Dry Goods Company beginning in 1927. The change to the name Hill's Department Store was made in 1950. Hills Department Store closed in 1969.

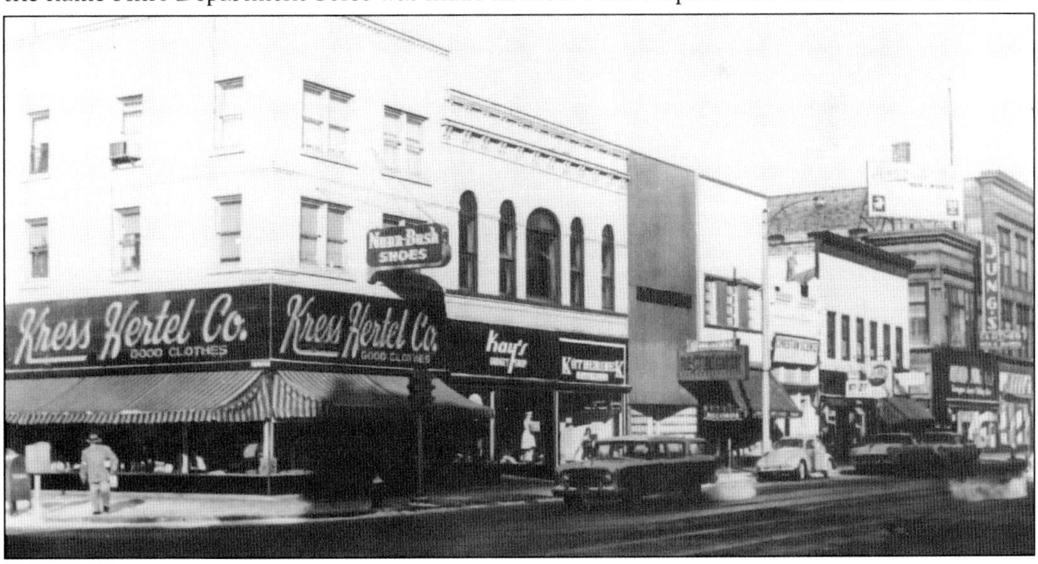

Once located in the block between Wisconsin and New York Avenues on the west side of the street, Kress-Hertel, Kay's Budget Shop, Katherine Kay's, Gmach's Restaurant, and the Christian Science Reading Room were busy places in this 1960s image. Katherine Kay's began as a corset studio in 1940, with Frances Lemkuil as proprietor. Kress Hertel moved to the Woolworth building in 1970.

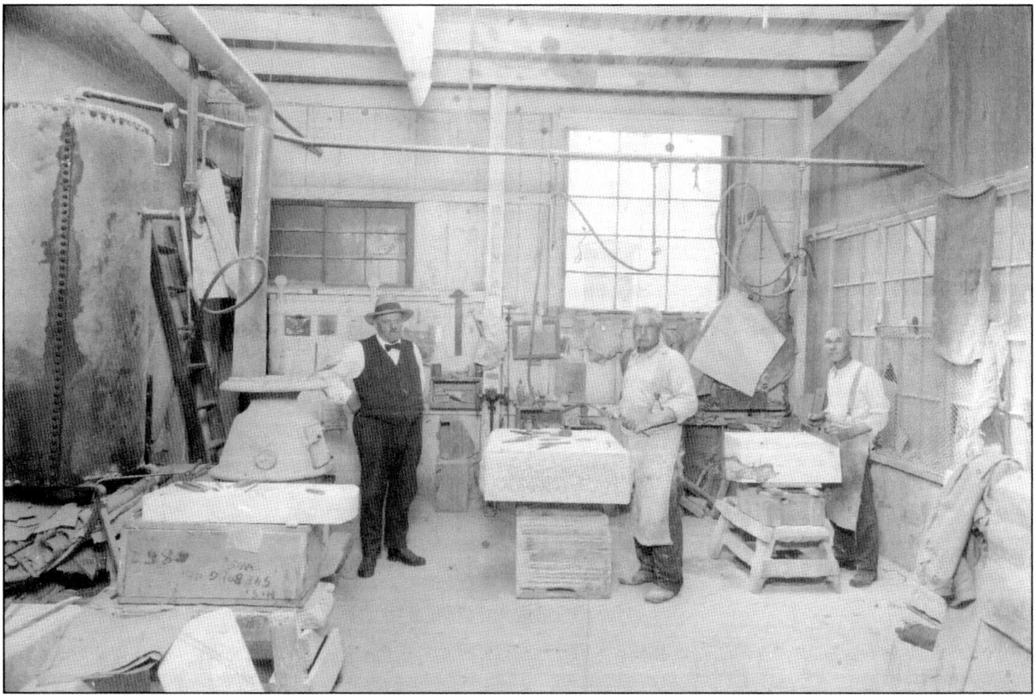

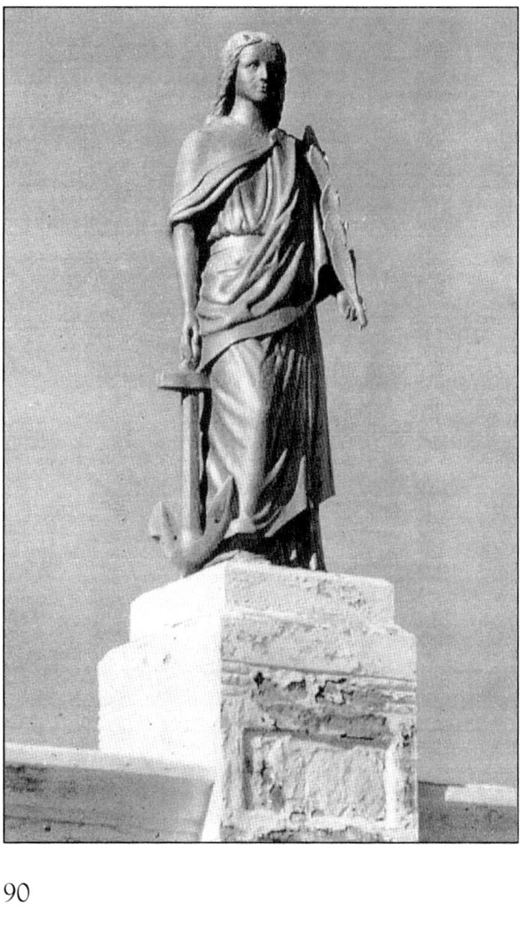

Henry Scheele operated a marble and stone cutting shop at 712 North Eighth Street on the west side of the street between Wisconsin and New York Avenues. The building was designed by William C. Weeks. Painted white, it was made of Illinois limestone. The oak floors were supported by heavy wooden timbers in order to support the 30 to 40 tons of marble and granite stocked by the firm.

The Scheele statue named Hope was cloaked in a flowing robe of marble and kept watch over Eighth Street for 72 years. Perched atop the Scheele Monument Company building, this 500-pound, 4.5-foot marble statue came from Italy and was put in place in 1885. The building later was used as the Christian Science Reading Room.

Richman Brothers, makers of men's clothes, opened for business on March 28, 1930. The store was located at 710 North Eighth Street between Wisconsin and New York Avenues. The building formerly housed the Gem Motion Picture Theater. Roy Lane was the first manager. His first employees were P.G. Fisher, Arwin Olson, John Alpert, and Bessie Steen.

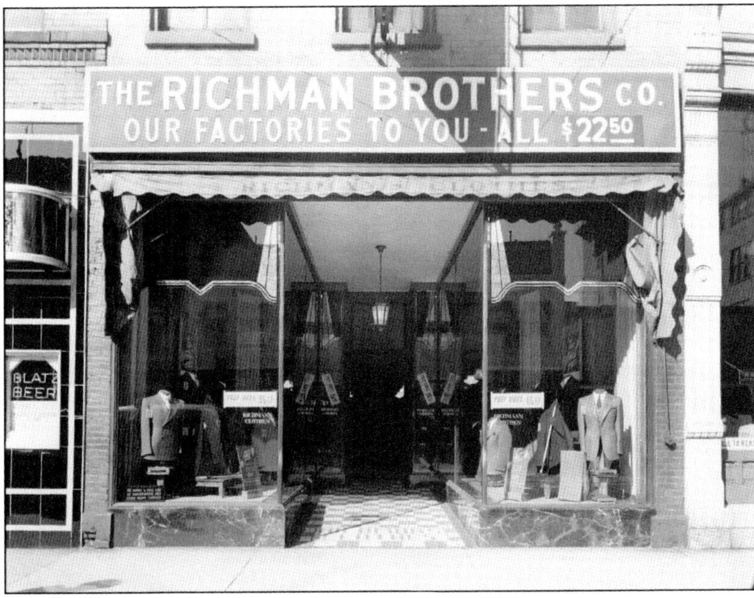

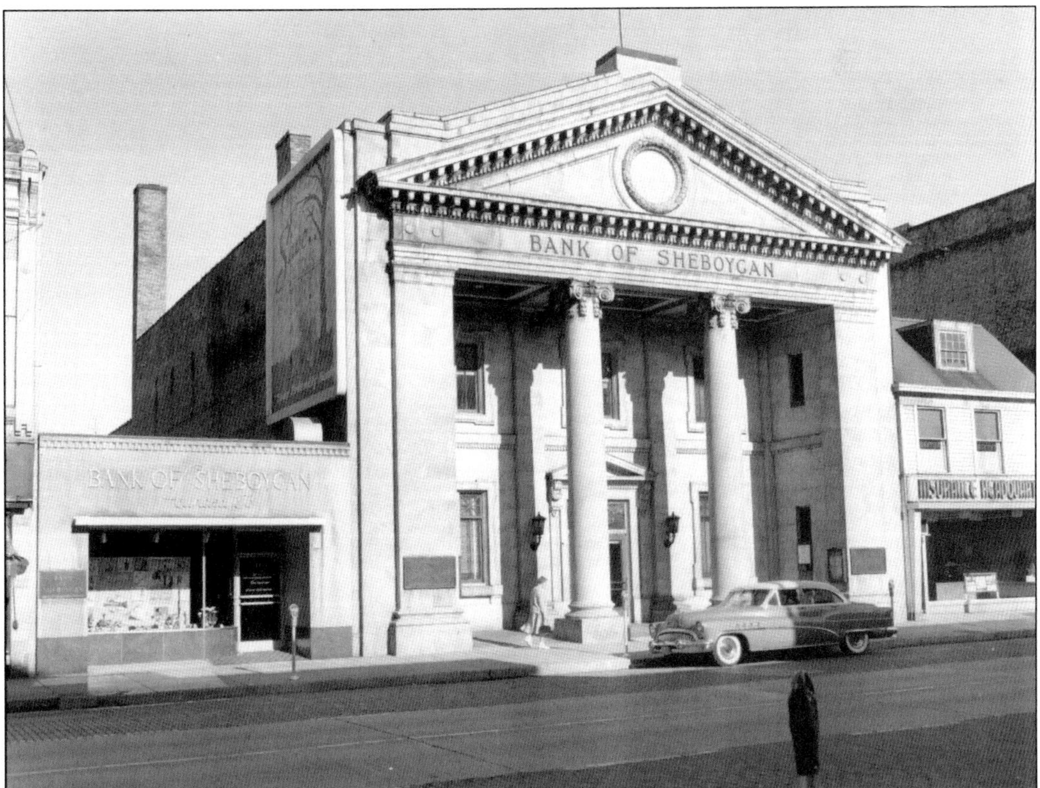

The Bank of Sheboygan, Greek Revival in style, was built in 1910 for $80,192. Henry Scheele and Company hauled the columns from the railroad station to the building site by horse-drawn drays. They set them upright using an A-frame, block and tackle and a hand-cranked windlass. When the building was demolished in the 1973, the 12-ton Georgia marble columns were unceremoniously dumped into Lake Michigan near the Reiss Coal property.

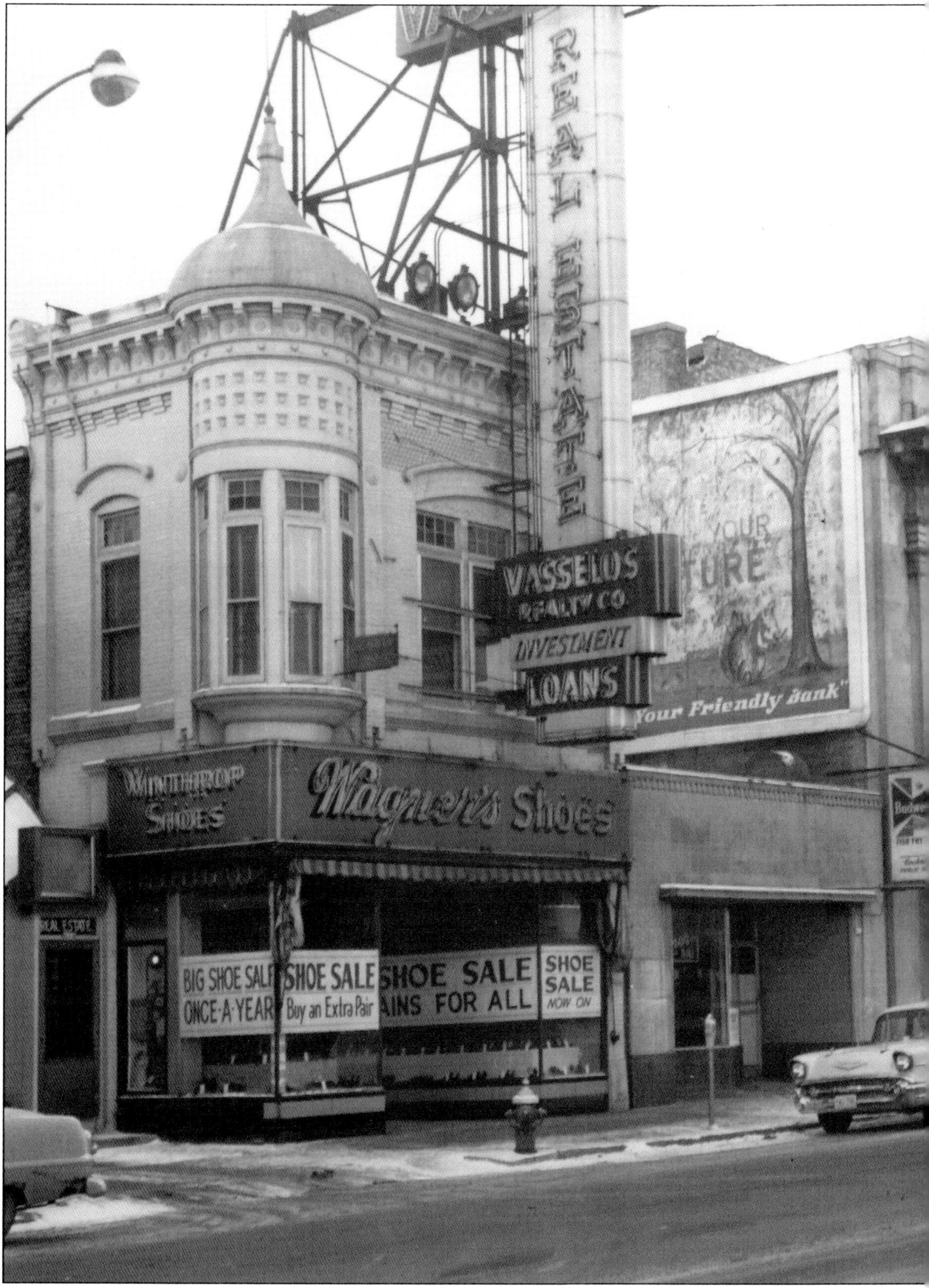
REAL ESTATE
VASSELOS REALTY CO.
INVESTMENT
LOANS
"Your Friendly Bank"
Wagner's Shoes
SHOE SALE
Buy an Extra Pair
BIG SHOE SALE
ONCE-A-YEAR
SHOE SALE
SHOE SALE
NOW ON

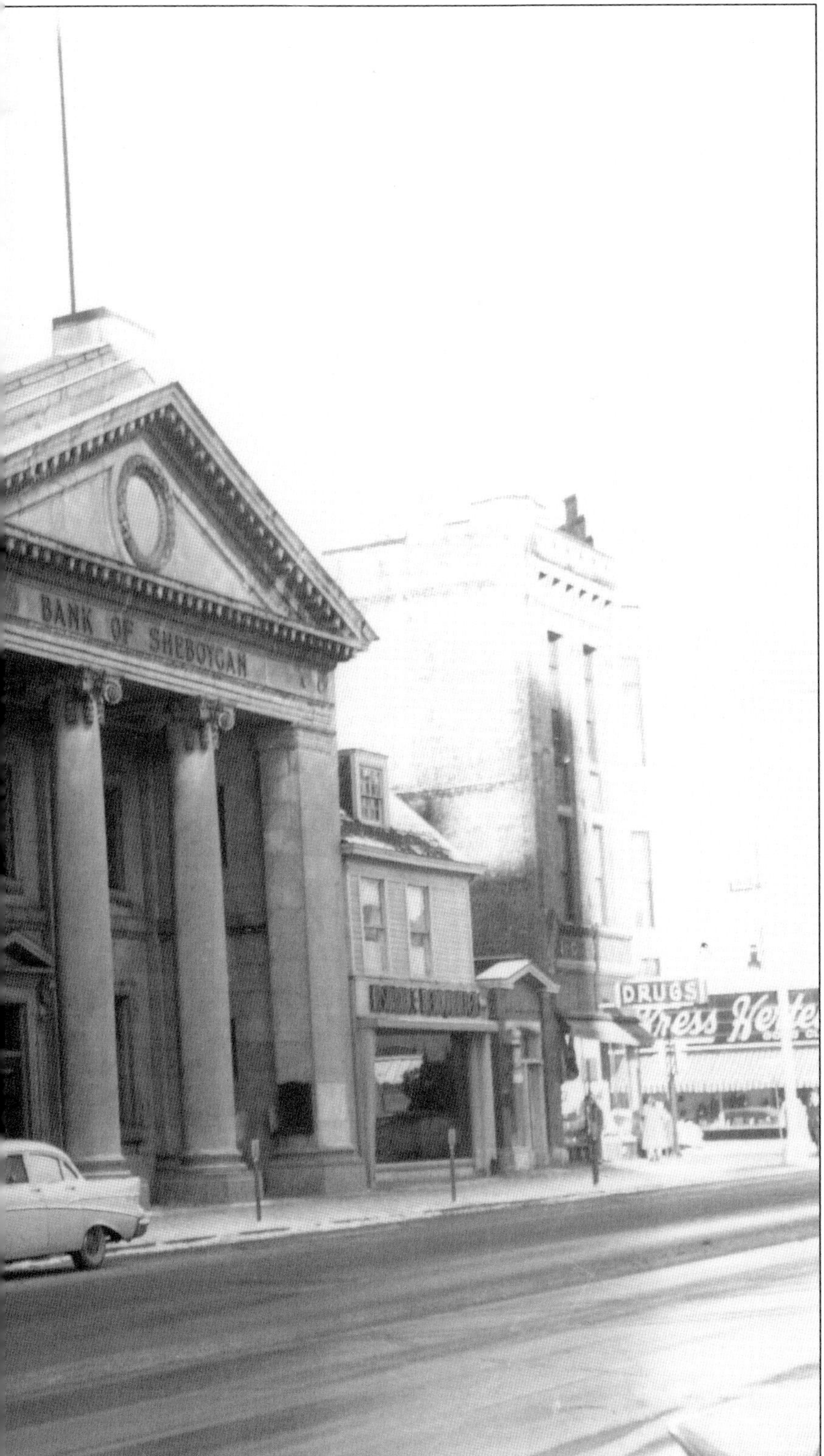

This c. 1957 image shows the west side of the block between New York and Center Avenues. From left to right are Wagner Shoes, Vasselos Investments, Schwartz Soft Drinks, Bank of Sheboygan, the Betsy Ross Building, Wisconsin Loan and Finance, and the I.C. Thomas Drug Store. The Thomas Building, also known as the Zaegel Building, was constructed in 1886. Zaegel used the ground floor as a drugstore. He established the first laboratory in Sheboygan making his medicinal preparation, which later became popular as a pain-relieving, healing oil known by the trademark of ZMO-Oil (Zaegel Magic Oil). He sold the drugstore in 1906 to I.C. Thomas, a clerk in his store. I.C. "Ike" Thomas admired Betsy Ross and built an ice cream parlor in her honor next to his store.

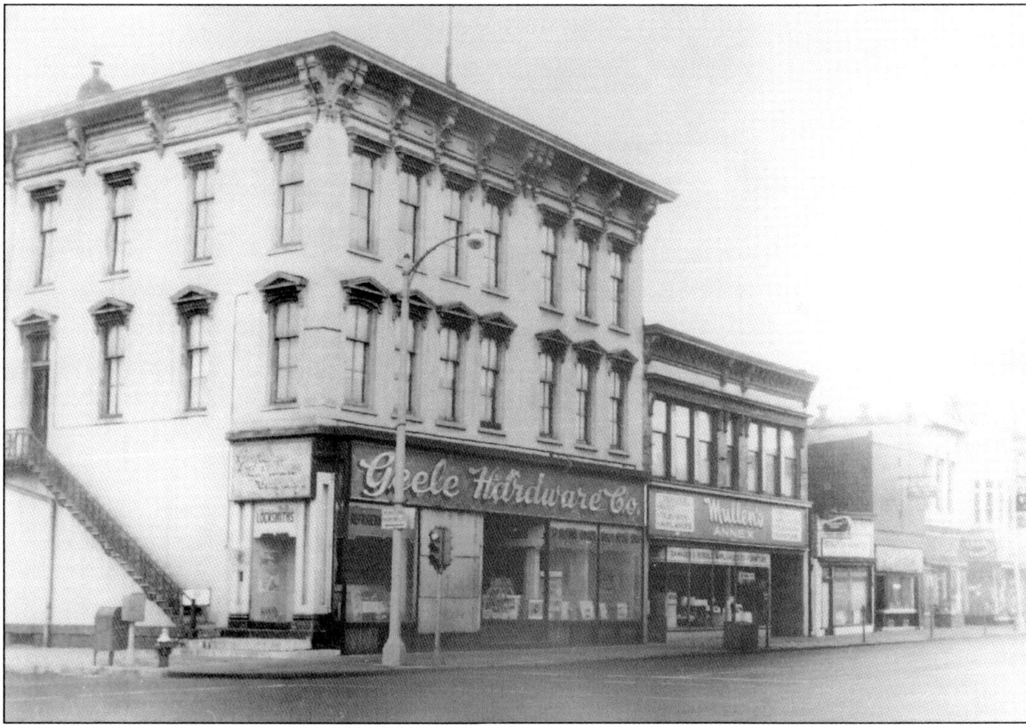

Geele Hardware was established in 1850 by Francis Geele, a young immigrant from Prussia. In 1867, the property on the northwest corner of Eighth Street and Center Avenue was purchased and a three-story building was erected on the site in 1868. Geele died in 1885. The company was run by his son Frank and then Emma Matton until the company was dissolved. The building was left vacant in 1956 and razed in 1961.

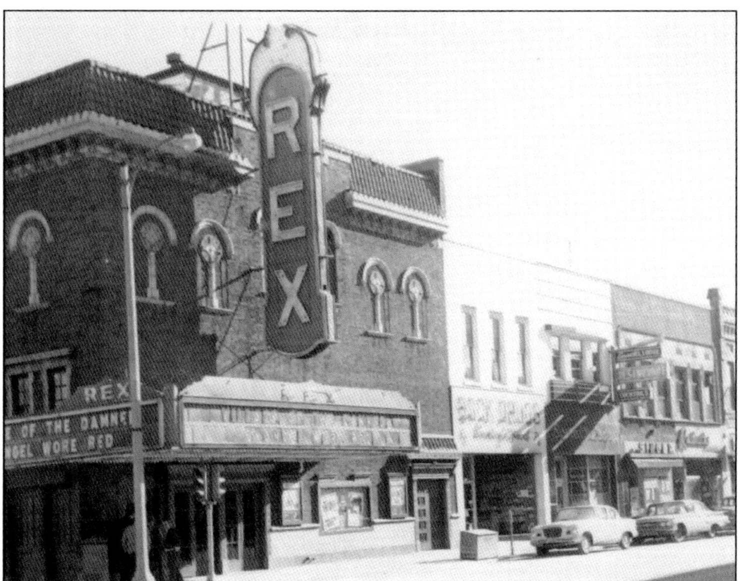

The Rex Theater was located at the southeast corner of North Eighth Street and Ontario Avenue. This second Rex Theater opened in 1923. For four years, from 1929 to 1933, it was known as the Fox. The Rex closed its doors in 1965. Directly south on the east side of Eighth Street were Bock Drugs, Everett's Lodge, Singer Sewing, Rudnick Jewelers, J&R Motor Supply, and Fisher's City News. Bock Drug was the Friday night hangout.

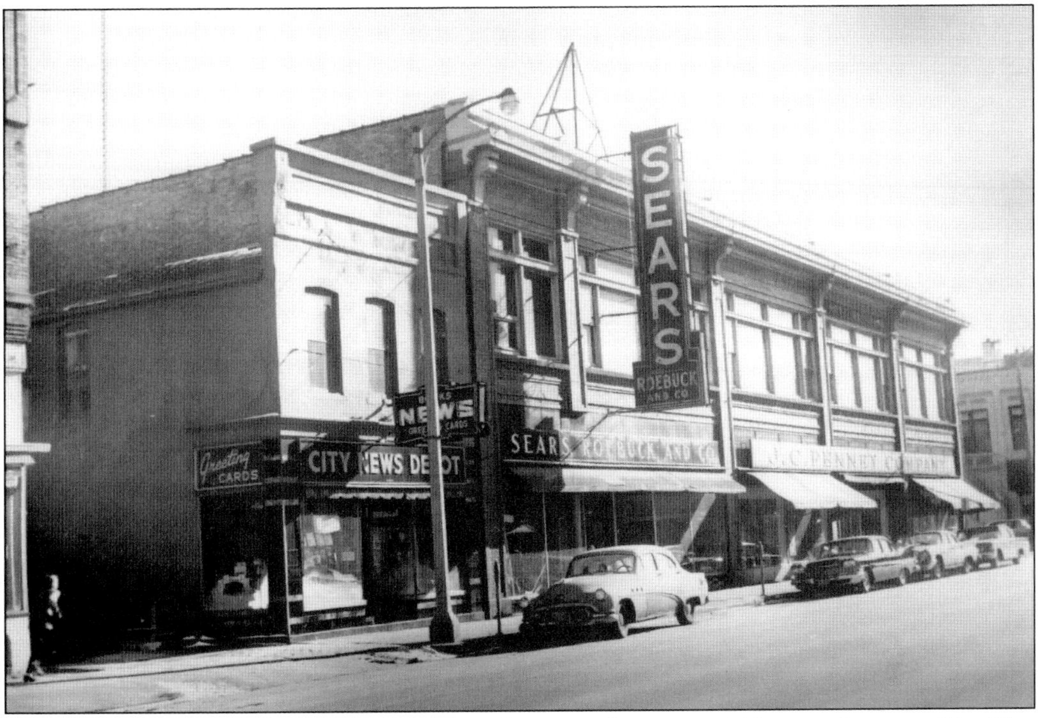

This is a view of the east side of Eighth Street between Ontario and Niagara Avenues. The City News Depot was started in 1910 by Elwood Fischer and Arthur Raab. The store handled wholesale and retail trade for newspapers and magazines. Raab also owned the news and cigar depot at the interurban station at North Eight Street and Pennsylvania Avenue. Directly south were Sears, Roebuck and Co. and J.C. Penney.

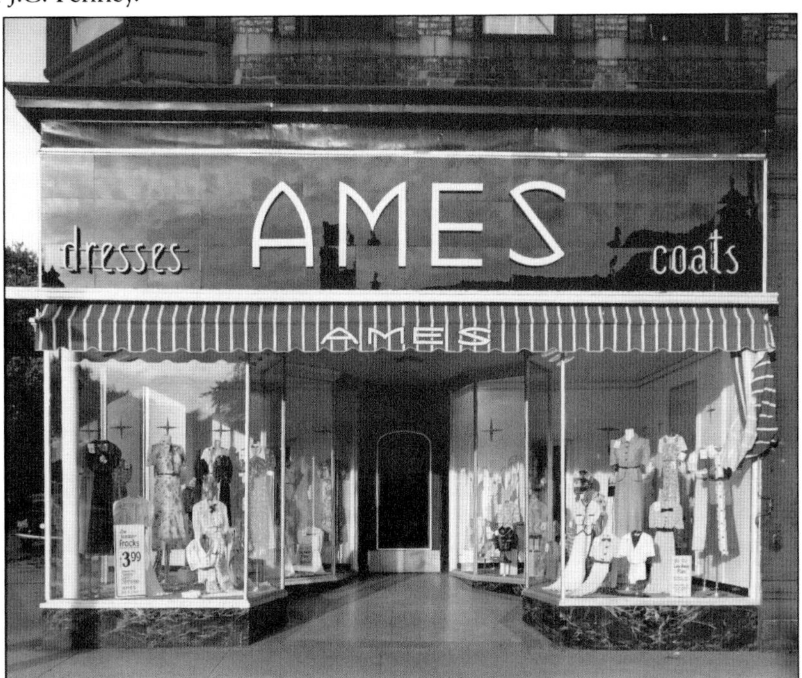

Ames Clothing and women's dress shop was located on the corner of Niagara Avenue and North Eighth Street in the 1940s. This store followed Klausen Clothing, a longtime staple of shopping on Eighth Street. It was followed by Erliens Jewelers.

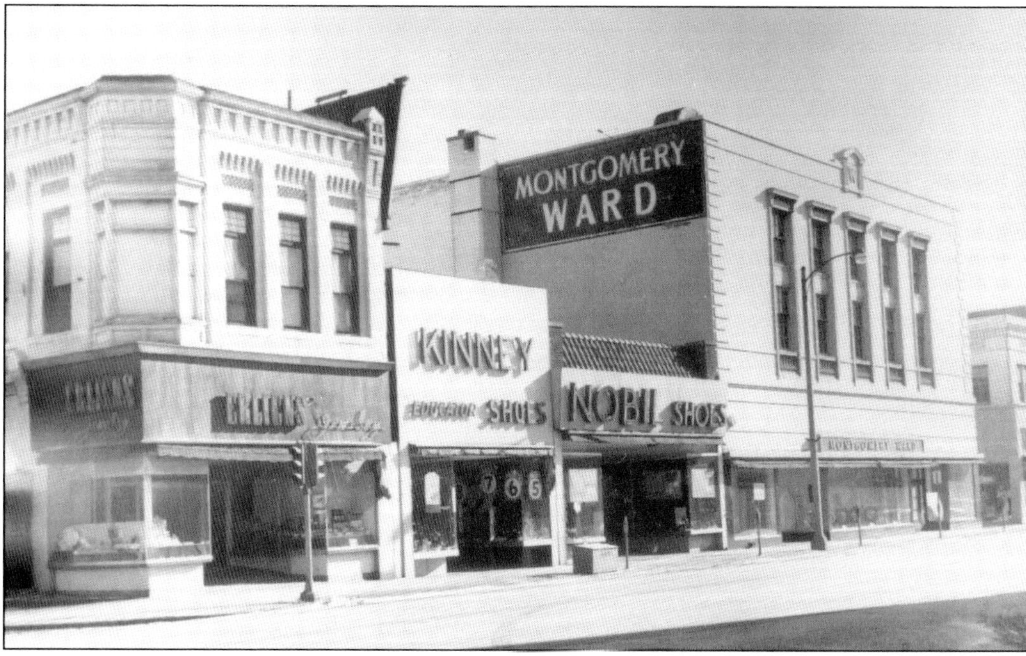

This view of the east side of the street from Niagara Avenue to Wisconsin Avenue shows Erliens Jewelers, Kinney Shoes, Nobil Shoes, and Montgomery Ward. Montgomery Ward opened its doors in Sheboygan in 1928, moving to this location in 1936. It closed its retail doors in 1960, replacing it with a catalog store.

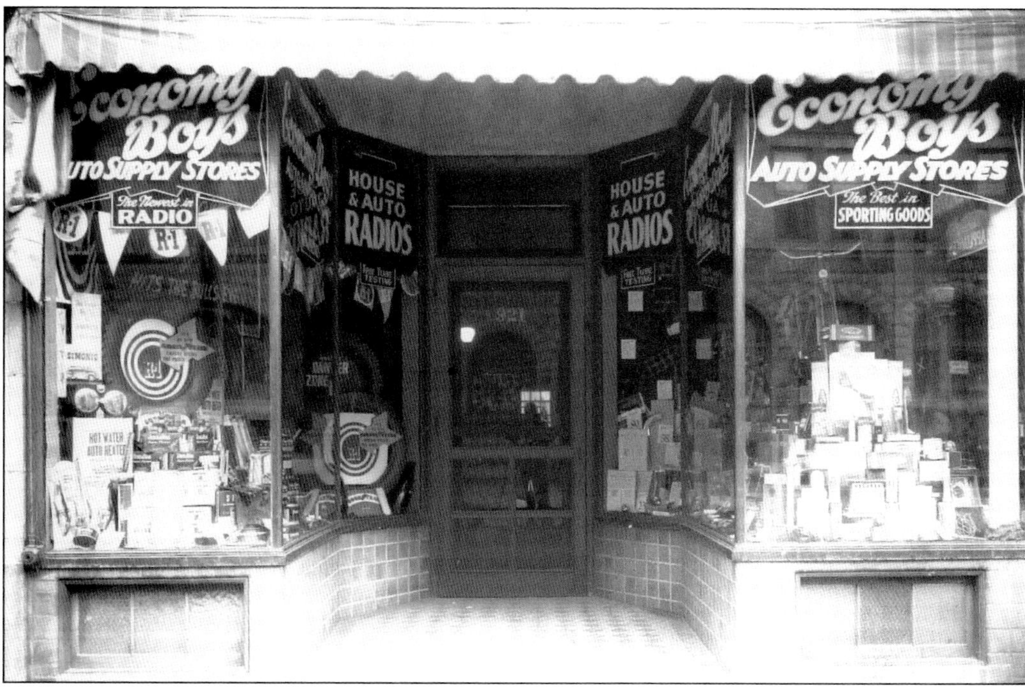

Economy Boys, once located at 921 North Eighth Street, was an automobile supply store. It also carried the newest in radios and the best in sporting goods. This building was also occupied at different times by Christopher and Pfund Shoe Store and a Singer Sewing Shop.

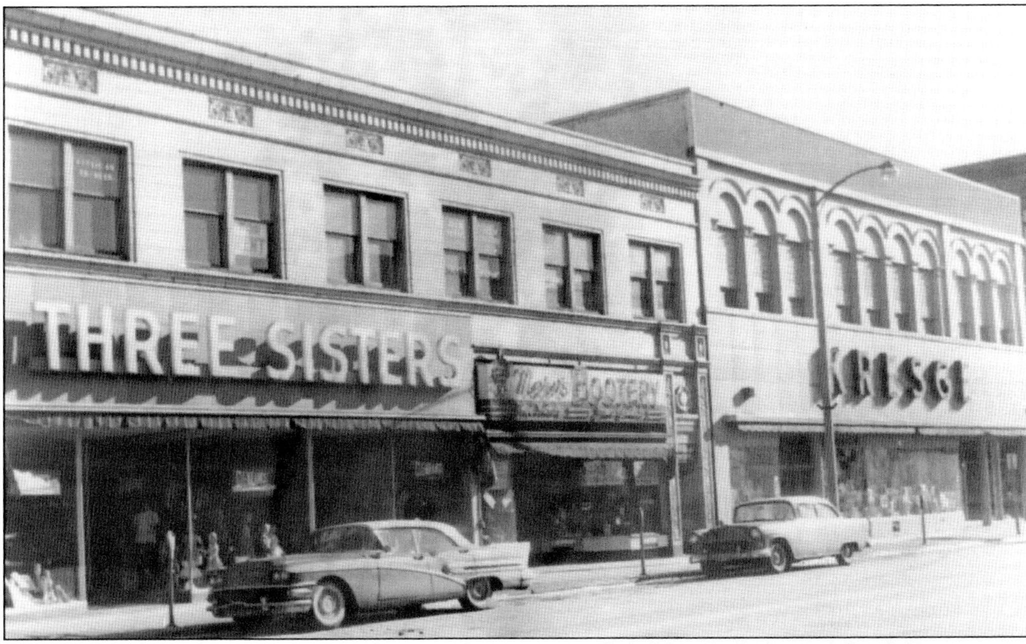

Three Sisters Clothing Store, which carried women's and children's clothing, Merv's Bootery and S.S. Kresge Company lined part of the east side of the street between Niagara and Wisconsin Avenues. Kresge's store took over the building where Victor Imig's Clothing store was formerly located. In August 1957, customers could get a low-calorie lunch of three Jell-O cubes, fresh fruit, and cottage cheese for 50¢ at Kresge's.

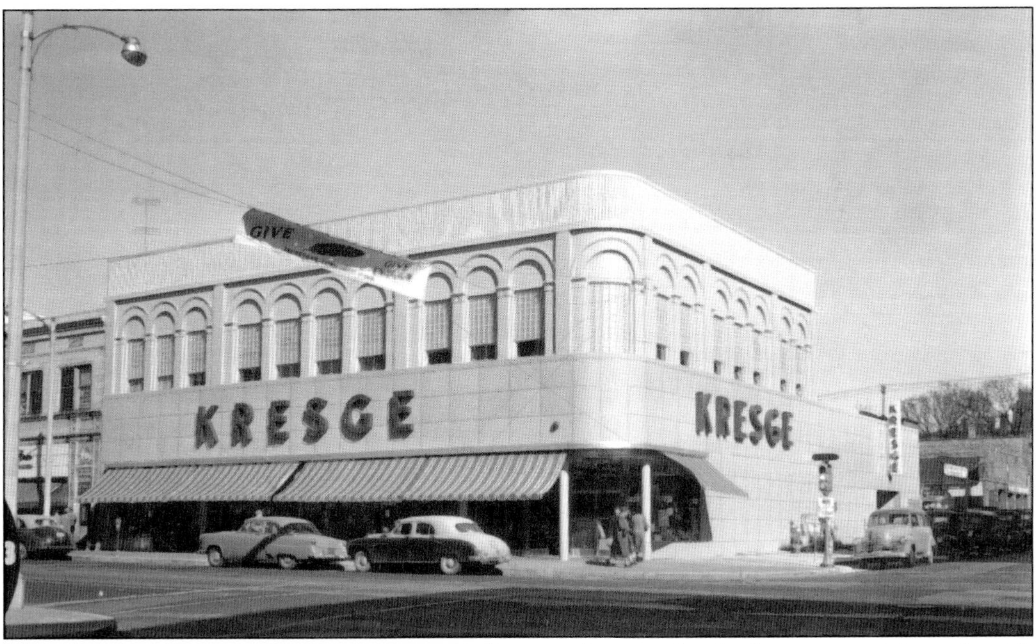

S.S. Kresge Company opened its doors to Sheboygan shoppers for the first time on November 13, 1924, in this location on the northeast corner of North Eighth Street and Wisconsin Avenue. The small five-and-dime added a luncheon fountain and food department in 1936. Newly remodeled in 1953, it was the first large store to be air-conditioned. This image was taken in 1957.

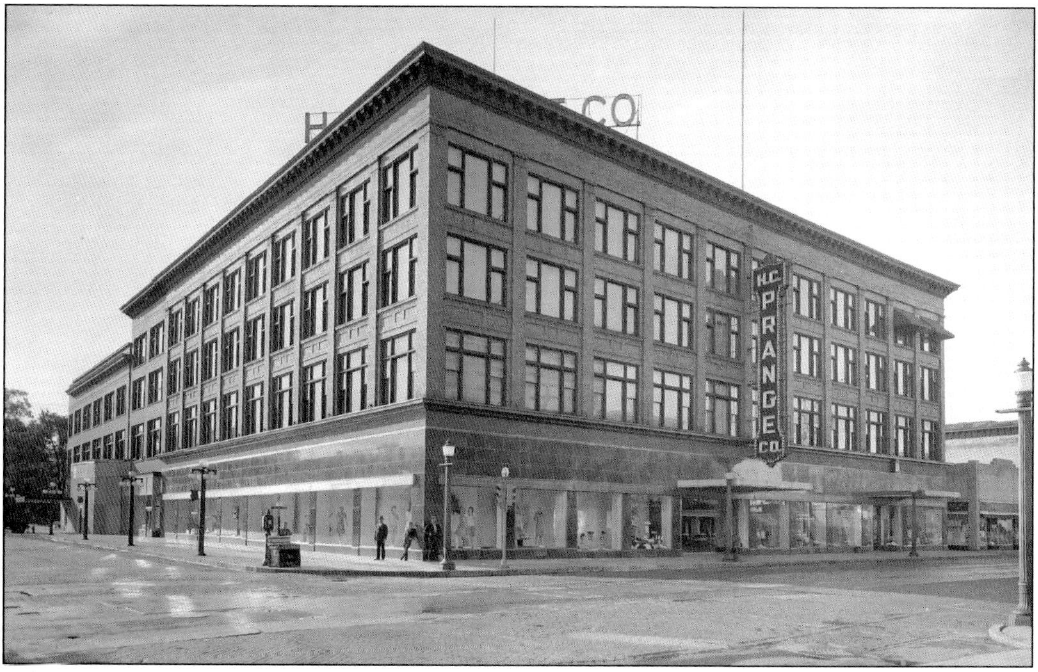

Whether it was for the freshly made caramel corn, the annual yearbook signing for high school seniors, or having groceries delivered by a horse-drawn sleigh, for 100 years H.C. Prange Co. in Sheboygan served as a hub for local commerce and socialization. Eventually taking up the entire east side of the block from Wisconsin Avenue to New York Avenue, Prange's first opened its doors in 1887.

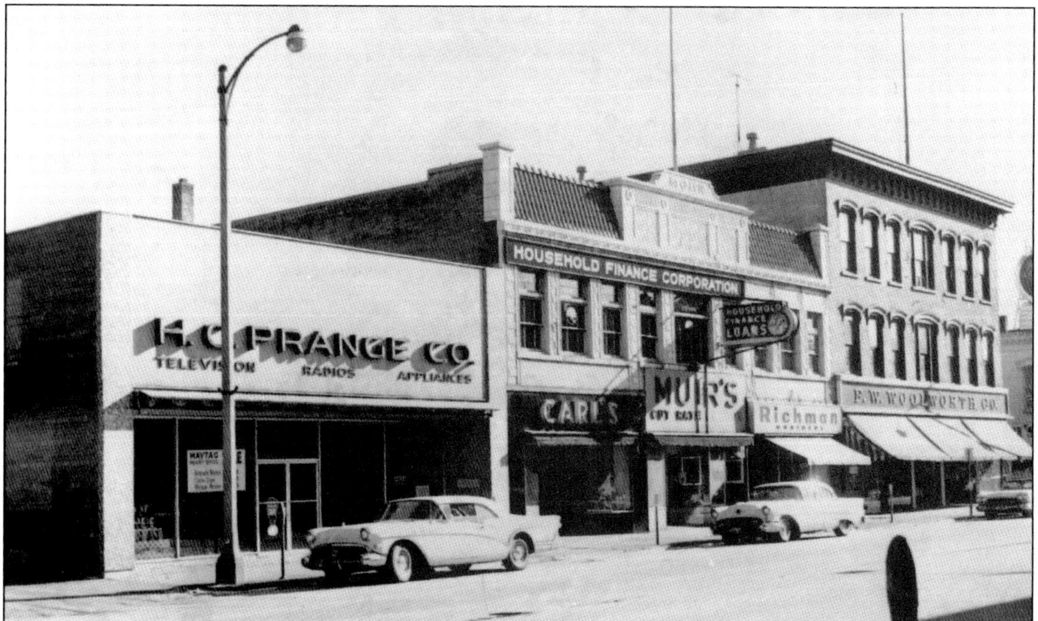

Connected to the H.C. Prange department store by a tunnel, this H.C. Prange annex carried household appliances for the company. South of Prange's on the east side of the street between Wisconsin Avenue and New York Avenue were Carl's, Muir's, Richman Brothers, and Woolworth's.

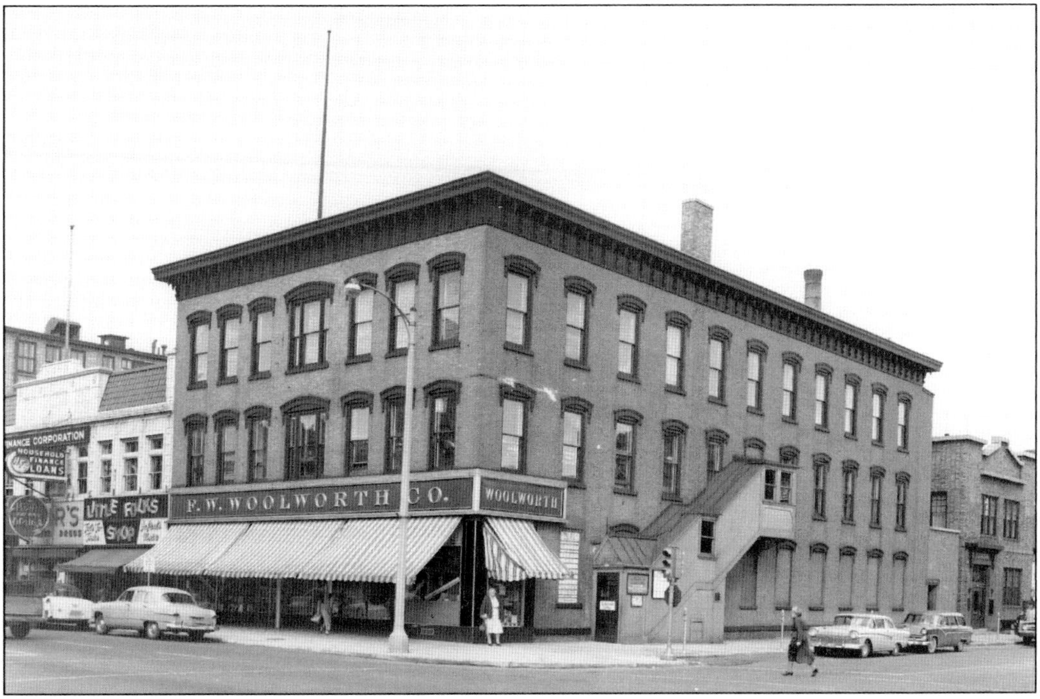

Woolworth's five-and-dime was located at 701–703 North Eighth Street. The first dime store in Sheboygan was opened in 1902 and was known as S.H. Knox Store. In 1912, the Knox stores were merged with other Woolworth stores and Sheboygan received its first Woolworth's. It quickly became a Sheboygan institution. In 1940, the store was given a face-lift with an entirely new facade. The five-and-ten was removed because higher priced items were offered.

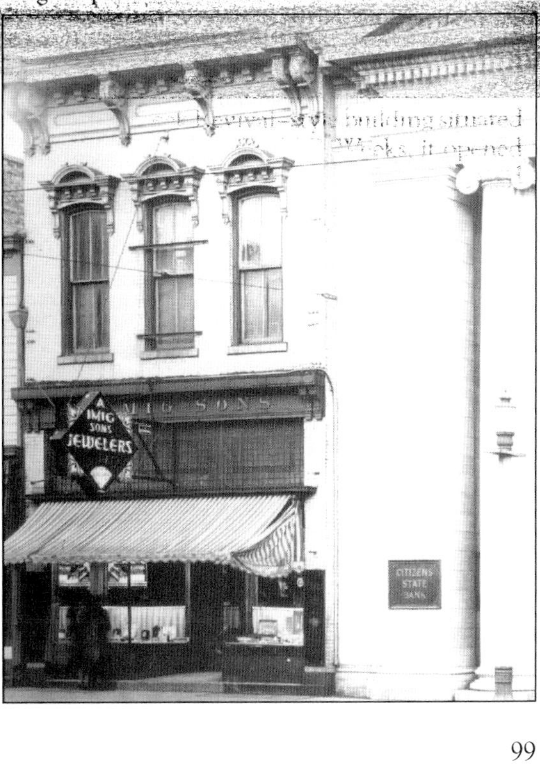

Imig Jewelers was located next to Citizens State Bank at 621 North Eighth Street. Started in 1872 by Adam Imig, a native of Simmens, Prussia, Imig learned the jeweler's trade in 1872. Both of Imig's sons, George and Edwin, learned the family business which expanded to carry not just jewelry and diamonds, but silver, dinnerware, and watches. George Imig was also an optometrist and provided eye testing in the back room.

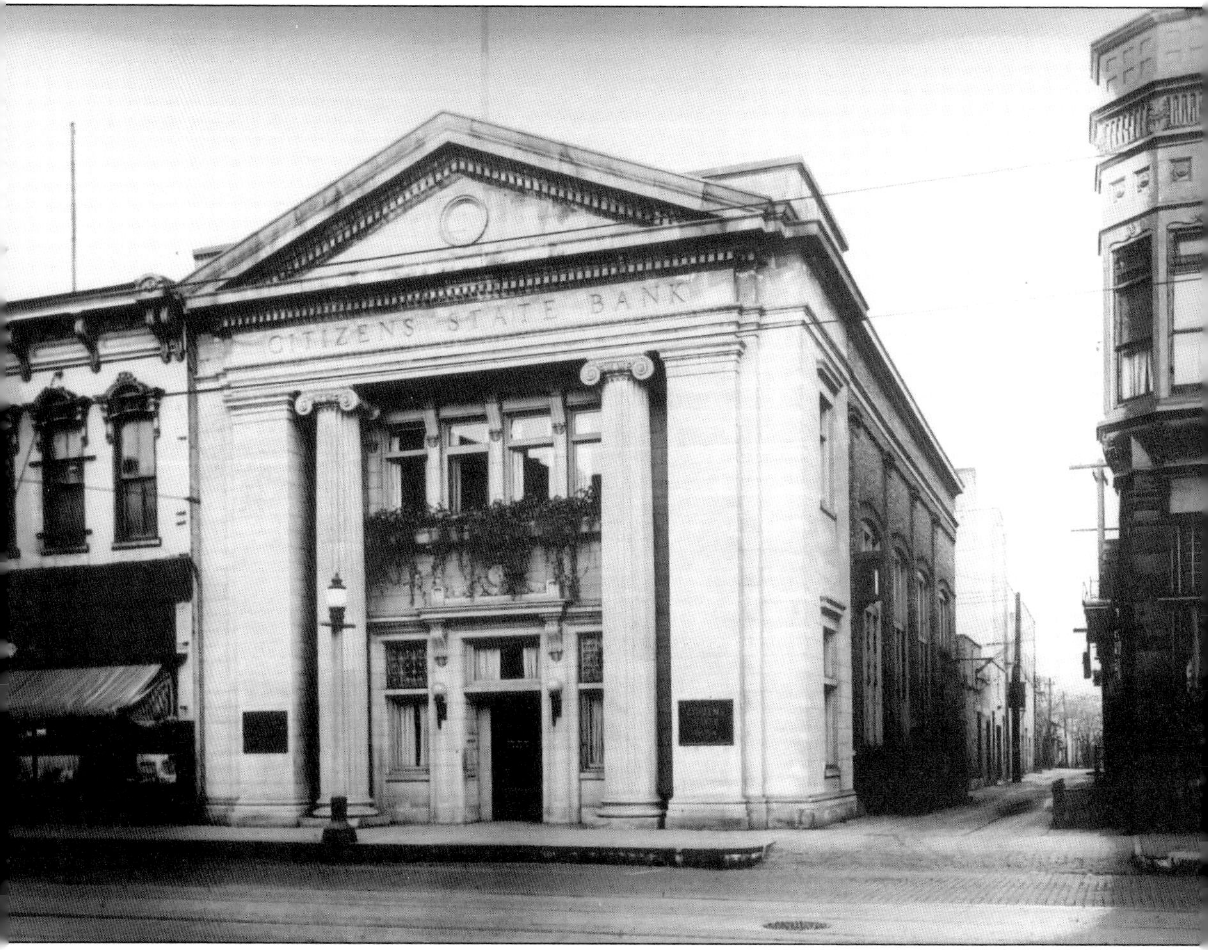

Citizens State Bank was originally located in this beautiful Greek Revival–style building situated at Eighth Street and Pennsylvania Avenue. Designed by local architect W.C. Weeks, it opened for business in 1910. After many years of service to the citizens of the city, the company merged with the Bank of Sheboygan in 1955. In 1957, the newly merged company, also known as Citizens State Bank, moved to a new location on the northeast corner of Seventh Street and Wisconsin Avenue. Today, that location is the main branch of Wells Fargo Bank in Sheboygan County.

Mullen's Annex at 616 North Eighth Street was located on the west side of the street south of Vasselos Realty and the old Bank of Sheboygan. This store specialized in the sales of rebuilt televisions, appliances and furniture. This 1960 image shows the local headquarters of Senator Kennedy for President to the right of Mullen's Annex.

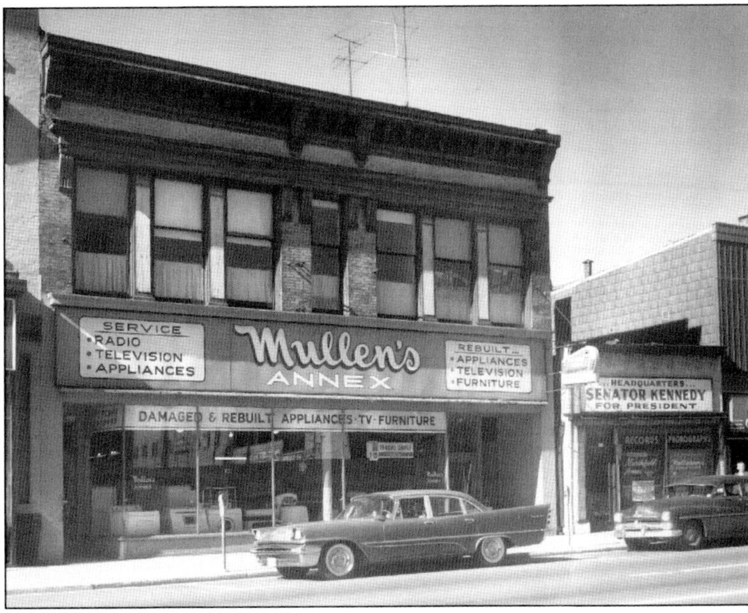

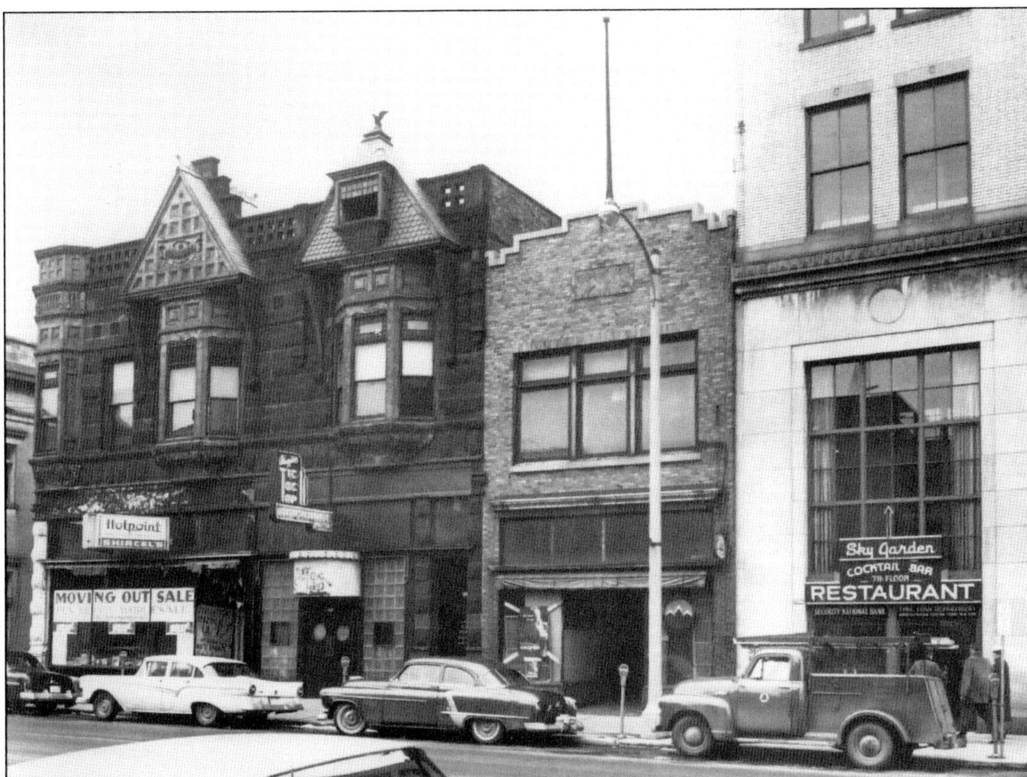

At left is the old Schlicht Building, once known as the "unofficial political headquarters" of the city. Seen here in the late 1950s, the building housed Mullen Appliances and the Tic Toc Tap. It was torn down in 1960. Maechtle's Flowers was previously located in the building in the center. At right is the seven-story Security National Bank building. Constructed in 1923, it housed the Sky Garden Restaurant and cocktail bar on the seventh floor.

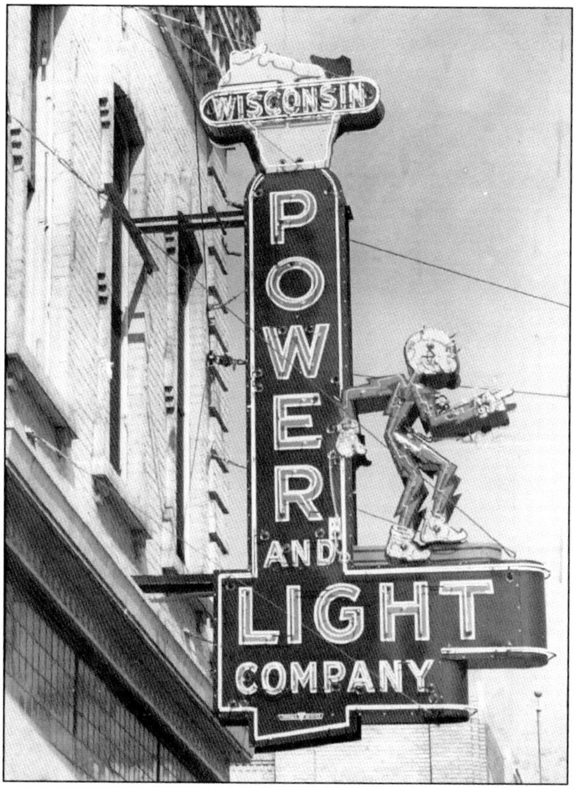

This iconic neon sign for the Wisconsin Power and Light Company formed in 1924 is seen here at its office in the 1940s located on the southeast corner of North Eighth Street and Center Avenue. This is the company that powered Sheboygan. The site was formerly occupied by the old German Bank organized by James Mead. Wisconsin Power and Light moved to its new offices at south Eighth Street.

The Majestic Theater was located at 523 North Eighth Street from 1911 to 1960. It was the first local theater to offer newsreel shorts with sound in 1926. The first talkie was the acceptance speech of presidential candidate Herbert Hoover. The theater soon became the most popular venue in town. It had special reserved seats in the balcony—for those in love—for 10¢. The structure was demolished in 1964.

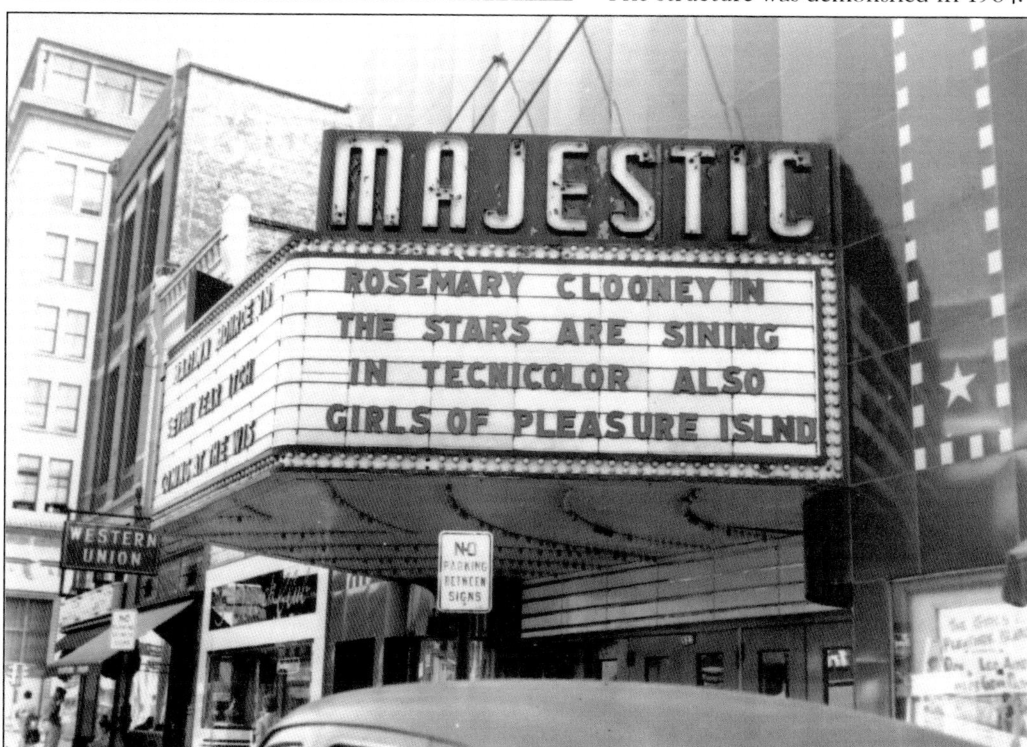

Seven

Parades, Festivals, and Events

Socially and culturally, Sheboygan has been, and is still, defined by its parades, festivals, and events. As early as 1852, a Fourth of July celebration took place in Sheboygan. The *Sheboygan Mercury* reported that a parade formed on Pennsylvania Avenue under the direction of Dr. Adolph St. Sure. The fire department decorated its new equipment with evergreens and flowers. Children from each church marched in the parade. The Declaration of Independence was read to the crowd at the public square, now Sheridan Park. A cannon was procured from Racine for entertainment, and it was reported to have been used liberally, like early fireworks. Sheboygan celebrated the centennial of its growth to village size and again as it reached city status. It sponsored at least two homecoming reunions to welcome back all who had roots here. The images in this chapter give just a glimpse into the social lives of Sheboyganites of the past.

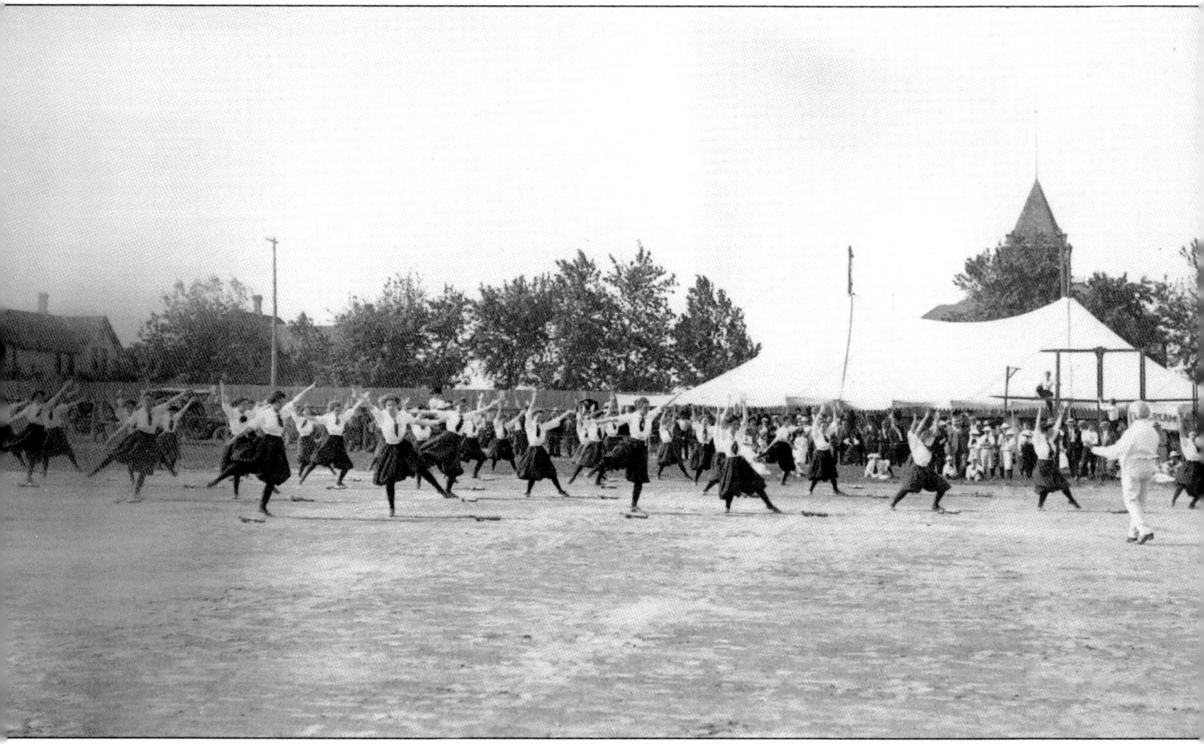

Friedrich Ludwig Jahr started the Turn Verein, or Turners Association, in Germany in 1811. The organization, which first came to America in 1923, promoted exercise for adults and children. Part of its original appeal for immigrants was that it was a good place for Germans to communicate with others who spoke their own language. The Turner chapter in Sheboygan was one of the first three in the country, holding classes in Fountain Park as early as 1848 and receiving their official charter in 1854. Many Olympic athletes got their start in the Turners. Stories tell that some members toughened their hands in pickle brine better enabling them to handle the acrobatic moves on ropes and trapezes. Turnfest competitions, like the one in this image, were held every four years, with competitors coming from all over the United States and Europe.

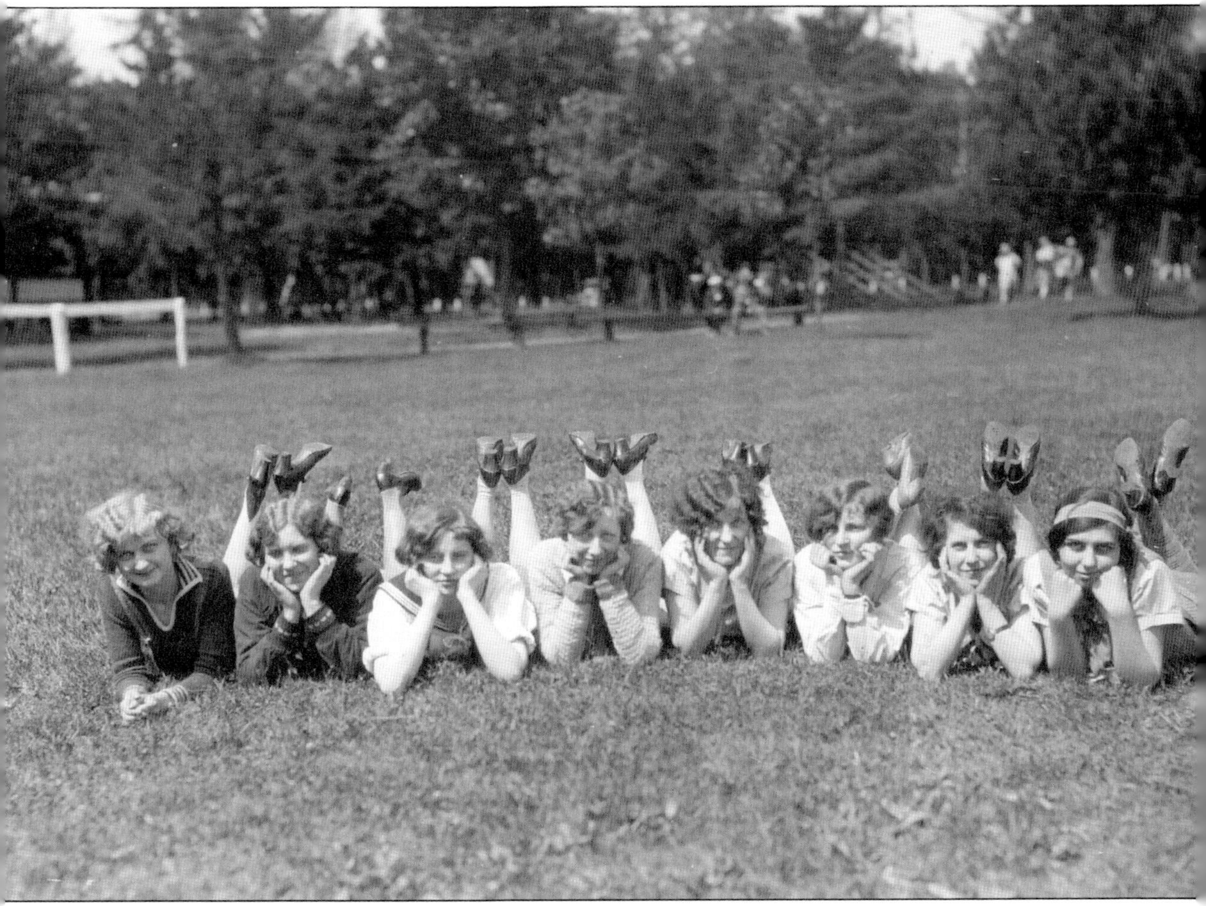

Sheboygan Press picnics were held annually into the 1990s at Evergreen, Shooting, and Roosevelt Parks. These girls are pictured at the 1926 celebration. Beer drinking and brat eating kept the adults busy. Activities, for adults and children alike, included softball, balloon-blowing contests, tug-of-war contests, and foot races. The 1930 picnic was another memorable one, as an African American jazz band provided the music, a different musical genre in Sheboygan. The *Sheboygan Press* started on December 17, 1907, in a print shop at 821 Pennsylvania Avenue. When Charles Broughton took over as editor in 1908, there were only 68 subscribers, but numbers grew quickly. From 1933 to 1941, the *Sheboygan Press* was the official state newspaper.

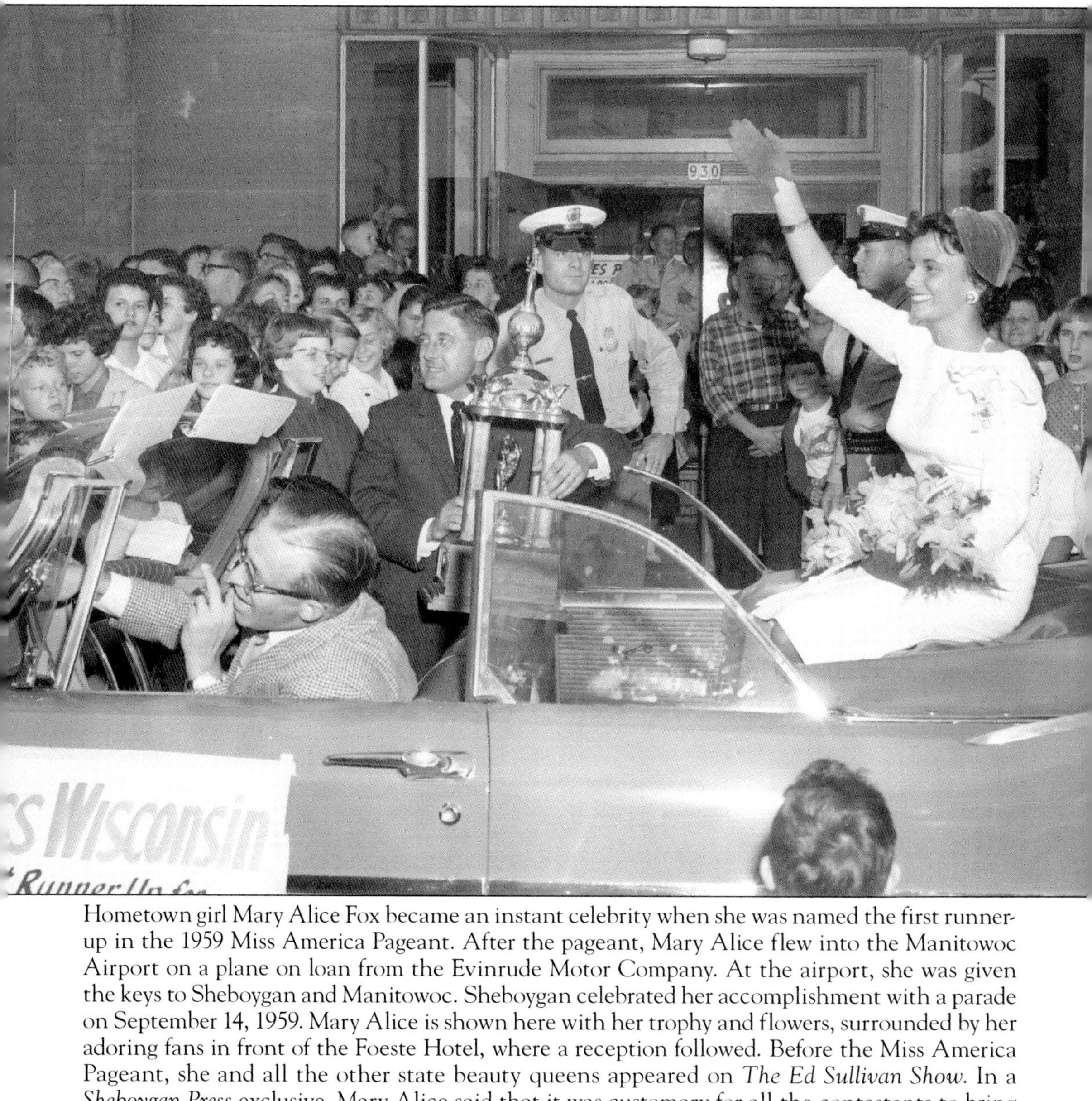

Hometown girl Mary Alice Fox became an instant celebrity when she was named the first runner-up in the 1959 Miss America Pageant. After the pageant, Mary Alice flew into the Manitowoc Airport on a plane on loan from the Evinrude Motor Company. At the airport, she was given the keys to Sheboygan and Manitowoc. Sheboygan celebrated her accomplishment with a parade on September 14, 1959. Mary Alice is shown here with her trophy and flowers, surrounded by her adoring fans in front of the Foeste Hotel, where a reception followed. Before the Miss America Pageant, she and all the other state beauty queens appeared on *The Ed Sullivan Show*. In a *Sheboygan Press* exclusive, Mary Alice said that it was customary for all the contestants to bring gifts from their home states for all the other contestants. She, of course, brought cheese. Later, she moved to California and became a successful product spokesperson, appearing in hundreds of commercials and on the television sitcom *Green Acres*.

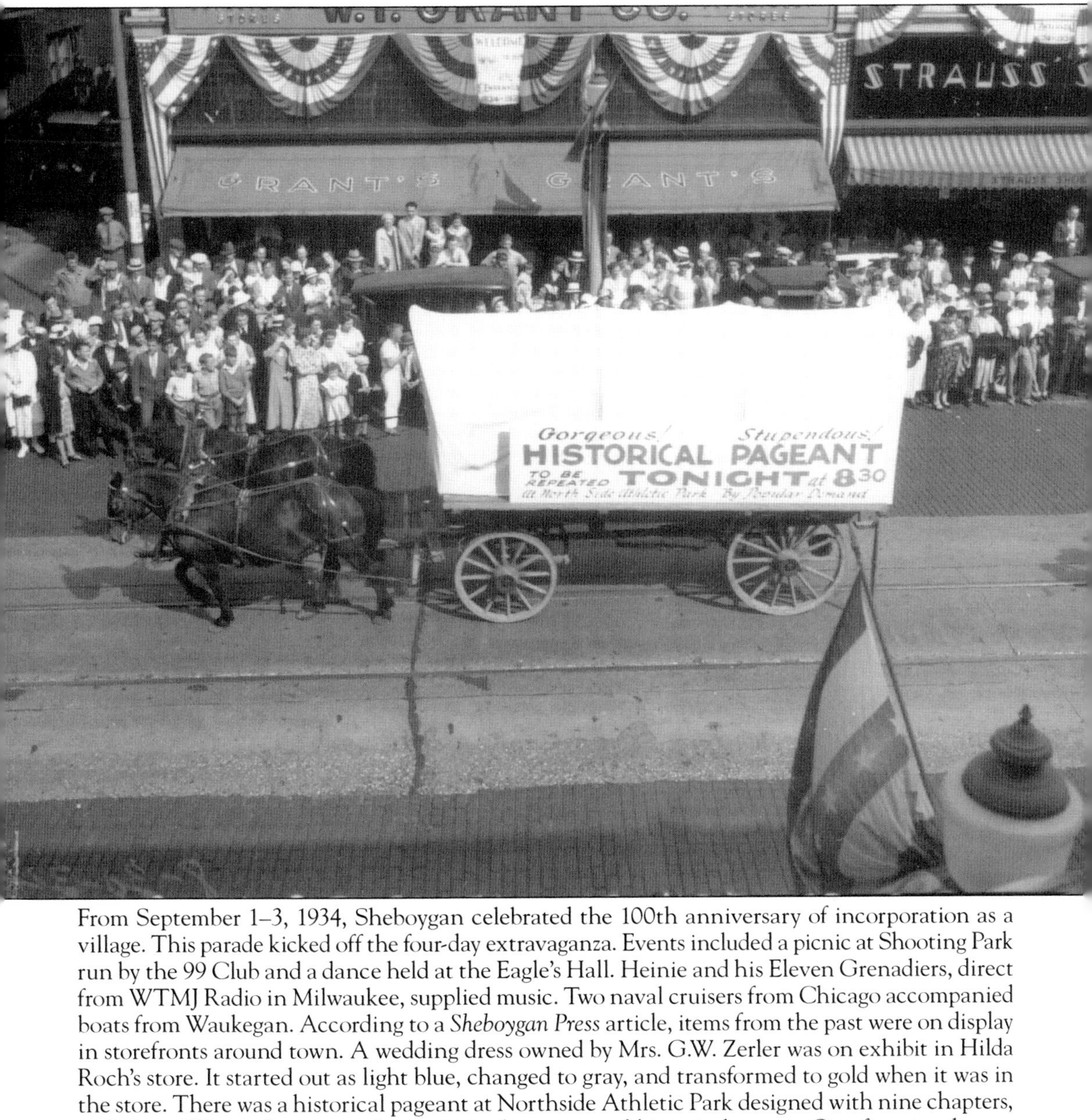

From September 1–3, 1934, Sheboygan celebrated the 100th anniversary of incorporation as a village. This parade kicked off the four-day extravaganza. Events included a picnic at Shooting Park run by the 99 Club and a dance held at the Eagle's Hall. Heinie and his Eleven Grenadiers, direct from WTMJ Radio in Milwaukee, supplied music. Two naval cruisers from Chicago accompanied boats from Waukegan. According to a *Sheboygan Press* article, items from the past were on display in storefronts around town. A wedding dress owned by Mrs. G.W. Zerler was on exhibit in Hilda Roch's store. It started out as light blue, changed to gray, and transformed to gold when it was in the store. There was a historical pageant at Northside Athletic Park designed with nine chapters, including 650 people in period costumes who reenacted historical events. One favorite chapter brought the first school in Sheboygan back to life and included spanking demonstrations and the proper use of the dunce cap.

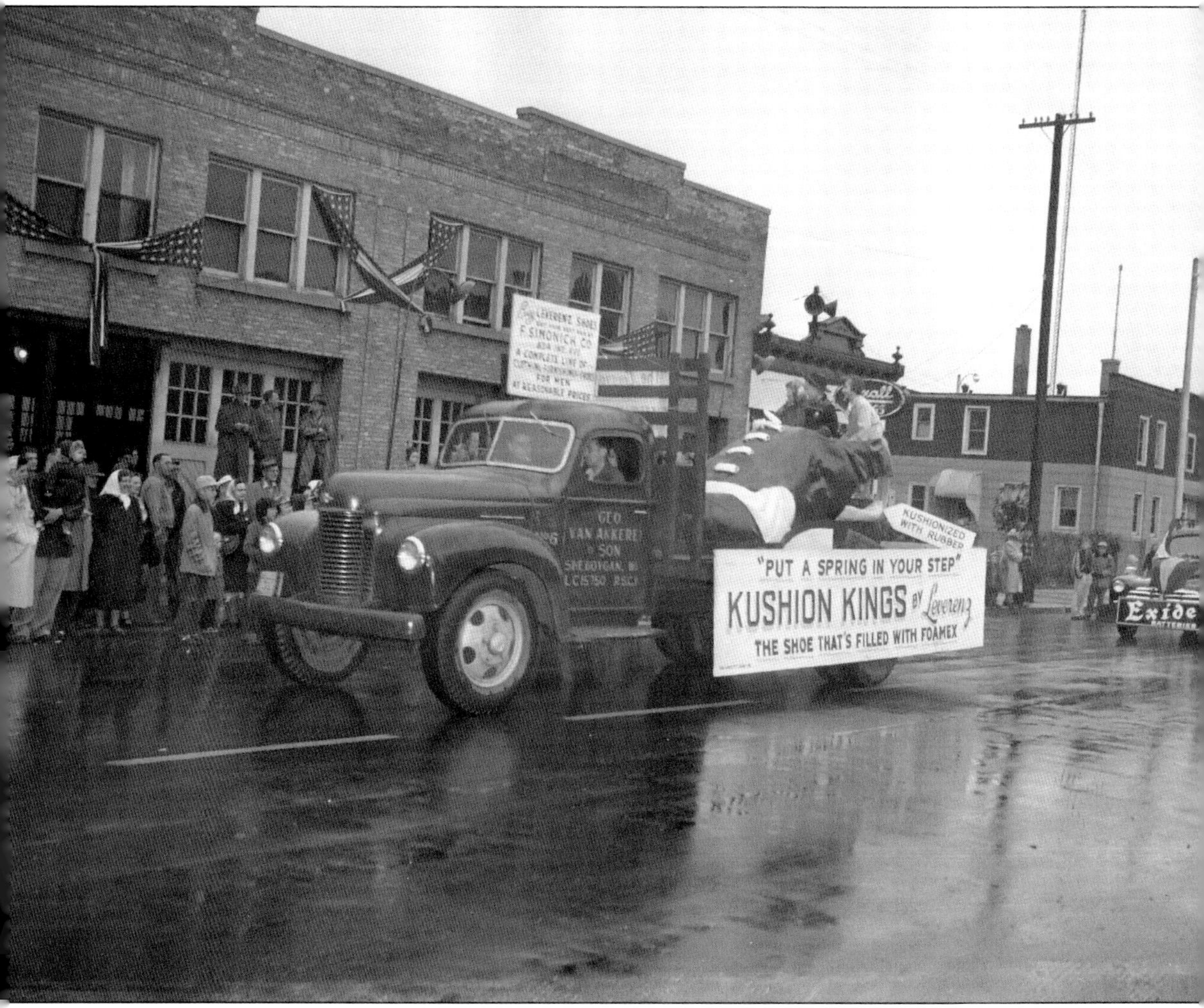

Sheboygan celebrated its second centennial in 1953, the anniversary of its becoming a city. More than 3,000 people participated in the parade. This image was taken on Indiana Avenue just east of Eighth Street. The float advertises shoes from the Leverenz Company. Well-known actor Charles Coburn appeared in Sheboygan as part of the celebration. Coburn got his first acting job at Lakeview Theatre, once located near Shooting Park. Cecil B. DeMille and his wife were invited to the celebration because they had spent their honeymoon in Sheboygan. They declined the offer because DeMille was filming *The Ten Commandments.* As part of the celebration, the mayor banned women from wearing makeup or jewelry without the purchase of a Sisters of the Swish permit. The Brothers of the Beard promoted all men to grow a beard for the centennial.

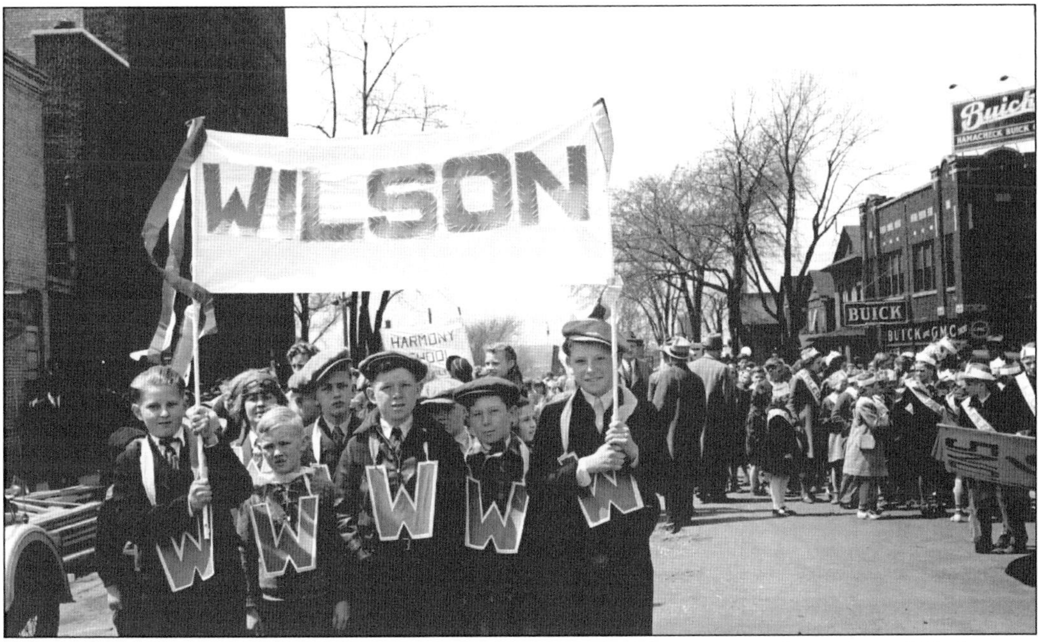

The first Rural Youth Day was held in 1939. More than 2,000 youngsters from around Sheboygan County participated. The junior chamber of commerce, along with the help of 4-H clubs and rural schools, sponsored the event. The first stop on the itinerary was the movie *Arizona Mahoney* and two cartoons at the Sheboygan Theater. Next, the kids marched in their groups in a parade that ended at Central High School. An entourage from the town of Wilson is pictured above in 1940. Lunch was served at Central High School. It consisted of 360 loaves of bread, 2,000 paper cups of ice cream, 2,000 bottles of milk, 22 pounds of butter, 60 pounds of sliced meat, and 125 pounds of cheese. The afternoon was spent taking tours of the Wisconsin Telephone Company, the *Sheboygan Press*, Radio Station WHBL, and the courthouse. The photograph below, also taken in 1940, shows cars made by kids participating in Rural Youth Day.

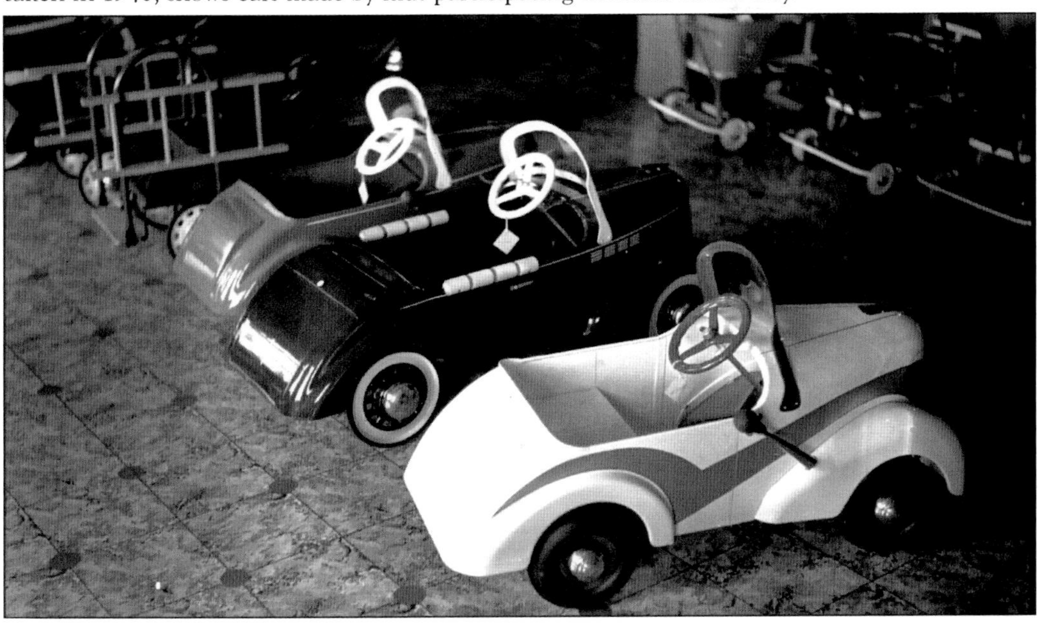

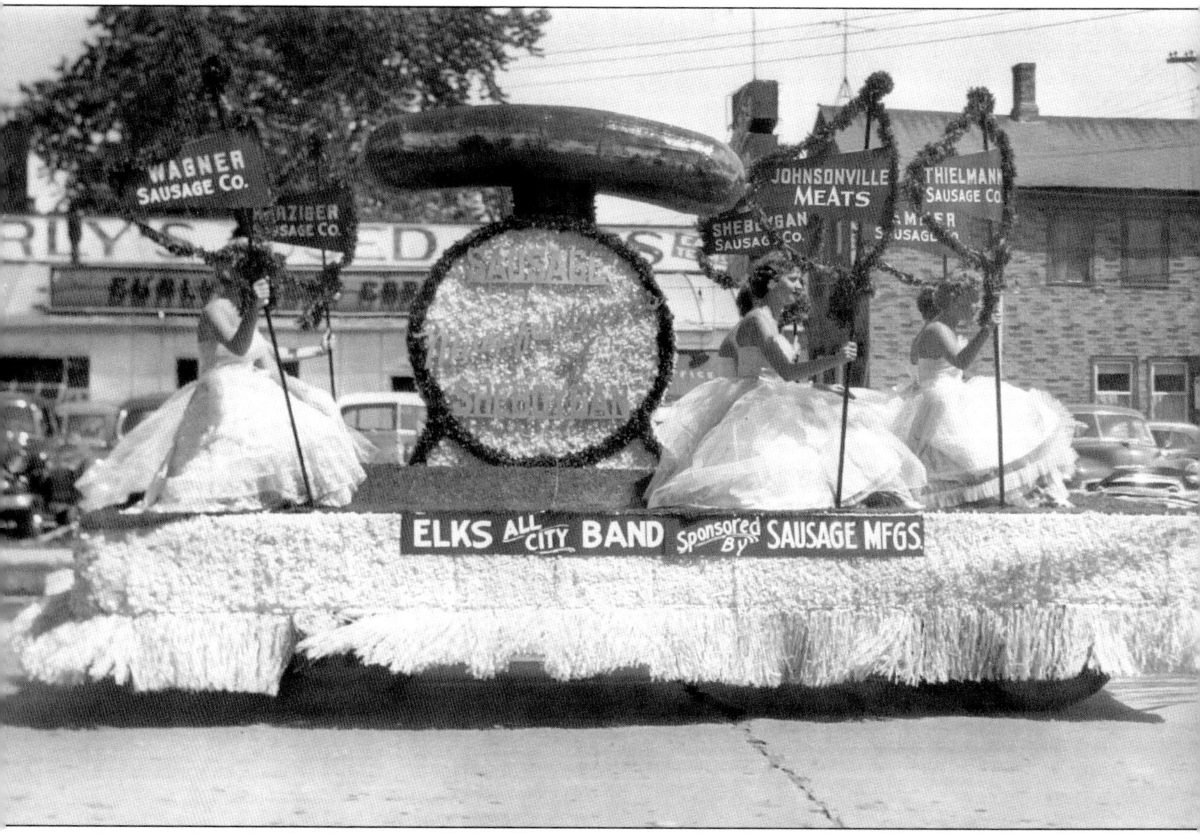

August 13, 1953, was a landmark day in the city of Sheboygan when a tradition that is truly Sheboygan's very own, Bratwurst Day, began. It was kicked off by a bratwurst breakfast and followed later by a bratwurst lunch. An accordion band made up of Olga Plesetz Saye's students provided musical entertainment in the afternoon. There was a bratwurst-eating contest and a pageant to choose the bratwurst queen. In the evening, music and fun was provided by the Balkan Serenaders and the Polka Rascals. As many as 150,000 people a year attended the festival at its peak in the 1960s. Bratwurst Day finished its first run in 1966 when a referendum abolished it because park benches, backyards, and the beach were used as hotel rooms and toilets. Replaced in 1969 by German Days, it returned in 1976. In 1991, the Jaycees tried for a Guinness world record by submitting two 130-pound brats on a 40-pound hard roll. The festival currently runs for three days in August, sponsored by longtime supporter Johnsonville Sausage.

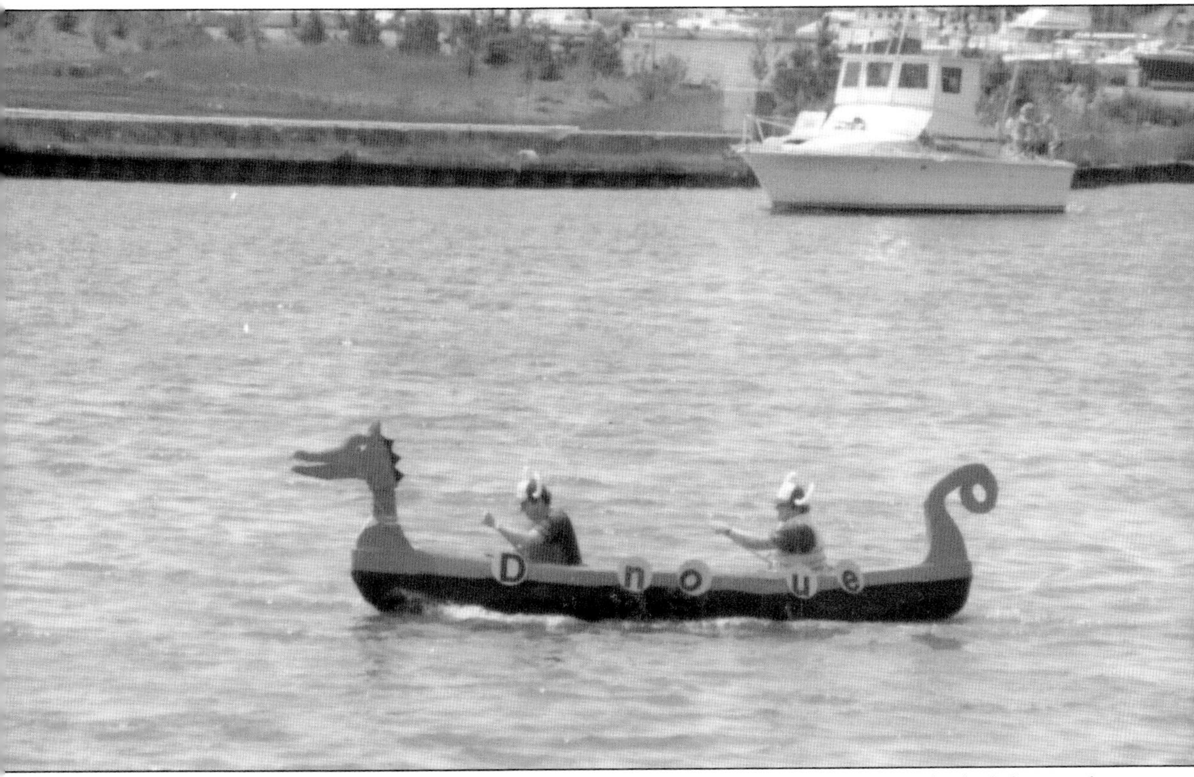

Independence Day in Sheboygan has always been celebrated in style. Starting the holiday on the evening of July 3 with a Venetian parade, local boat owners decorated their vessels with lights and sailed up and down the Sheboygan River for all to see. A total of 1,600 Chinese lanterns were lit in Fountain Park to create a magical effect. A huge parade has always been a part of the day. A crowd favorite in a past parade was a wagon drawn by four horses topped by 38 women in white dresses, one for each state in the union (in the 1880s). In 1976, Sheboygan's bicentennial parade was a special one, bigger than usual, with 120 units participating. The fireworks were also longer than the usual 50 minutes, tripling the cost from $2,500 in 1975 to $7,500. A recent addition to the holiday celebration is the Cardboard Boat Regatta sponsored by the John Michael Kohler Arts Center. Teams of ship builders construct boats made of cardboard that may or may not prove to be seaworthy, like the Viking contraption pictured here.

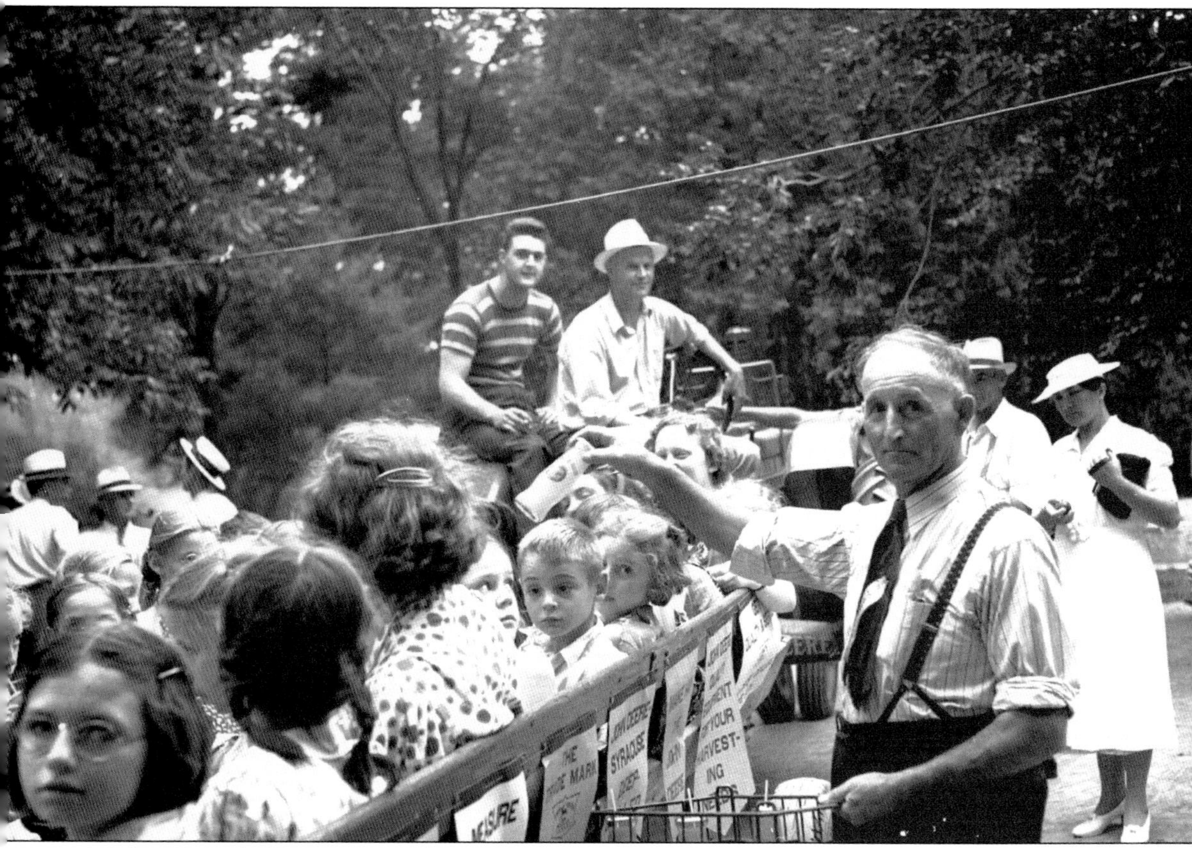

Modern Dairy held a picnic on July 20, 1940, at Evergreen Park. The 200 farmers brought their friends and families along for the occasion. The weather was perfect on that day, as ordered by weather committee chairman Henry Tasche. Sixty kids from the Kiddies Camp were brought over on hay wagons and given hamburgers and milk. The picnic ended early, because the farmers had to get back home and milk at night. The picnic also had a softball game with a team of farmers competing against the board of directors. When the game was over, no one was sure who had won.

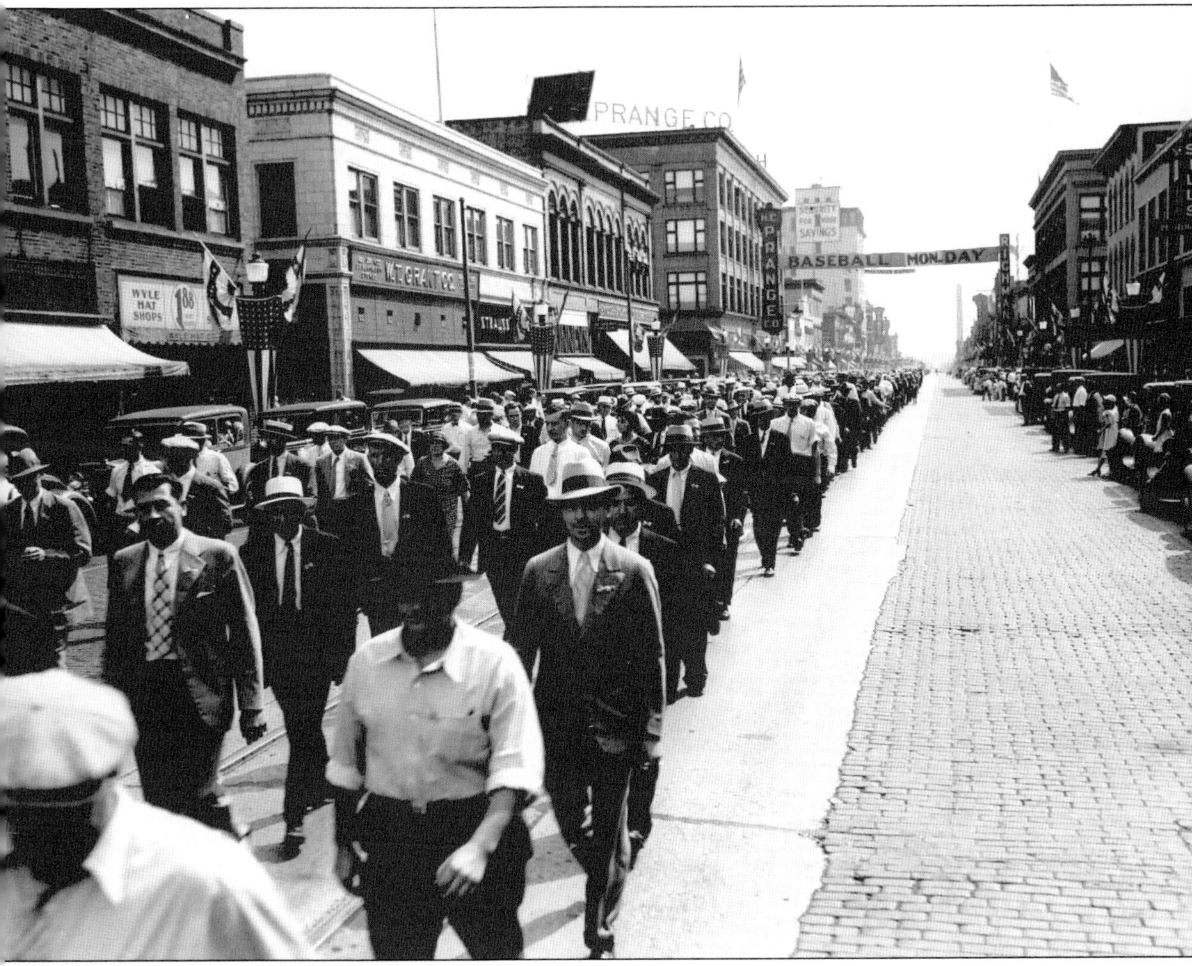

Labor Day 1933 saw one of the largest parades and picnics celebrating the union worker. According to the *Sheboygan Press*, more than 7,000 people marched up North Eighth Street, seen here, to Vollrath Park for the gathering. Mayor Willard Sonnenburg was the first speaker. Sonnenburg talked about the history of the country and the hard times it had been through. Arthur Gruhle, city attorney, talked about the history of Labor Day. In 1894, Congress passed a law making the day a holiday in the District of Columbia and for all federal employees.

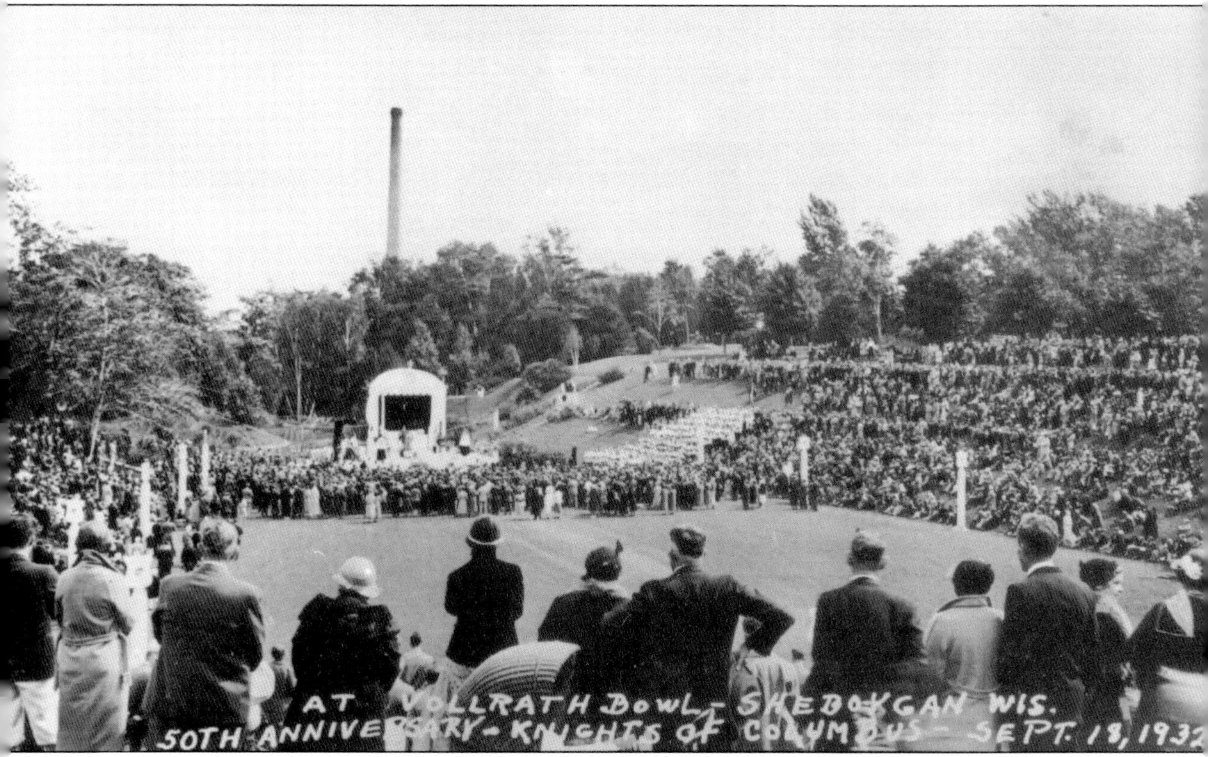

On September 18, 1932, thousands of people attended a field mass at Vollrath Bowl commemorating the 50th anniversary of the Knights of Columbus, seen here. Started in 1882, the organization was founded on three basic principles: love of country, love of God, and love of humanity. At the time of the 1932 celebration, the Knights of Columbus had 7,000 chapters serving over 1.5 million members. On May 18, 1953, the Sheboygan chapter of the Knights of Columbus observed their 50th anniversary. Formed on January 4, 1903, with 45 members, Simon Gillen, a former district attorney and judge, was the first grand knight of the Sheboygan chapter. The festivities concluded with a dance. Reggie Barber and his orchestra provided music.

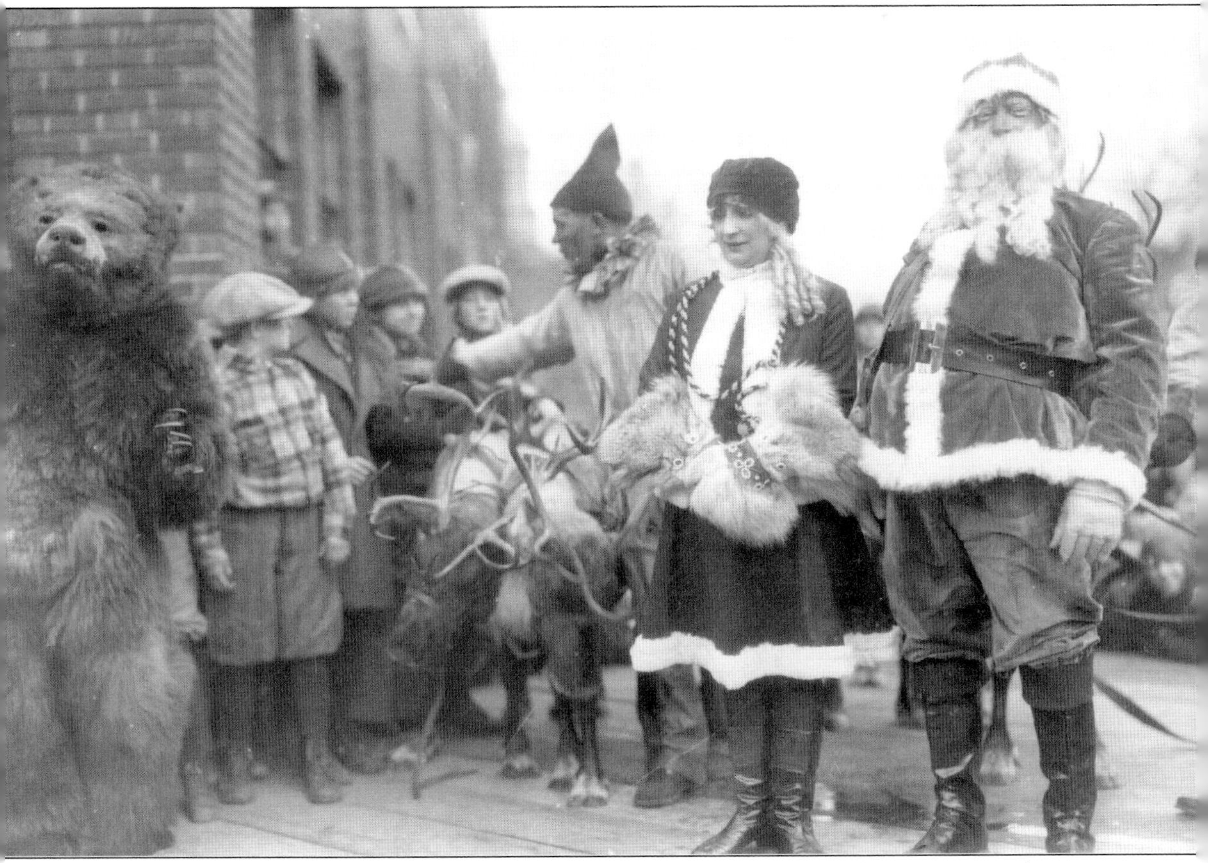

Pictured here are some of the characters who appeared in the November 20, 1929, Christmas parade in Sheboygan. Residents of the city, along with people from as far away as Watertown, Oshkosh, and Green Bay, lined the streets to greet Santa at the train station. Those who went to the train station were treated to an extra show. The reindeer handler, who was responsible for hitching the animals to Santa's sleigh, was involved in a boxing match with a particularly feisty reindeer. Happily, no one was injured. Once the reindeer calmed down, children welcomed Santa Claus, his Mary Christmas, and their companions, Spirit of Love and Little Quen. Dr. Louis Wolf, noted Alaskan explorer, along with his trusty Malmute, Kusko, accompanied Santa as well. The Santa Claus Band entertained people with holiday songs. A big, brown bear amused children with his dancing. Other unusual and inexplicable creatures in the parade were grotesque figures with heads twice as big as their bodies, pigs with large heads that walked upright, a 20-foot-long dog, and walking trees.

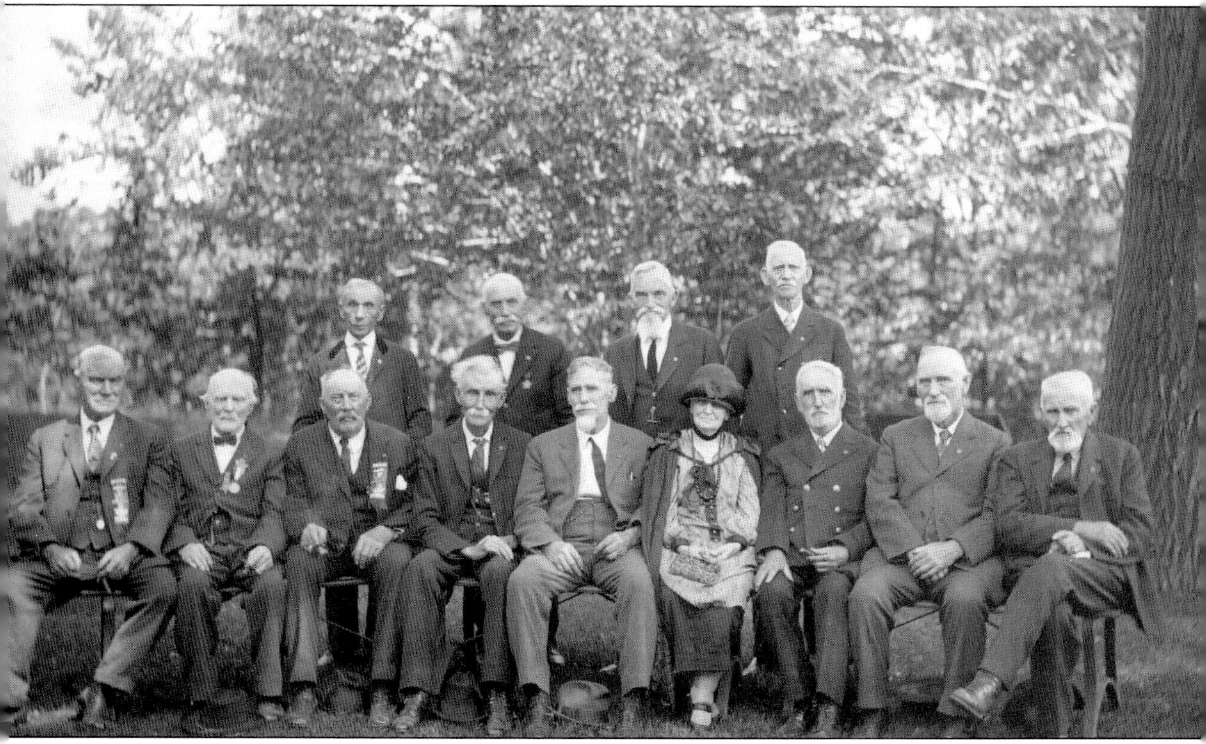

Civil War soldier reunions started as early as 1869. Officially known as the Grand Army of the Republic, the GAR was a fraternal organization composed of veterans of the Union Army, US Navy, US Marines, and US Revenue Cutter Service who served in the American Civil War. The local chapter was organized in Sheboygan on November 28, 1884. Soldiers from Sheboygan served in Company C, mustering for duty on June 17, 1861. Only seven of the company's original members survived to return in 1866. Helen Brainerd Cole, the only surviving Civil War nurse in Sheboygan, gave a moving speech at the 1926 reunion. The surviving veterans are pictured here with Helen Cole. The 1937 parade was special because W.H. Chesebro, one of the area's last remaining Civil War veterans, marched in it.

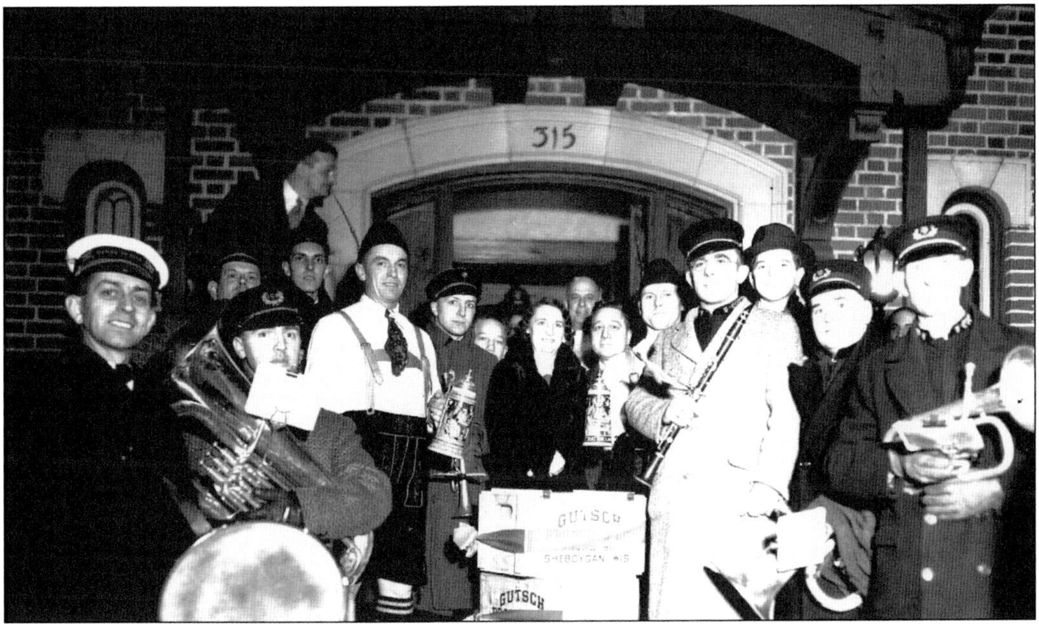

While Milwaukee waited until Lent was finished, a river of beer flowed through Sheboygan at 12:01 a.m. on April 7, 1933, the first possible minute it was legal to again sell beer when Prohibition ended. Surveys showed 10-to-1 that Sheboyganites were in favor of changing the Dry Laws. In early 1933, President Roosevelt legalized the sale of 3.2 beer, modifying the Volstead Act—done in part because it would raise tax revenue. Pictured above, Charles Broughton, at center rear, editor of the *Sheboygan Press*, received the first case of Gutsch or Kingsbury off the line because of his strong appeals for the end of Prohibition. The restart of beer production allowed thousands of workers to find jobs again. In the image below, trucks are lined up and waiting for the go-ahead to deliver. Hard liquor was not legal until August 1933.

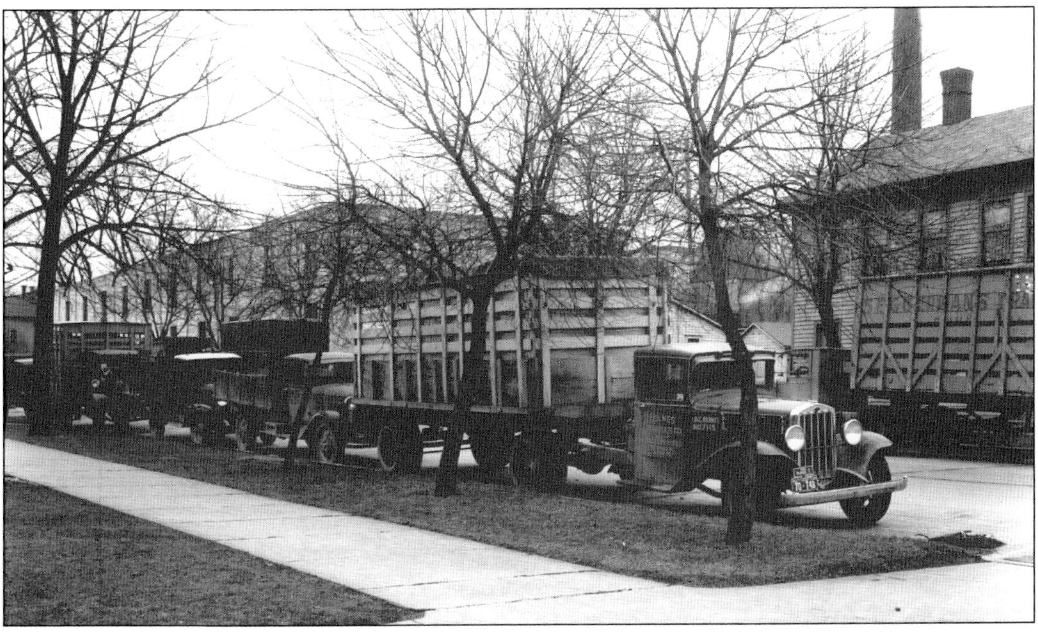

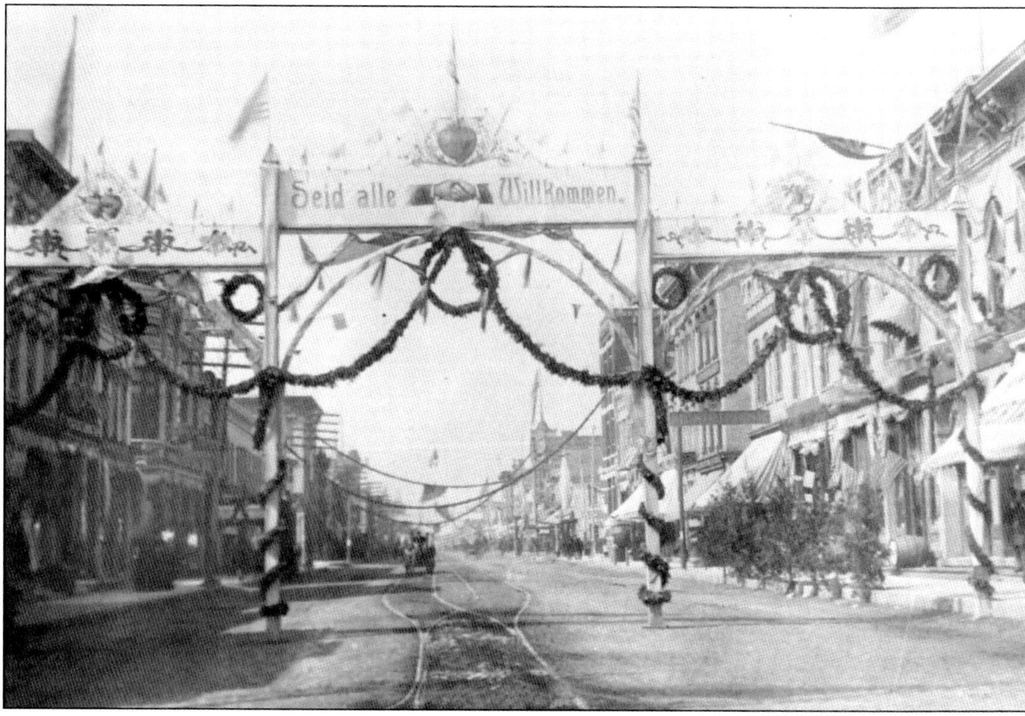

Catholic Mayfest was held in 1894. It was the largest gathering of Catholics in Wisconsin up to that time, with 15,000 attending. A train with 11 coach cars holding 1,000 people came on Sunday. Many enterprising tavern owners displayed signs claiming that their establishment was the official headquarters of a particular delegation. This image shows Eighth Street decorated, with the sign welcoming everyone.

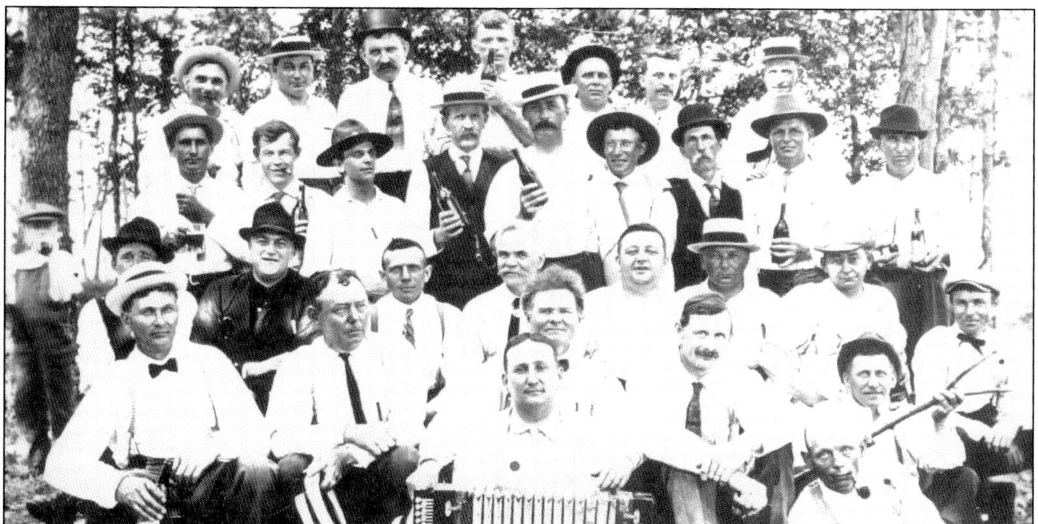

In 1915, the local Spanish-American War Veterans group from the Doege Trier Post held a picnic at Taylor Park. This local group formed on May 15, 1900. In December 1926, it declared 100 percent membership. Every eligible man in the city had joined. Past national commander William H. Armstrong gave a speech at the event calling for a cleanup in this country and reform to veterans' pension problems.

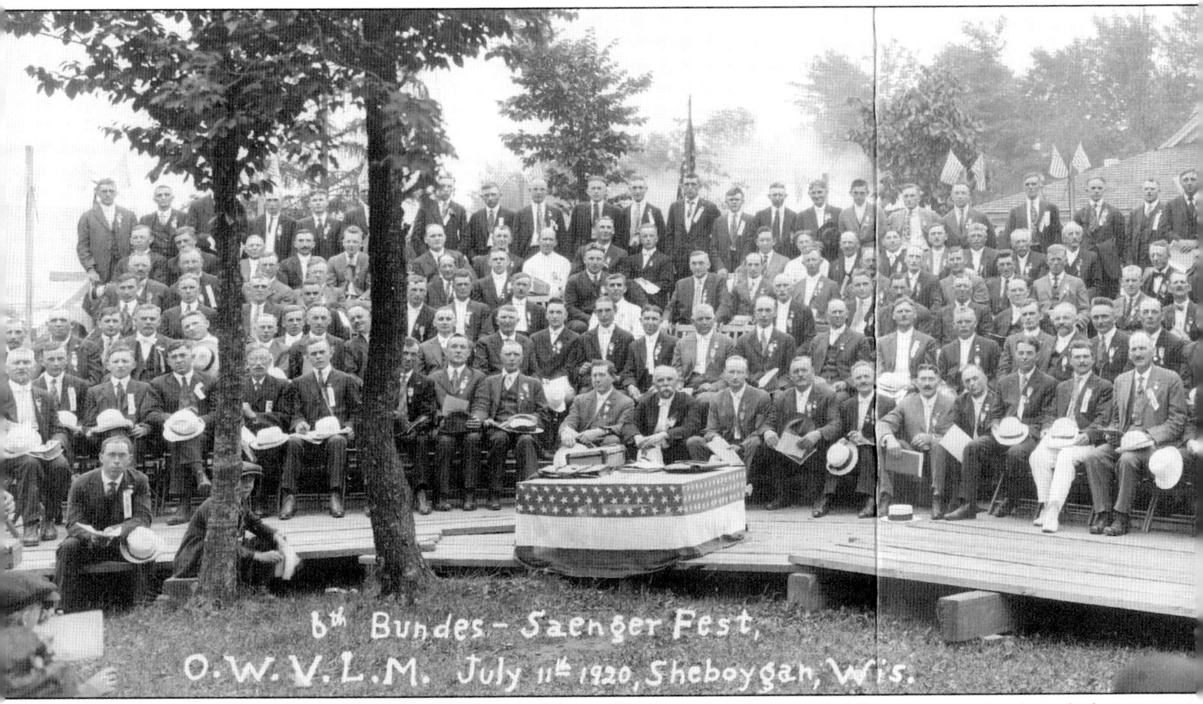

In 1892, the Ost-Wisconsin Saengerbund (East Wisconsin singing club) was organized and the first Saengerfest was held in Sheboygan. It was a competition among choirs from different cities. Held in Binz Hall, which later became Born's Sanitarium, the event was hosted by the Concordia Singing Society. A memorable Saengerfest was held on July 21 and 22, 1929. The highlight was a 400-voice choir accompanied by the Sheboygan Symphony at a concert at Central High School. The image seen here shows the choir at the 1920 Saengerfest.

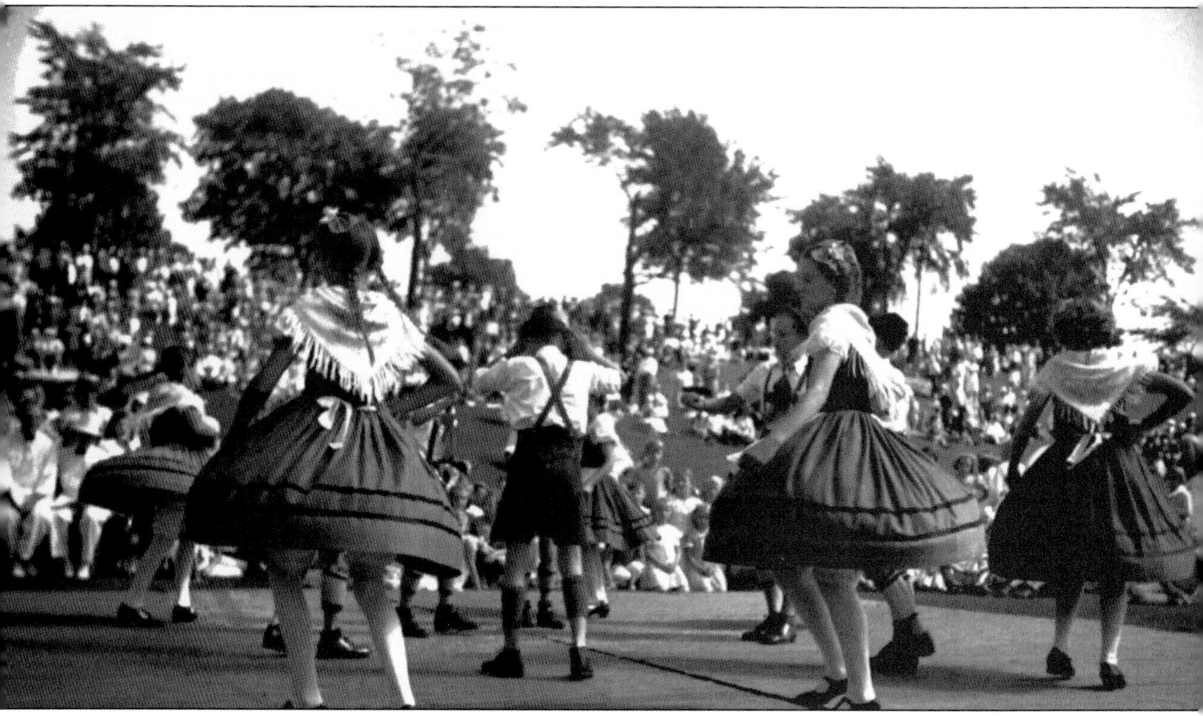

Sheboygan's German immigrants honored their heritage on August 8, 1934. The German Day celebration was held at Vollrath Bowl. The Wuerl Band played only German music for the event. Other entertainment included performances by the Bavarian Entertainers, a dance group accompanied by an accordionist, and the Werdenfelser Schuhplattlers, who performed dances in native costumes, seen in this image. Attorney Andrew Brunhart, president of the Muehlenburg Unit of the Steuben Society, gave the only speech in English.

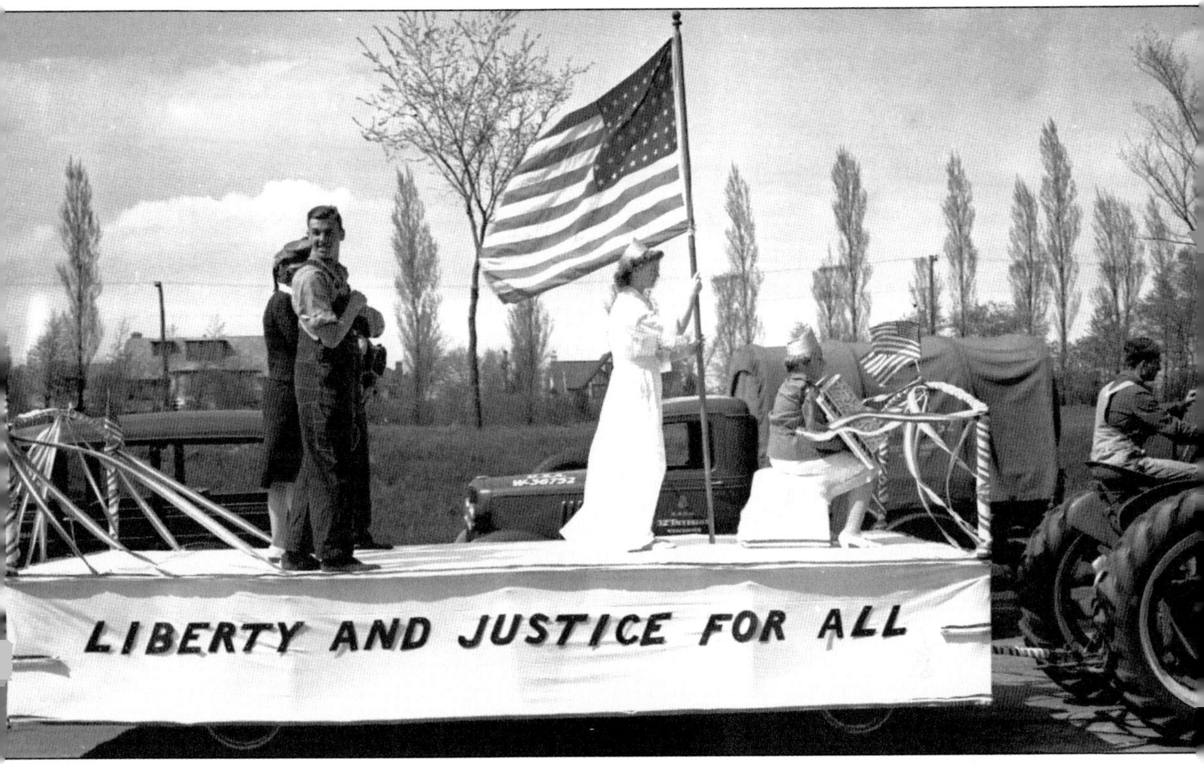

May 25, 1940, was known as Citizenship Day in Sheboygan. This event welcomed new 21-year-old voters into citizenship. The downtown was decorated with flags and banners. There was a parade featuring patriotic floats. "Liberty and justice for all" was the theme of the float seen in this image. In a ceremony at Vollrath Bowl, new voters took an oath of citizenship. County board chairman James Gannon read a message from Pres. Franklin Delano Roosevelt. Out of 1,085 new voters, 98 showed up for the ceremony, according to a *Sheboygan Press* account.

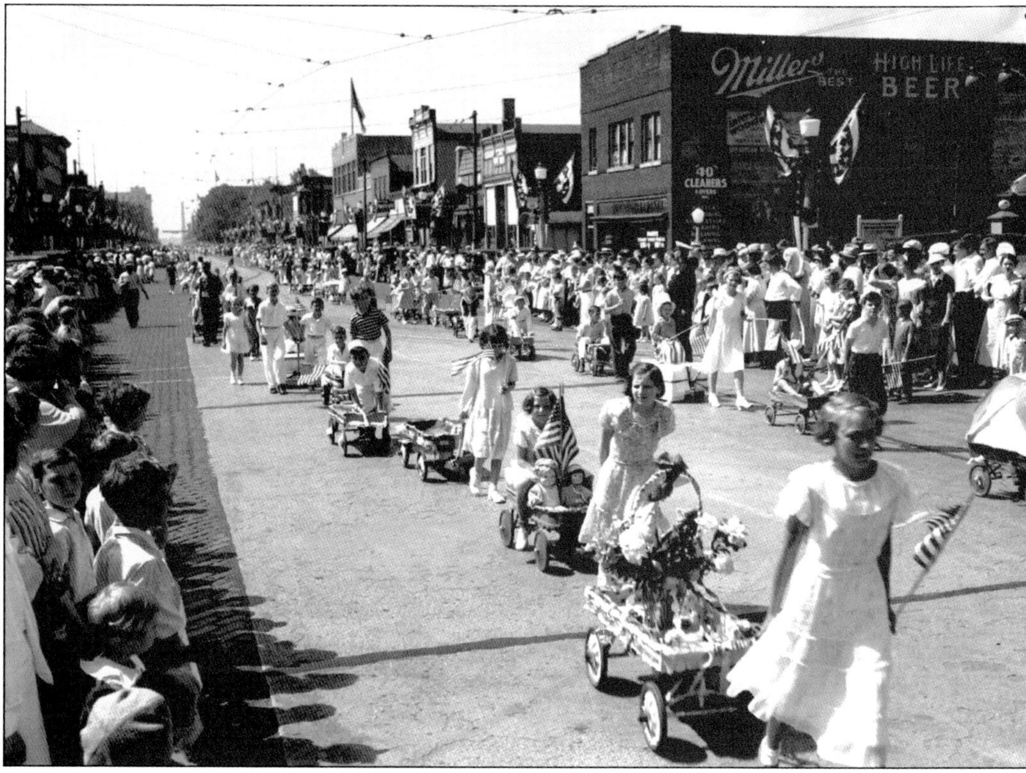

The Children's May Day Parade was an event sponsored by the *Sheboygan Press* and held on May 19, 1934. Thousands of spectators attended, and 1,400 children participated. Over 1,000 balloons were given out, along with 1,400 Eskimo Pies, and 73 merchandise prizes were awarded. Girls pushing buggies led the parade, seen here at Eighth Street and Michigan Avenue. An imaginative group of kids called themselves the Dillinger Gang. The Sheridan School Harmonica Band marched in the parade as well. Scooters and wagons were decorated with balloons, crepe paper, flowers, and flags. Children brought their kittens, rabbits, and mice along in cages and wagons. Ponies and would-be zebras marched in the parade. Dogs were wearing dresses and hats for the occasion. There was even a pink dog in the parade. The image below of tots on tricycles was taken in front of Geele Hardware Store on North Eighth Street.

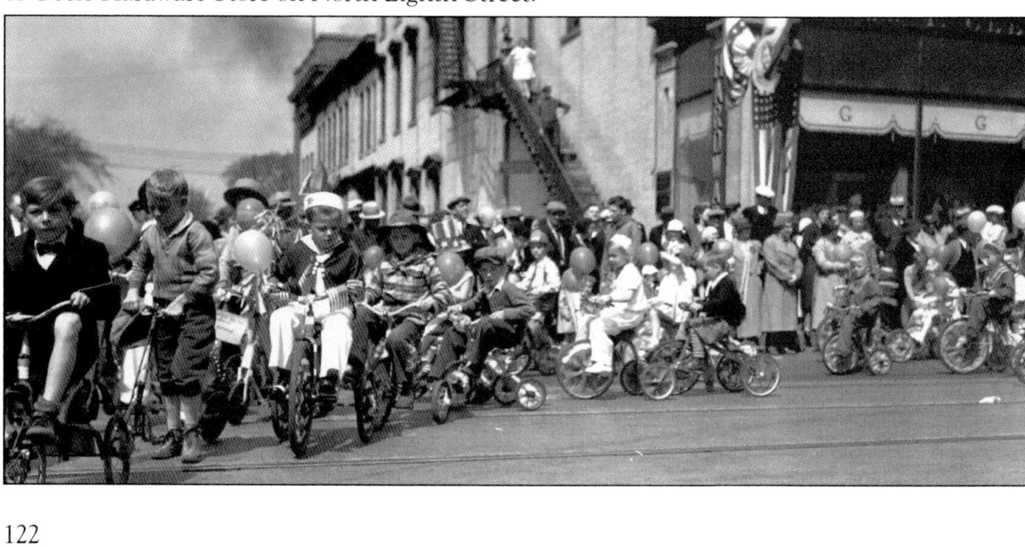

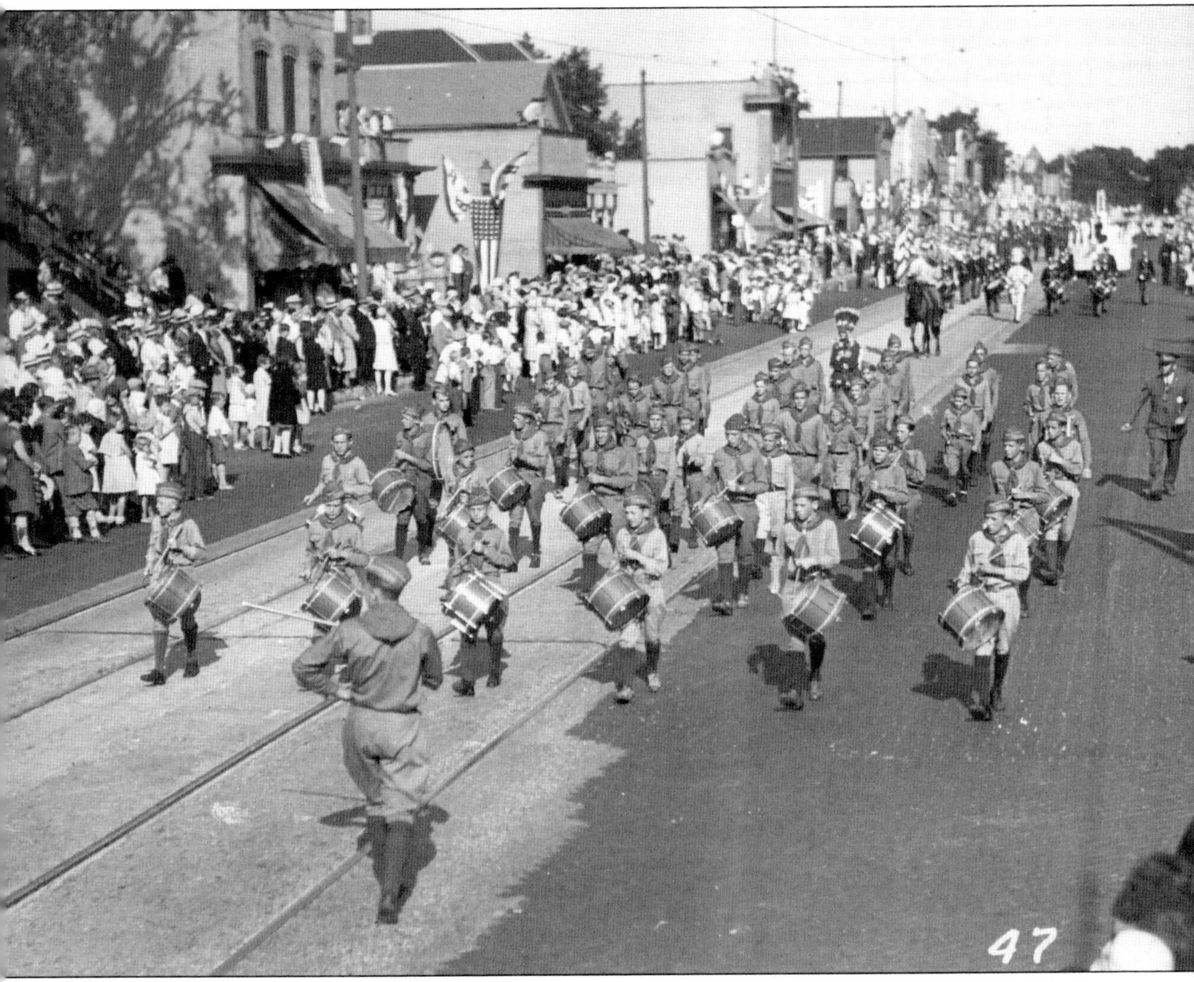

The American Legion National Convention was held in Sheboygan from August 17 to August 20, 1930. Events around the area included a parade in downtown Sheboygan, an air show at the Kohler Airport, and a drum corps competition at the Legion Baseball Park. This image was taken at Twelfth Street and Michigan Avenue and shows a troop of Boy Scouts performing. Possibly the most unique event of the convention was the Initiation of the Ceremonial Grand and Noble Order of Bananas. On Memorial Day 1923, the organization moved into a house at 609 Wisconsin Avenue, which was donated by the Kohler family. In November 1974, the American Legion moved into the former Odd Fellows at South Fifteenth Street and New Jersey Avenue.

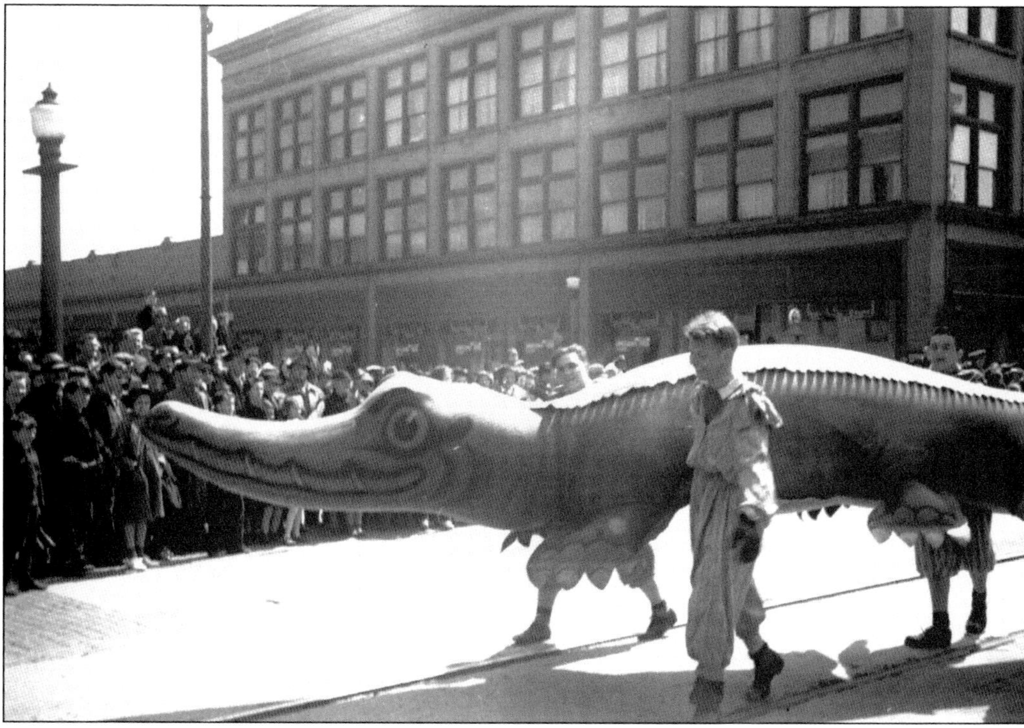

The Parade of the Giant Balloons was sponsored by the retail division of the chamber of commerce and was held on April 15, 1939. According to the *Sheboygan Press*, there was a dragon with red eyes and red and blue flames coming out of his nose. There was an elephant, an alligator, and a blue hippopotamus. Felix the Cat and Donald Duck showed up for the occasion. For fun, a big pig blew a horn that tooted. Possibly the most spectacular sight was a set of huge letters spelling Gulliver, followed by the 80-foot man himself. Pictured here are the giant crocodile, an elephant, and a monkey.

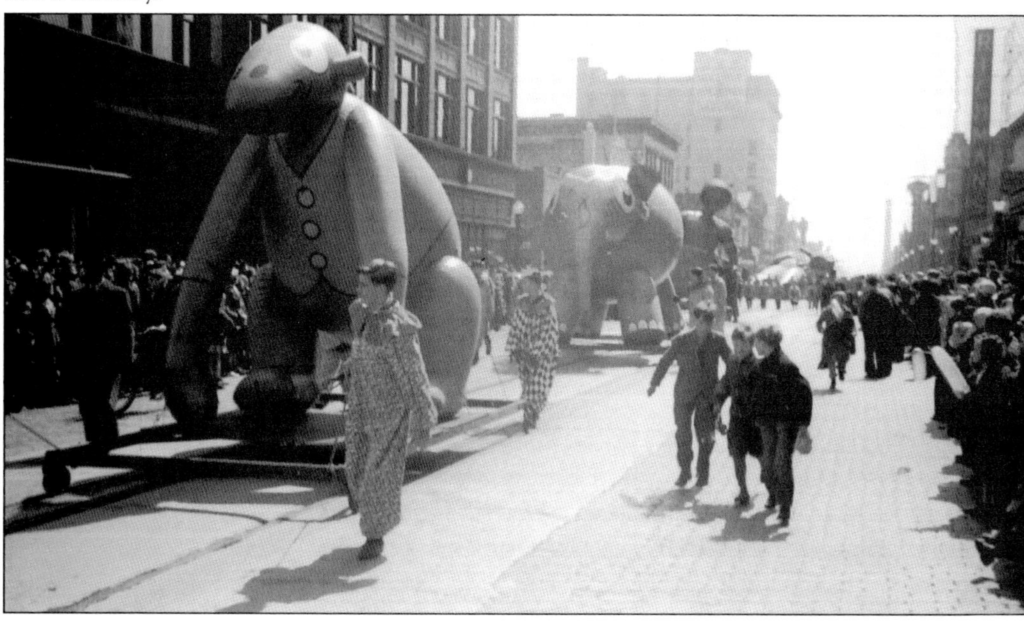

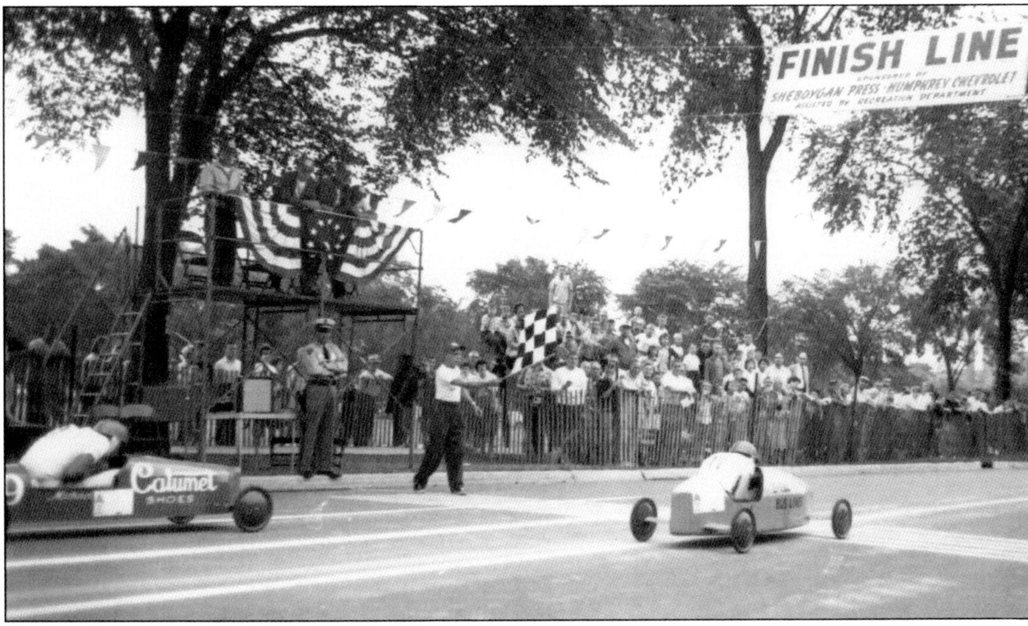

The first Soap Box Derby in Sheboygan was held in 1959. The *Sheboygan Press* and Humphrey Chevrolet were sponsors of the local contest. There were 38 contestants, and the race was held on North Seventeenth Street next to Kiwanis Park. The 1965 derby was filmed and shown across America and around the world to publicize the race. In an interview in the *Sheboygan Press*, 1965 winner Ron DeTroye revealed his winning secret. Between races, he covered his wheels with rags soaked in dry ice and antifreeze to make the rubber harder and faster. Local celebrities, such as Mayor Joseph Browne, Mayor John Bolgert, and WITI Channel 6 sportscaster Earl Gillespie, participated in the races. The final derby was held in 1970. These images were taken July 22, 1961.

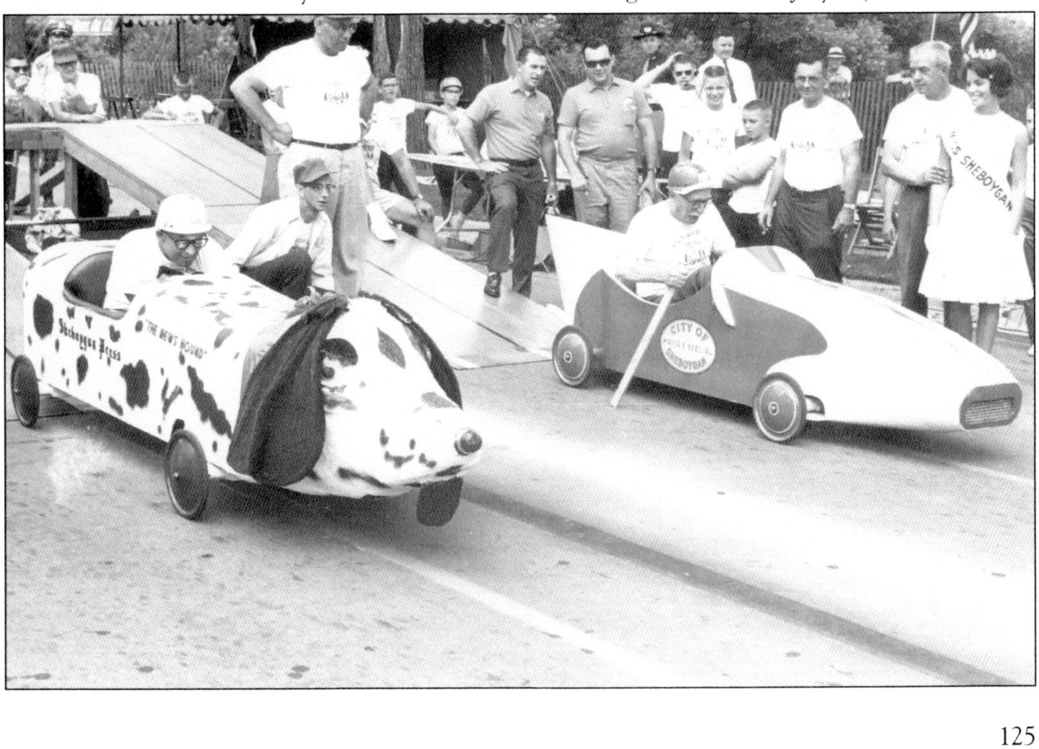

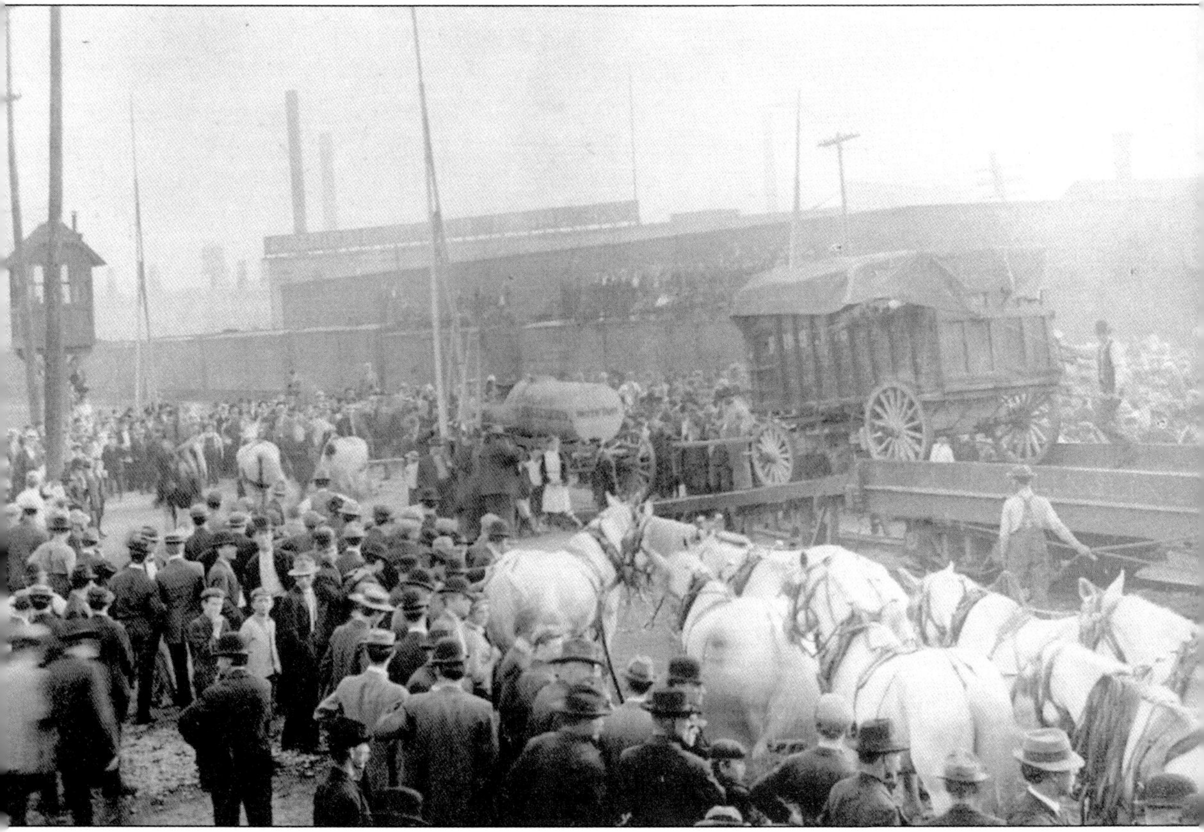

The Yankee American Shows, Carson Barnes, Clyde Beatty-Russell Brothers, Kelly Miller, the Dailey Brothers, and the Cole Brothers were just a few of the many circuses to come through Sheboygan. A Sells-Floyd Circus parade on August 4, 1909, included bandwagons, floats, and Roman chariots. Over 400 horses were used in the parade. The Ringling Bros. Circus staged a parade on August 17, 1910, and it was estimated that it was at least three miles long. About 1,300 people, 656 horses, 40 elephants, and several floats were part of the parade. Over 1,000 animals were also on display. The star of the parade was Darwin, the Missing Link, who lived in a house, ate with a knife and fork, and wore a watch. This image shows the Ringling Bros. Circus unloading at the depot in 1907.

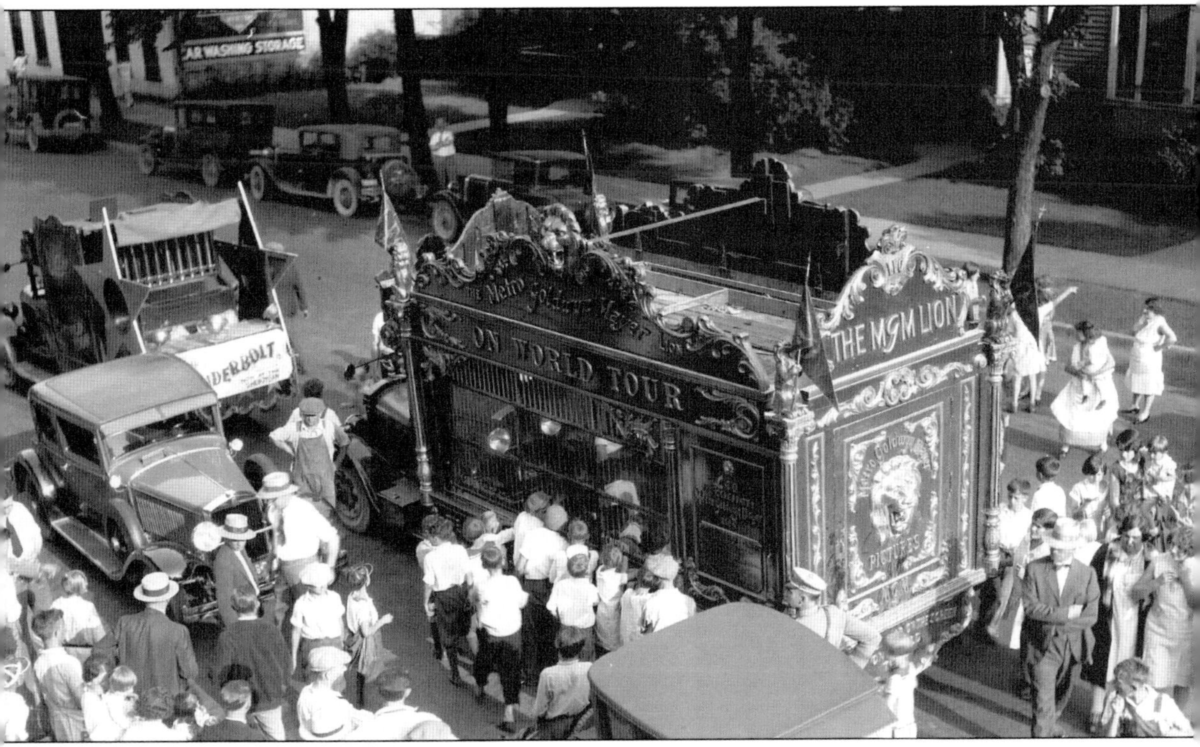

Leo, a black Nubian lion, was the living trademark of Metro-Goldwyn-Mayer Pictures. He was insured for $1 million and was purported to be the heaviest and longest lion in captivity. On Monday, July 22, 1929 he stopped in Sheboygan as part of a five-year world tour. Leo traveled from stop to stop in his cage that was mounted on an REO Speedwagon truck, pictured here. At the *Sheboygan Press*, a photographer entered the cage to take his picture. At the Sheboygan Theater, he performed stunts for the audience, including kneeling and saying his prayers. Leo split his usual rations of 25 pounds of meat a day into meals at Joe Bensman's Meat Market, Diamond Meat Market, and the Sanitary Cash Meat Market.